English/Cambodian Edition

The New Oxford Picture Dictionary

E. C. Parnwell

Translated by Im and Sivone Proum

Illustrations by:
Ray Burns
Bob Giuliani
Laura Hartman
Pamela Johnson
Melodye Rosales
Raymond Skibinski
Joel Snyder

Oxford University Press

Oxford University Press

200 Madison Avenue
New York, NY 10016 USA

Walton Street
Oxford OX2 6DP England

OXFORD is a trademark of Oxford University Press.

ISBN 0-19-434359-6

Associate Editor: Mary Lynne Nielsen
Assistant Editor: Mary Sutherland
Art Director: Lynn Luchetti
Production Co-ordinator: Claire Nicholl
The publishers would like to thank the following agents for their co-operation:
Carol Bancroft and Friends, representing Bob Giuliani,
Laura Hartman, and Melodye Rosales.

Publishers Graphics Inc., representing Ray Burns,
Pamela Johnson, and Joel Snyder.

Cover illustration by Laura Hartman.

Printing (last digit): 10 9 8 7 6

Printed in Hong Kong

The New Oxford Picture Dictionary contextually illustrates over 2,400 words. The book is a unique language learning tool for students of English. It provides students with a glance at American lifestyle, as well as a compendium of useful vocabulary.

The Dictionary is organized thematically, beginning with topics that are most useful for the "survival" needs of students in an English-speaking country. However, pages may be used at random, depending on the students' particular needs. The book need not be taught in order. A complete index with pronunciation guide in English is in the Appendix.

The New Oxford Picture Dictionary contextualizes vocabulary whenever possible. Verbs have been included on separate pages, but within a topic area where they are most likely to occur. However, this does not imply that these verbs only appear within these contexts.

For further ideas using The New Oxford Picture Dictionary, see the Listening and Speaking Activity Book, the Teacher's Guide, and the two workbooks: Beginner's and Intermediate levels. Also available in the program are a complete set of Cassettes, offering a reading of all of the words in the Dictionary; Vocabulary Playing Cards, featuring 40 words and the corresponding pictures on 80 cards, with ideas for many games; and sets of Wall Charts, available in one complete package or in three smaller packages. All of these items are available in English only.

វចនានុក្រមខុកស្វិតថ្មីដោយរូបភាព មានពាក្យជាង ២.៤០០ គូរូបជារូបប្រើនៅក្នុងកាល:- ទេស:ប៉ុស្តានការណ៍អ្វីមួយ ។ សៀវភៅនេះជាខុបករណ៍ដ៏ពិសេសសំរាប់កូនសិស្សដែលរៀន ភាសាអង់គ្លេស ។ សៀវភៅនេះបង្ហាញកូនសិស្សនូវរបៀបរស់នៅរបស់ប្រជាជនអាមេរិកាំង ផង ហើយផ្តល់នូវរកម្រងពាក្យមានប្រយោជន៍ដ៏សង្ខេបមួយផង ។

វចនានុក្រមនេះ ចែកជាផ្នែកទៅតាមប្រធាន, ចាប់ផ្តើមឡើងនឹងប្រធានណា ដែលមានប្រ- យោជន៍ចំពោះសេចក្តីត្រូវការអាយុជីវិតរបស់កូនសិស្សដែលរស់នៅក្នុងប្រទេសដែលនិយាយ ភាសាអង់គ្លេស ។ ក៏ប៉ុន្តែកូនសិស្សអាចចាប់រៀនទំព័រណាក៏បានស្រេចតែគេត្រូវការ ។ សៀវភៅនេះមិនបាច់ចាប់ពីដើមហូរហែរទេ (គីចាប់ពីទំព័រណាក៏បាន) ។

វចនានុក្រមខុកស្វិតថ្មីដោយរូបភាព ប្រើពាក្យនៅក្នុងកាល:ទេស:ប៉ុស្តានការណ៍មួយបើអាចធ្វើ ទៅបាន ។ យើងដាក់កិរិយាសព្ទក្នុងទំព័រផ្សេងៗ តែនៅក្នុងប្រធានណាដែលកិរិយាសព្ទ នោះអាចយកមកប្រើ ។ នេះមិនមែនបានសេចក្តីថាកិរិយាសព្ទទាំងនោះ អាចប្រើបានតែក្នុង កាល:ទេស:នោះទេ ។

បរិសិដ្ឋ (ផ្នែកបន្ថែម) មានលិបិក្រម (តារាងពាក្យតាមលំដាប់អក្សរ) នៃពាក្យទាំងនោះ និង របៀបអាន ក្រៅពីនេះមានលិបិក្រមនៃពាក្យខ្មែរដាក់បញ្ចូលផងដែរ ។

ចំពោះមធ្យោបាយប្រើប្រាស់វចនានុក្រមខុកស្វិតថ្មីដោយរូបភាព បន្ថែមទៀតសូមអញ្ជើញទៅ មើលនៅក្នុងមគ្គុទេសក៍សម្រាប់គ្រូបង្រៀននៅក្នុងសៀវភៅកិច្ចការទាំងពីរ: ថ្នាក់ចាប់ផ្តើម និង ថ្នាក់មធ្យម ។ នៅក្នុងកំរោងការណ៍យើងមានការស្តែង (ខ្សែអាត់)នៃការអានពាក្យនៅ ក្នុង វចនានុក្រម មួយឈុត ហើយនឹងផ្ទាំងគំនូរ ដែលមានជាមួយកញ្ចប់ធំ ឬជាបីកញ្ចប់តូច តូច ។ របស់ទាំងប៉ុន្មាននេះមានតែជាភាសាអង់គ្លេសទេ ៕

II Contents

មាតិការរឿង

People and Relationships	មនុស្សនិងញាតិសន្លាន	Page	2
The Family	គ្រួសារ		3
The Human Body	ខ្លួនមនុស្ស		4–5
Vegetables	បន្លែ		6–7
Fruits	ផ្លែឈើ		8–9
Meat, Poultry, and Seafood	សាច់(គោ, ជ្រូកៗល។, មាន់ទា, និងមួបសមុទ្រ		10–11
Containers, Quantities, and Money	ប្រដាប់សំរាប់ច្រកខ្ចប់ទុកឬដាក់, ចមន្ននិងប្រាក់កាស		12–13
The Supermarket	ស៊ុបផែរម៉ារកេត, កន្លែងលក់មួប		14–15
Family Restaurant and Cocktail Lounge	ភោជនីយដ្ឋាននិងកន្លែងញាំុស្រាកំសាន្ត		16
Restaurant Verbs	កិរិយាសព្ទទាក់ទងនឹងភោជនីយដ្ឋាន		17
Common Prepared Foods	មួបសាមញ្ញធ្វើស្រេច		18
Outdoor Clothes	សំលៀកបំពាក់នៅក្រៅផ្ទះ		19
Everyday Clothes	សំលៀកបំពាក់ប្រចាំថ្ងៃ		20–21
Underwear and Sleepwear	ខោអាវទ្រនាប់និងខោអាវស្លៀកពាក់គេង		22
Jewelry and Cosmetics	គ្រឿងអលង្ការនិងទឹកអប់ប្រេងម្សៅៗតុបតែងខ្លួន		23
Describing Clothes	ពណ៌នាអំពីសំលៀកបំពាក់		24
Describing the Weather	ពណ៌នាអំពីធាតុអាកាស		25
Seasonal Verbs	កិរិយាសព្ទទាក់ទងនឹងរដូវ		26
Houses	ផ្ទះសំបែង		27
The Living Room	បន្ទប់ទទួលភ្ញៀវ		28
The Dining Room	បន្ទប់ទទួលទានបាយ		29
The Kitchen	ផ្ទះបាយ		30
Kitchen Verbs	កិរិយាសព្ទទាក់ទងនឹងផ្ទះបាយ		31
The Bedroom	បន្ទប់គេង		32
The Baby's Room	បន្ទប់កូនង៉ា		33
The Bathroom	បន្ទប់ទឹក		34
The Utility Room	បន្ទប់ដាក់ឥវ៉ាន់		35
A Workshop	រោងជាង, បន្ទប់គ្រឿងជាង		36–37
Housework and Repair Verbs	កិច្ចការក្នុងផ្ទះនិងកិរិយាសព្ទទាក់ទងនឹងការជួសជុល		38
Medical and Dental Care	ការព្យាបាលរោគនិងការថែទាំធ្មេញ		39
Ailments and Injuries	ជម្ងឺនិងរបួស		40
Treatments and Remedies	ការព្យាបាលនិងថ្នាំព្យាបាលរោគ		41
Firefighting and Rescue	ការពន្លត់ភ្លើងឆេះផ្ទះនិងជួយសង្គ្រោះ		42
Crime and Punishment	បទឧក្រិដ្ឋនិងទណ្ឌកម្ម		43
The City	ទីក្រុង		44–45
The U.S. Postal System	ប្រៃសណីយនៅសហរដ្ឋអាមេរិក		46
The Public Library	បណ្ណាល័យសាធារណៈ		47
The Armed Forces	កងប្រដាប់អាវុធ		48
Trucks	រថយន្ត(ធមូតា)		50–51
Bikes	កង់ជិះ		52
Highway Travel	ការធ្វើដំណើរតាមយន្តបថ		53
Public Transportation	យានជំនិះសាធារណៈ		54–55

Air Travel	ការធ្វើដំណើរតាមអាកាស	*Page* 56
Aircraft	អាកាសយាន	57
In Port	នៅផែកប៉ាល់	58
Pleasure Boating	ជិះទូកឬកាណូតលេង	59
Plants and Trees	រុក្ខជាតិគូចធំ	60–61
Simple Animals	សត្វថ្នាក់ទាប(មិនទាន់វិវឌ្ឍ)	62
Insects	សត្វល្អិត	63
Birds	សត្វស្លាប	64
Fish and Reptiles	ត្រីនិងសត្វលូន	65
Mammals I	ថនិកសត្វ (សត្វបំបៅដោះកូន) ភាគ១	66–67
Mammals II	ថនិកសត្វ (សត្វបំបៅដោះកូន) ភាគ២	68–69
Map of the World	ផែនទីពិភពលោក	70–71
The United States of America	សហរដ្ឋអាមេរិក	72–73
The Universe	សាកលលោក	74
The Space Program	កម្មវិធីអាវកាស	75
A Classroom	បន្ទប់រៀន	76
School Verbs	កិរិយាសព្ទទាក់ទងនឹងសាលារៀន	77
A Science Lab	បន្ទប់ពិសោធនវិទ្យាសាស្ត្រ	78
Math	គណិតសាស្ត្រ	79
Energy	ថាមពល	80
Farming and Ranching	ការធ្វើស្រែនិងការចិញ្ចឹមសត្វ	81
Construction	ការសង់សំណង់	82
An Office	ការិយាល័យ	83
Occupations I: Main Street USA	របររកស៊ី១៖នៅតាមទីក្រុងគូចធំ ក្នុងស.រ.អ.	84
Occupations II	របររកស៊ី ២	85
Occupations III	របររកស៊ី ៣	86
Neighborhood Parks	សួនលំហែរជិតៗផ្ទះ	87
Outdoor Activities	សកម្មភាពក្រៅផ្ទះ	88–89
At the Beach	នៅមាត់សមុទ្រ	90–91
Team Sports	កីឡាជាក្រុម	92
Ballfields	កន្លែងលេងបាល់	93
Individual Sports	កីឡាឯកជន	94
Fields and Courses	វាលនិងទីលេងកីឡា	95
Sports Verbs	កិរិយាសព្ទទាក់ទងនឹងកីឡា	96–97
Musical Instruments	គ្រឿងភ្លេង	98
Music, Dance, and Theater	តន្ត្រី, របាំ, និងល្ខោន	99
Electronics and Photography	អេឡិចត្រូនិចហើយនិងការថតរូប	100
Handicrafts	សិប្បកម្ម	101
Prepositions of Description	អាយតនិបាតសំរាប់ពណ៌នា	102
Prepositions of Motion	អាយនិបាតទាក់ទងនឹងចលនា	103
Appendix	បរិសិដ្ឋ	104
Index	បញ្ជីក្រម	105

មនុស្សនិងញាតិសន្តាន

ស្ត្រី, មនុស្សស្រី	**1.** woman		កូន	**7.** children
មនុស្សប្រុស	**2.** man		ក្មេងប្រុស	**8.** boy
ប្ដី	**3.** husband		ក្មេងស្រី	**9.** girl
ប្រពន្ធ	**4.** wife		ជីដូនជីតា	**10.** grandparents
កូនង៉ែត, ទារក	**5.** baby		ចៅស្រី	**11.** granddaughter
និពុកម្ដាយ	**6.** parents		ចៅប្រុស	**12.** grandson

Virginia (Taylor) Bates ①
Joseph Bates ②
Ellen (Dalton) Bates
Peter Bates ③
Elizabeth (Bates) Jones ④
Tom Jones ⑤
Helen Jones ⑥
Joan Bates ⑦
Betty (Collins) Jones ⑧
Jack Jones ⑨
Jane (Jones) Carter ⑩
Tom Carter ⑪
Mary (Jones) Smith
Bob Smith ⑫
Jimmy Lee Jones ⑬
Peg Carter ⑭
Sally Ann Smith ⑮
Tim Smith ⑯

គ្រួសាររបស់លោកស្រីម៉ារីស្មីធ

Mary Smith's Family

ជីដូន	**1.** grandmother	
ជីតា	**2.** grandfather	
ពូ, មា, ធំ, អ៊ំ	**3.** uncle	
ម្តាយ	**4.** mother	
ឪពុក	**5.** father	
ម្តាយមីង, ម្តាយធំ	**6.** aunt	
បងប្អូនជីដូនមួយ	**7.** cousin	
បងថ្លៃស្រី, ប្អូនថ្លៃស្រី	**8.** sister-in-law	

បងប្រុស, ប្អូនប្រុស	**9.** brother
បងស្រី, ប្អូនស្រី	**10.** sister
បងថ្លៃប្រុស, ប្អូនថ្លៃប្រុស	**11.** brother-in-law
ប្តី	**12.** husband
ក្មួយប្រុស	**13.** nephew
ក្មួយស្រី	**14.** niece
កូនស្រី	**15.** daughter
កូនប្រុស	**16.** son

ខ្លួនមនុស្ស

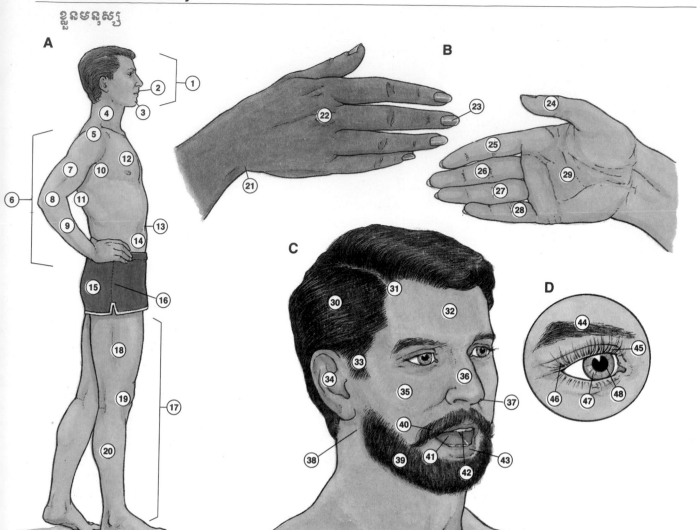

ដងខ្លួន	A. The Body		
មុខ	1. face		
មាត់	2. mouth		
ចង្កា	3. chin		
ក	4. neck		
ស្មា	5. shoulder		
ដៃ	6. arm		
ដើមដៃ	7. upper arm		
កែងដៃ	8. elbow		
កំភួនដៃ	9. forearm		
ក្លៀក	10. armpit		
ខ្នង	11. back		
ទ្រូង	12. chest		
ចង្កេះ	13. waist		
ពោះ	14. abdomen		
គូទ	15. buttocks		

ត្រគាក	16. hip
ជើង	17. leg
ភ្លៅ	18. thigh
ជង្គង់	19. knee
កំភួនជើង	20. calf

ដៃ	B. The Hand
កដៃ	21. wrist
គន្លាក់ម្រាមដៃ	22. knuckle
ក្រចកដៃ	23. fingernail
មេដៃ	24. thumb
ចង្អុលដៃ	25. (index) finger
ចង្អុលដៃកណ្ដាល	26. middle finger
នាងដៃ	27. ring finger
កូនដៃ	28. little finger
បាតដៃ	29. palm

ក្បាល	C. The Head
សក់	30. hair
វៃកចំហៀង	31. part
ថ្ងាស	32. forehead
ជើងសក់ (ត្រង់ថ្ពាល់)	33. sideburn
ត្រចៀក	34. ear
ថ្ពាល់	35. cheek
ច្រមុះ	36. nose
រន្ធច្រមុះ	37. nostril
ថ្គាម	38. jaw
ពុកចង្កា	39. beard
ពុកមាត់	40. mustache
អណ្ដាត	41. tongue
ធ្មេញ	42. tooth
បបូរមាត់	43. lip

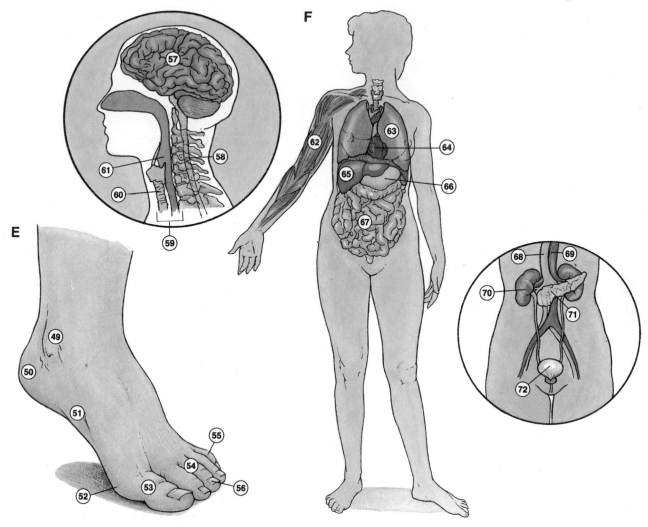

វ៉ាភ្នែក	**D. The Eye**		សរីរាង្គក្នុងខ្លួន	**F. The Internal Organs**
ចិញ្ចើម	**44.** eyebrow		ខួរក្បាល	**57.** brain
ត្របកភ្នែក	**45.** eyelid		សរសៃក្នុងឆ្អឹងខ្នង	**58.** spinal cord
រោមភ្នែក	**46.** eyelashes		បំពង់ក	**59.** throat
ប្រស្រីភ្នែក	**47.** iris		បំពង់ខ្យល់	**60.** windpipe
រន្ធប្រស្រី	**48.** pupil		បំពង់អាហារ	**61.** esophagus
			សាច់ដុំ	**62.** muscle
			សួត	**63.** lung
ជើង(ចាប់ពីកជើងនៅក្រោម)	**E. The Foot**		បេះដូង	**64.** heart
កជើង	**49.** ankle		ថ្លើម	**65.** liver
កែងជើង	**50.** heel		ក្រពះ	**66.** stomach
ខ្នងជើង	**51.** instep		ពោះវៀន	**67.** intestines
កន្លែងត្រង់ខ្នងជើងជាប់និងមេជើង	**52.** ball		សរសៃឈាមខ្ចៅ	**68.** vein
មេជើង	**53.** big toe		សរសៃឈាមក្រហម	**69.** artery
ម្រាមជើង	**54.** toe		តម្រងមូត្រ, វ៉ក្កៈ	**70.** kidney
កូនជើង	**55.** little toe		លំពែង	**71.** pancreas
ក្រចកជើង	**56.** toenail		ក្រពះនោម	**72.** bladder

បន្លែ

ស្ទ្វេផ្កាស (មួយផ្ទុំ)	1. (head of) cauliflower	អាទីឆ្លុក	11. artichoke
ស្ទ្វេផ្កាខ្ចៀវ	2. broccoli	(ផ្លែ) ពោត	12. (ear of) corn
ស្ទ្វេក្តោប	3. cabbage	បណ្តូល	a. cob
កូនស្ទ្វេក្តោប	4. brussels sprouts	សណ្តែកអង្កុយ	13. kidney bean(s)
ក្រេះសុង	5. watercress	សណ្តែកអង្កុយខ្មៅ	14. black bean(s)
សាឡាត់	6. lettuce	សណ្តែកកួ	15. string bean(s)
អេស្ការ៉ូល	7. escarole	សណ្តែកអង្កុយម្យ៉ាង	16. lima bean(s)
ស្ពីណាត់	8. spinach	សណ្តែកបារាំង	17. pea(s)
តិណទេសប្រើជាគ្រឿងសម្ល ឬ ថ្នាំ	9. herb(s)	ក្រ	a. pod
សែលឡ្យូរី	10. celery	អាស្ប៉ារ៉ាហ្គុស, ទំពាំងបារាំង	18. asparagus

បេ៉ងប៉ោះ	**19.** tomato(es)		ល្ពៅ	**26.** pumpkin
ត្រសក់	**20.** cucumber(s)		ហ្ស៊ូគីនី	**27.** zucchini
ត្រប់	**21.** eggplant		ល្ពៅម្យ៉ាងតូចៗ	**28.** acorn squash
ម្ទេស	**22.** pepper(s)		រ៉ាឌី	**29.** radish(es)
ដំឡូងបារាំង	**23.** potato(es)		ផ្សិត	**30.** mushroom(s)
ដំឡូងជ្វា	**24.** yam		ខ្ទឹមបារាំង	**31.** onion(s)
ខ្ទឹមស	**25.** garlic		ការ៉ុត	**32.** carrot(s)
កំពីស	**a.** clove		បែតតីរ៉ាវ	**33.** beet(s)
			ឆៃថាវបារាំង	**34.** turnip

ទំពាំងបាយជួរ (មួយចង្កោម)	**1.**	(a bunch of) grapes
ប៉ោម	**2.**	apple
ទង		**a.** stem
បណ្ដូល		**b.** core
ដូង	**3.**	coconut
ម្នាស់	**4.**	pineapple
ស្វាយ	**5.**	mango
ល្ហុង	**6.**	papaya

Khmer		**Citrus Fruits**
ក្រូច		
ក្រូចថ្លុងអាមេរិកាំង	**7.**	grapefruit
ក្រូចពោធិសាត់	**8.**	orange
ខ្ញែប		**a.** section
សំបក		**b.** rind
គ្រាប់		**c.** seed
ក្រូចឆ្មារលឿង	**9.**	lemon
ក្រូចឆ្មារ	**10.**	lime

Khmer		**Berries**
ផ្លែឈើផ្សេងៗ		
ហ្គូហ្គូបែរី	**11.**	gooseberries
ប្ល៉ាក់បែរី	**12.**	blackberries
ក្រានបែរី	**13.**	cranberries
ប្លូបែរី	**14.**	blueberries
ស្ត្រប៊ែរី	**15.**	strawberry
រ៉ាស់បែរី	**16.**	raspberries
ណិចតារ៊ីន	**17.**	nectarine
ព័រ	**18.**	pear

សិរីហ្សី	**19.** cherries	ទំពាំងបាយជូរក្រៀម	**24.** raisin(s)	អាម៉ង់, អាម៉ុន	**31.** almond(s)
ចេក (មួយស្និត)	**20.** (a bunch of) bananas	អាប្រ៊ីកុតក្រៀម	**25.** apricot	គ្រាប់ឆិសណាណិត	**32.** chestnut(s)
សំបក	**a.** peel	ឪឡឹកក្រៀម	**26.** watermelon	អាវ៉ូកាដូ	**33.** avocado
				ផ្លែផ្លុំ	**34.** plum

ផ្លែឈើក្រៀម	**Dried Fruits**	ក្រាប់ (ផ្លែឈើដែលគេឧទ្ធលទាន)	**Nuts**	ត្រសក់ស្រូវហុនណេខូ	**35.** honeydew melon
ផ្លែល្វាបារាំងក្រៀម	**21.** fig	គ្រាប់ស្វាយចន្ទី	**27.** cashew(s)	ត្រសក់ស្រូវកង់តីឡុប	**36.** cantaloupe
ផ្លែព្រូនក្រៀម	**22.** prune	សណ្តែកដី	**28.** peanut(s)	ប៉ែស	**37.** peach
ល្មើ	**23.** date	គ្រាប់វល់ណាណិត	**29.** walnut(s)	គ្រាប់	**a.** pit
		គ្រាប់ហេបប្រ៊ីលណាណិត	**30.** hazelnut(s)	សំបក	**b.** skin

សាច់ (គោ ជ្រូក ៩ល៩), សាច់ មាន់ទា និងមច្ឆបសមុទ្រ

A

សាច់ គោ, ជ្រូក ៩ល៩	**A. Meat**	សាច់ជ្រូកចងជាដុំសំរាប់យកទៅដុតក្នុងឡ	**8. roast**
សាច់គោ	**1. beef**	សាច់ជាប់ឆ្អឹងជំនីរ	**9. chops**
សាច់គោកិន	**2. ground beef**	ឆ្អឹងជំនីរ	**10. spare ribs**
សាច់គោកាត់ជាដុំសំរាប់ដុត	**3. roast**	បេកុន, សាច់បីជាន់ហាន់ជាបន្ទះស្ដើងៗ	**11. bacon**
សាច់គោកាត់ជាដុំតូចៗ	**4. stewing meat**	សាច់ភ្លៅ (ភ្លៅជ្រូកខាងក្រោយ)	**12. ham**
ស្ទេក	**5. steak**	សាច់ចៀម	**13. lamb**
សាច់ជ្រូក	**6. pork**	ភ្លៅ	**14. leg**
សាច់ក្រកអាមេរិកាំង	**7. sausage**	សាច់ជាប់ឆ្អឹងជំនីរ	**15. chops**

សាច់, មាន់-ទា បសុ, និង មូបសមុទ្រ

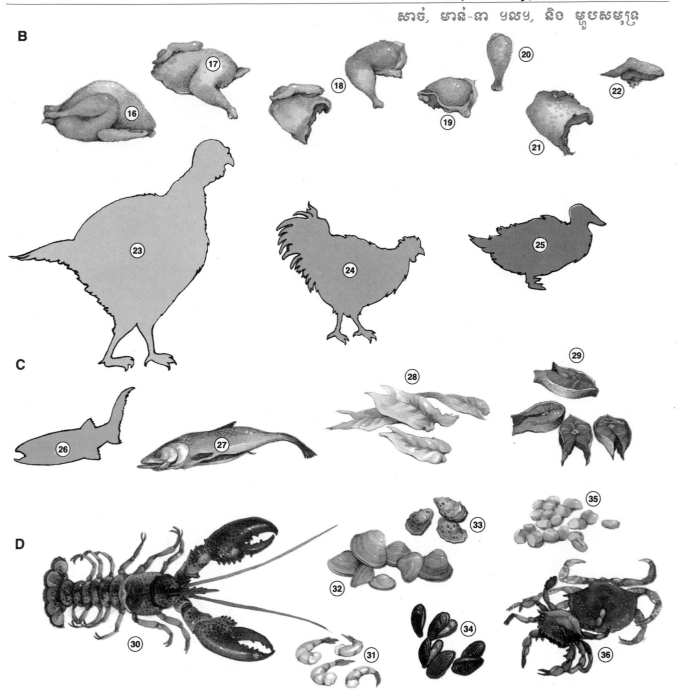

សាច់, មាន់, ទា បសុ	**B. Poultry**			
(មាន់) ទាំងមូល	**16.** whole (chicken)	មាន់ឫាវាំង	**23.** turkey	សត្វជំពូកសាសខ្លួងគ្រំបឡូង	**D. Shellfish**
ពុះជាពីរ	**17.** split	មាន់	**24.** chicken	បង្កង (សមុទ្រ)	**30.** lobster
កាត់ជាបួន	**18.** quarter	ទា	**25.** duck	ព្រាន	**31.** shrimp
ភ្លៅ	**19.** thigh			លាស	**32.** clam(s)
ដើង	**20.** leg	មូបសមុទ្រ	**C. Seafood**	ខ្យងស្ងិត, នាវ	**33.** oyster(s)
ទ្រូង	**21.** breast	ត្រី	**26.** fish	ចំពុះទា	**34.** mussel(s)
ស្លាប	**22.** wing	ទាំងមូល	**27.** whole	ស្កាឡុប, គ្រំសមុទ្រ (ម្យ៉ាង)	**35.** scallop(s)
		សាច់ពនះ	**28.** filet	ក្តាម	**36.** crab(s)
		ត្រីកាត់ជាកង់ៗ	**29.** steak		

ប្រដាប់ច្រក ឬ ដាក់ទុក, ចំនួន, និងប្រាក់កាស

កាតុង, ប្រអប់	**1.** carton			ដុំ	**7.** loaf
ប្រដាប់ច្រក ឬដាក់ទុក	**2.** container			កញ្ចប់	**8.** bag
ផប	**3.** bottle			កែវ, ក្រឡ	**9.** jar
ប្រអប់, កញ្ចប់	**4.** package			កំប៉ុង	**10.** can
ដុំ	**5.** stick			ដុំ	**11.** roll
ធុង, ចាំង	**6.** tub				

ប្រអប់	**12.** box	ថែង	**19.** cup	ប្រាក់កាស, លុយ	**Money**
ឌប ឬ កំប៉ុងប្រាំមួយស្រោក់ជាប់គ្នា	**13.** six-pack	កែវ	**20.** glass	ក្រដាសប្រាក់ដុល្លារ	**25.** dollar bills
ប្រដាប់ឬមបញ្ចេញ	**14.** pump	ចំណិត	**21.** slice	កាក់	**26.** coins
ប្រអប់ច្របាច់, ទូប	**15.** tube	ជ្រុង, ដុំ	**22.** piece	សេន	**27.** penny
កញ្ចប់	**16.** pack	ចាន	**23.** bowl	ប្រាំសេន	**28.** nickel
កញ្ចប់, ប្រអប់	**17.** book	កំប៉ុងបាញ់	**24.** spray can	ដប់សេន, មួយកាក់	**29.** dime
ដុំ	**18.** bar			ម្ភៃប្រាំសេន	**30.** quarter

កន្លែងលក់មួប

កន្លែងលក់មួបឆ្អិនស្រេច	**1.** deli counter		កន្ត្រក	**8.** shopping basket
មួបកក	**2.** frozen foods		បន្លែផ្លែឈើ	**9.** produce
ម៉ាស៊ីនធ្វើឱ្យកក	**3.** freezer		ច្រកដើរ	**10.** aisle
មួបធ្វើអំពីទឹកដោះគោ	**4.** dairy products		នំចំណីដុតក្នុងឡ	**11.** baked goods
ទឹកដោះគោ	**5.** milk		នំប៉័ង	**12.** bread
ធ្នើរ	**6.** shelf		មួបកំប៉ុង	**13.** canned goods
ជញ្ជីង	**7.** scale		ភេសជ្ជៈ	**14.** beverages

FISH MEAT POULTRY

EXPRESS LANE 10 ITEMS OR LESS

គ្រឿងប្រើប្រាស់ក្នុងផ្ទះ	**15.** household items	អ្នកគិតលុយ	**22.** cashier
ធុង	**16.** bin	ប្រដាប់ដាក់ទំនិញឲ្យទៅខ្លួនឯង	**23.** conveyor belt
អ្នកទិញ	**17.** customer	មួបអាហារ	**24.** groceries
គ្រឿងបរិភោគកំសាន្ត	**18.** snacks	កញ្ចប់ដាក់ឥវ៉ាន់	**25.** bag
រទេះដាក់ឥវ៉ាន់	**19.** shopping cart	កន្លែងគិតលុយ	**26.** checkout counter
រ៉ឺស៊ីប, បង្កាន់ដៃ	**20.** receipt	ឈែក, សែក	**27.** check
ម៉ាស៊ីនគិតលុយ	**21.** cash register		

Family Restaurant and Cocktail Lounge

ភោជនីយដ្ឋានគ្រួសារ និង កន្លែងញ៉ាំស្រាក់សាន្ត

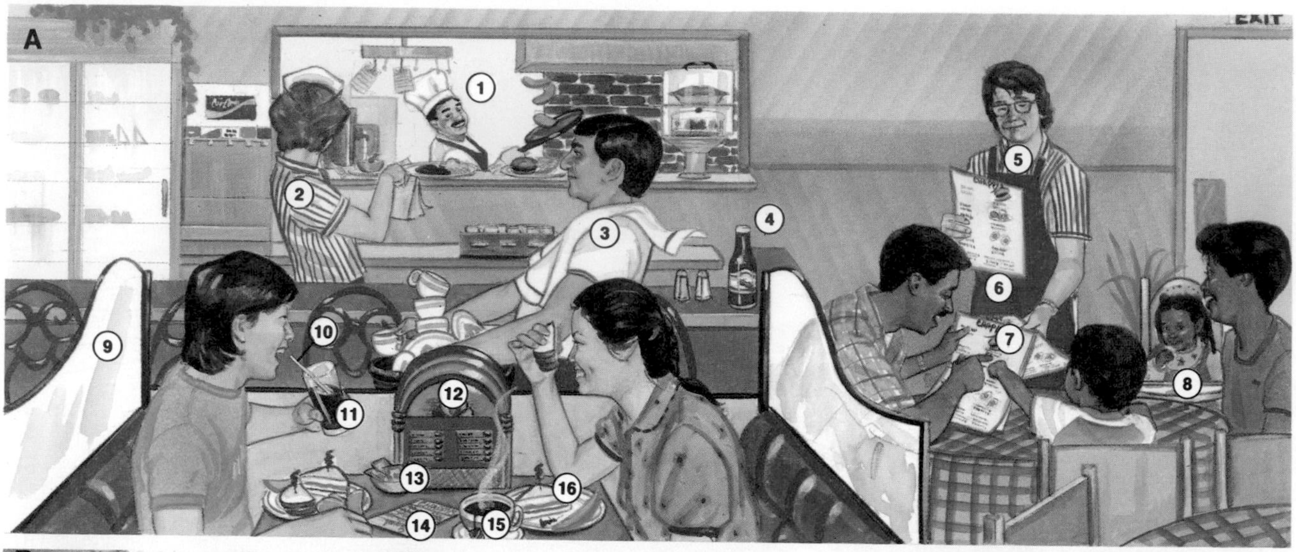

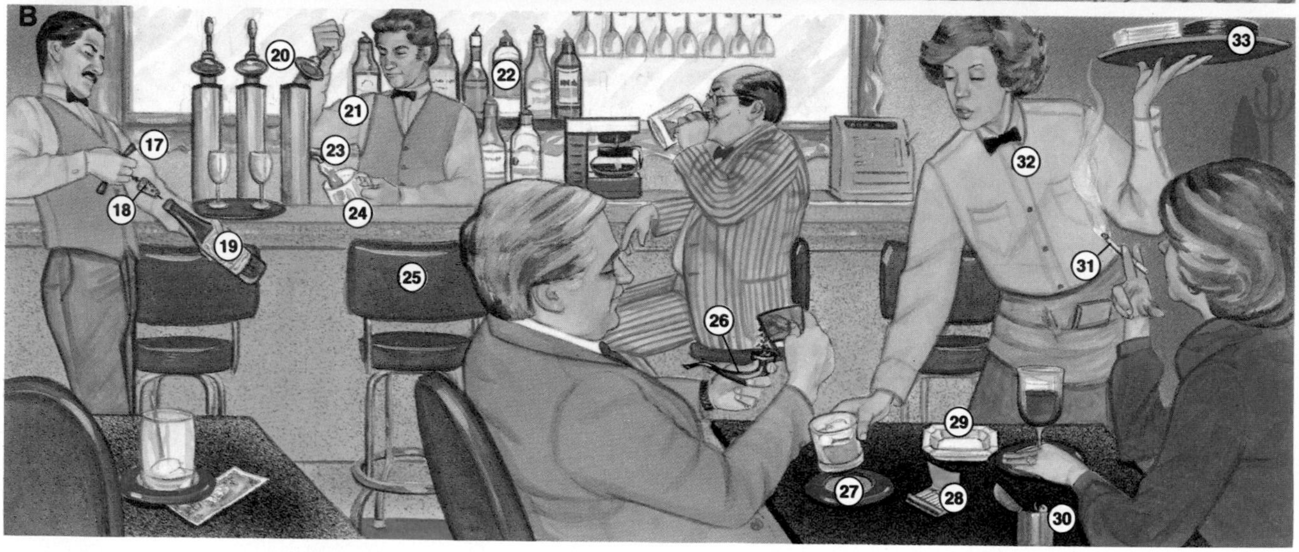

ភោជនីយដ្ឋានគ្រួសារ A. Family Restaurant

- អ្នកធ្វើបាយ **1.** cook
- អ្នកបំរើស្រី **2.** waitress
- ជំនួយអ្នកបំរើ **3.** busboy
- ទឹកប៉េងប៉ោះ, ខិតឈឹប **4.** ketchup
- អ្នកបំរើប្រុស **5.** waiter
- ប្រដាប់ពាក់ការពារខោអាវ **6.** apron
- បញ្ជីឈ្មោះម្ហូប **7.** menu
- កៅអីកូនក្មេង **8.** high chair
- កន្លែងអង្គុយឃាំងដាច់គ្នា **9.** booth
- បំពង់បឺត **10.** straw
- ភេសជ្ជៈឥតមានស្រា **11.** soft drink
- ប្រដាប់ចាក់ភ្លេងដាក់លុយ **12.** jukebox
- ស្ករ (កញ្ចប់) **13.** sugar (packet)
- ក្រដាសគិតលុយ **14.** check
- តែ **15.** tea
- សាន់វិច **16.** sandwich

កន្លែងញ៉ាំស្រាក់សាន្ត B. Cocktail Lounge

- ប្រដាប់បើកឆ្នុកដប **17.** corkscrew
- ឆ្នុកដប **18.** cork
- ស្រាទំពាំងបាយជូរ **19.** wine
- ប្រដាប់បូមភេសជ្ជៈ **20.** tap
- អ្នកលាយស្រា **21.** bartender
- ស្រា (ដប) **22.** liquor (bottle)
- ប៊ីយែរ **23.** beer
- កន្លែងអង្គុយញ៉ាំស្រា **24.** bar
- កៅអីខ្ពស់ **25.** bar stool
- ខ្សៀ **26.** pipe
- ទ្រនាប់កែវ **27.** coaster
- (ប្រអប់) ឈើគូស **28.** (book of) matches
- ចានគោះបារី **29.** ashtray
- ដែកកេះ **30.** lighter
- បារី **31.** cigarette
- ស្រីបំរើស្រា **32.** cocktail waitress
- ថាស, ស្លក **33.** tray

កិរិយាសព្ទនាក់ទងនឹងភោជនីយដ្ឋាន

ញ៉ាំ, ស៊ី, ទទួលទាន, បរិភោគ	**1.** eat	រៀបតុ, រៀបចានស្លាបព្រា (លើតុ)	**8.** set (the table)
ញ៉ាំ, ផឹក	**2.** drink	អោយ,ឲ្យ	**9.** give
យកមកឲ្យ, បម្រើ	**3.** serve	យក	**10.** take
ចំអិន, ធ្វើម្ហូប	**4.** cook	ប៉ាត, លាប	**11.** spread
ហៅ	**5.** order	កាន់	**12.** hold
យកចេញ	**6.** clear	អុជ	**13.** light
ចេញលុយ, បង់	**7.** pay	ធ្វើឲ្យខ្លោច, ខ្លោច	**14.** burn

មូបសាមញ្ញភ្លិនស្រាប់

មូតាត	**1.** mustard	ដាក់សាច់)	**13.** tossed salad	នំស្ត្រូបែរីសតកេក	**26.** strawberry shortcake
ហុតដក	**2.** hot dog	ស៊ុបសាច់គោ, រាហ្គូ	**14.** beef stew	នំបីស្គី	**27.** biscuit
សណ្ណែកអុយចំអិនក្នុងឡ	**3.** baked beans	សាច់ជ្រកជាប់ឆ្អឹងជំនីរច្បៀន	**15.** pork chops	ដំឡូងច្បៀន	**28.** french fries
ប៉ុតេតូឈិប	**4.** potato chips	បន្លែច្រើនមុខលាយគ្នា	**16.** mixed vegetables	មាន់ច្បៀន	**29.** fried chicken
ប៉ាន់ខេក	**5.** pancakes	ដំឡូងស្មោះកិន	**17.** mashed potatoes	ពិតហ្សា	**30.** pizza
ស៊ីរ៉ូ	**6.** syrup	ប៊ីរ	**18.** butter	ចេល្លើ	**31.** jelly
នំប៉័ង	**7.** bun	នំប៉័ងមូលៗតូចៗ	**19.** roll	ពងមាន់ច្បៀនឥតប្រែ	**32.** (sunnyside-up) egg
ត្រសក់ជ្រក់	**8.** pickle	ដំឡូងដុតដុតឡ	**20.** baked potato	សាច់ជ្រកបន្ទះស្ដើងៗ,	**33.** bacon
ហាំប៊ឺហ្គឺរ	**9.** hamburger	ស្ដេក	**21.** steak	បេកុន	
ស្ប៉ាហ្គេទី	**10.** spaghetti	គុកគី	**22.** cookie	នំប៉័ងអាំង	**34.** toast
សាច់លញ (ជាដុំ)	**11.** meatballs	ការេ៉មដាក់ផ្លែឈើ	**23.** sundae	ការហេ	**35.** coffee
ទឹកសាឡាត់ សាឡាត់	**12.** salad dressing	តាកូ	**24.** taco	នំសំរាប់ប៉ាត់ការេ៉ម	**36.** ice cream cone
(មានបន្លែលាយគ្រប់មុខឥតមាន)		ឡុកសម័យ, ផៃយ៉ចិន	**25.** egg roll		

សំលេវិកបំពាក់ក្រៅផ្ទះ

ស្រោមដៃ	1. gloves	ខោរីប	14. tights
កាតិប	2. cap	ប៉ាតាំង, ស្បែក	15. ice skates
អាវហ្គាណែល	3. flannel shirt	កាតិបពាក់លេងស្គី	16. ski cap
សំពាយ	4. backpack	អាវហ្គាក់កែត	17. jacket
អាវការពារខ្យល់	5. windbreaker	មួក	18. hat
ខោកូវបោយ	6. (blue) jeans	កន្សែងរុំក	19. scarf
អាវយឺតកមួល	7. (crewneck) sweater	អាវរងា	20. overcoat
អាវផាកា, អាវរងាក្រាស់ម្ប៉ៀង	8. parka	ស្បែកជើងកវែង, ប៊ុត	21. boots
ស្បែកជើងដើរព្រៃ	9. hiking boots	បេរេ	22. beret
ស្រោមត្រចៀក	10. earmuffs	អាវយឺតកស្រួច	23. (V-neck) sweater
ស្រោមដៃគ្មានម្រាម	11. mittens	អាវធំ	24. coat
អាវញ្ញាត់ស្វាបសត្វ	12. down vest	ស្បែកជើងកវែងពាក់ពេលភ្លៀង	25. rain boots
អាវយឺតពណ្លាក់ក	13. (turtleneck) sweater		

សំលៀកបំពាក់ប្រចាំថ្ងៃ

កអាវ	**1.**	lapel
អាវត្រួសរហ្សេ	**2.**	blazer
ឡេវ	**3.**	button
ខោជើងវែង	**4.**	slacks
កែងស្បែកជើង	**5.**	heel
បាតស្បែកជើង	**6.**	sole
ខ្សែស្បែកជើង	**7.**	shoelace
អាវយឺតកីឡាដៃវែង	**8.**	sweatshirt
កាបូប	**9.**	wallet
ខោកីឡាជើងវែង	**10.**	sweatpants
ស្បែកជើងបាតា	**11.**	sneakers
ឆ្នូតញើស	**12.**	sweatband
អាវវៀលក្លៀក	**13.**	tank top

ខោខ្លី	**14.**	shorts
អាវដៃវែង	**15.**	long sleeve
ខ្សែក្រវាត់	**16.**	belt
ក្បាលខ្សែក្រវាត់	**17.**	buckle
ស្បៀង, ថង់	**18.**	shopping bag
ស្បែកជើងសង្ក្រែក	**19.**	sandal
កអាវ	**20.**	collar
អាវដៃខ្លី	**21.**	short sleeve
អាវម៉ាដាម, រៀម	**22.**	dress
កាបូប	**23.**	purse
ឆ័ត្រ	**24.**	umbrella
ស្បែកជើងកែងចោត	**25.**	(high) heels

សំលៀកបំពាក់ប្រចាំថ្ងៃ

អារយ៉ឺតរលុងមានឡេ្យវខាងមុខ	**26.** cardigan		អារភ្លៀង	**38.** raincoat
ខោគ័រដ៍រវ័យ	**27.** (corduroy) pants		អារកាក់ (ពាក់ជាមួយអារធំ)	**39.** vest
មួកដែក	**28.** hard hat		អារធំមានទាំងអារកាក់	**40.** three-piece suit
អារយ៉ឺតស្លើងៗ	**29.** T-shirt		ហោប៉ៅ	**41.** pocket
ខោរៀម (សំរាប់ពាក់ធ្វើការ)	**30.** overalls		ស្បែកជើងយួបឥតមានខ្សែ	**42.** loafer
ប្រដាប់ដាក់បាយទៅធ្វើការ	**31.** lunch box		មួកមានរប៉ាំងមុខ	**43.** cap
ស្បែកជើងពាក់ធ្វើការ	**32.** (construction) boots		វ៉ែនតា	**44.** glasses
បហ្រាក់កែត, អារពាក់ពីក្រៅ	**33.** jacket		ឯកសណ្ឋាន	**45.** uniform
អារស្រី	**34.** blouse		អារស៊ីមីបហ្ស៍	**46.** shirt
កាប៊ូបស្ពាយ	**35.** (shoulder) bag		ក្រវ៉ាត់ក	**47.** tie
សំពត់	**36.** skirt		កាសែត, សារពត៌មាន	**48.** newspaper
កាតាប	**37.** briefcase		ស្បែកជើង	**49.** shoe

ខោអាវទ្រនាប់និងខោអាវស្លៀកពាក់គេង

អាវទ្រនាប់	**1.** undershirt	សំពត់ទ្រនាប់ខ្លី	**8.** half slip	ប្រដាប់ស្ពៀករឹបត្រគាក	**15.** girdle
ខោស្លាប់ភ្លៅ	**2.** boxer shorts	អាវទ្រនាប់វែង	**9.** camisole	ស្រោមជើងវែង, បា	**16.** knee socks
ខោទ្រនាប់	**3.** underpants	អាវនិងសំពត់ទ្រនាប់ជាប់គ្នា	**10.** full slip	ស្រោមជើង	**17.** socks
ខោទ្រនាប់អ្នកកម្សួលកម្ម	**4.** athletic supporter	ខោទ្រនាប់បីគីនី	**11.** (bikini) panties	ស្បែកជើងពាក់ក្នុងផ្ទះ	**18.** slippers
ស្រោមជើងស្ពៀកដួចខោ (ស្ត្រី)	**5.** pantyhose	ខោទ្រនាប់រឹប	**12.** briefs	ភិសាម៉ា	**19.** pajamas
ស្រោមជើង	**6.** stockings	អាវទ្រនាប់ស្ត្រី	**13.** bra(ssiere)	អាវពាក់ទៅបន្ទប់ទឹក	**20.** bathrobe
(ស្ត្រី), ស្រោមជើងនីឡុង		ខ្សែក្រវាត់ពាក់ជាមួយស្រោមជើងនីឡុង	**14.** garter belt	អៀមពាក់គេង	**21.** nightgown
ខោអាវស្ពៀកពីក្នុងកំឡុងរងា	**7.** long johns				

គ្រឿងអលង្ការ និងគ្រឿងប្រដាប់តែងខ្លួន

គ្រឿងអលង្ការ	A. Jewelry		មូលខ្លាស់ក្រវ៉ាត់	13. tie pin	ផ្លែកាំបិតការពុកមាត់	23. razor blades
ក្រវិល, ទំហុ	1. earrings		ដង្កៀបខ្លាស់ក្រវ៉ាត់	14. tie clip	ប្រដាប់ខាត់ក្រចក	24. emery board
ចិញ្ចៀន	2. ring(s)		ក្រវិលគីប	15. clip-on earring	ថ្នាំលាបក្រចក	25. nail polish
ចិញ្ចៀនភ្ជាប់ពាក្យ	3. engagement ring		ក្រវិលសំរាប់ត្រចៀកចោះ	16. pierced earring	ខ្មៅដៃគូសចិញ្ចើម	26. eyebrow pencil
ចិញ្ចៀនអាពាហ៍ពិពាហ៍	4. wedding ring		ទម្ពក់	17. clasp	ទឹកអប់	27. perfume
ខ្សែមាស	5. chain		ផ្លែទំហុ	18. post	ថ្នាំលាបរោមភ្នែក, ម៉ាស្ការ៉ា	28. mascara
ខ្សែក	6. necklace		ប្រដាប់មូលភ្ជាប់ទំហុទៅនឹងត្រចៀក	19. back	ក្រែមលាបបូរមាត់	29. lipstick
(ខ្សែ) អង្កាំ	7. (strand of) beads				ថ្នាំលាបគ្របភ្នែក	30. eye shadow
ក្រង្កាស់ខ្លាស់	8. pin		គ្រឿងសំអិតសំអាងខ្លួន		ប្រដាប់កាត់ក្រចក	31. nail clippers
ខ្សែដៃ	9. bracelet			B. Toiletries	ថ្នាំក្រហម	32. blush
នាឡិកា	10. watch			and Makeup	(សំរាប់ផាត់ថ្ពាល់)	
ខ្សែនាឡិកា	11. watchband		ប្រដាប់ការពុកមាត់	20. razor	ថ្នាំគូរភ្នែក	33. eyeliner
ឡេវអាវកដៃនុប	12. cuff links		ទឹកអប់សំរាប់លាបក្រោយពេលការពុកមាត់	21. after-shave lotion		
			សាប៊ូការពុកមាត់	22. shaving cream		

ពណ៌នាអំពីសំលៀកបំពាក់

ខ្លី	1. short	មិនស្រអាប់	9. light	ឆ្នូត	17. striped
វែង	2. long	ស្រអាប់	10. dark	ក្រឡាឈើត្រង់	18. checked
រឹប, តឹង, ចង្អៀត	3. tight	ខ្ពស់	11. high	មានផ្កាមូលៗ (ពាសពេញ)	19. polka dot
ទូលាយ	4. loose	ទាប	12. low	លាត	20. solid
ក្រខ្វក់	5. dirty	ថ្មី	13. new	ផ្កា, បោះពុម្ព	21. print
ស្អាត	6. clean	ចាស់	14. old	ឆ្នូតខ្វែងគ្នា	22. plaid
តូច	7. small	បើក, ចំហ	15. open		
ធំ	8. big	បិទ	16. closed		

ពណ៌នាអំពីធាតុអាកាស

ភ្លៀង, មានភ្លៀង	**1.** rainy		ត្រជាក់បន្តិច	**9.** cool
មានពពកច្រើន	**2.** cloudy		ត្រជាក់	**10.** cold
ធ្លាក់ទឹកកក	**3.** snowy		ដែលកក, ត្រជាក់ខ្លាំង	**11.** freezing
ថ្ងៃ, មានថ្ងៃល្អ	**4.** sunny		ចុះអ័ព្រ	**12.** foggy
ទែរម៉ូម៉ែត្រ	**5.** thermometer		ខ្យល់ខ្លាំង	**13.** windy
កំដៅ	**6.** temperature		មិនសើម, ស្ងួត	**14.** dry
ក្ដៅ	**7.** hot		សើម	**15.** wet
ក្ដៅបន្តិចៗ, ក្ដៅឧណ្ហៗ	**8.** warm		ដែលមានទឹកកកកក	**16.** icy

ភិរិយាសព្ទនាក់ទងនឹងរដូវ

រដូវផ្ការីក, រដូវស្លឹកឈើលាស់	Spring	រដូវក្តៅ	Summer	រដូវស្លឹកឈើជ្រុះ	Fall	រដូវរងា, រដូវត្រជាក់	Winter
លាបថ្នាំ	1. paint	ស្រោចទឹក	5. water	បំពេញ	9. fill	ជីក, ចូក, ឈូស	13. shovel
សំអាត	2. clean	កាត់ស្មៅ	6. mow	រាស់	10. rake	បាចដីខ្សាច់	14. sand
ជីក	3. dig	បេះ	7. pick	ពុះ	11. chop	កោស, ឈូស	15. scrape
ដាំ	4. plant	តម្រឹម, ច្រិប	8. trim	រុញ	12. push	លី, សែង	16. carry

ផ្ទះ

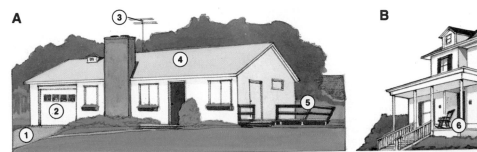

ផ្ទះតម្រួម, ផ្ទះមានតែមួយជាន់	**A. Ranch House**	ឆ្នាក្រោយផ្ទះ	**C. The Backyard**	ធ្យូងសំរាប់អាំងសាច់	**23.** charcoal briquettes
		១ **10.** gutter		កៅអីអង្គុយសណ្ដូក	**24.** lounge chair
ផ្លូវឡានចូល	**1.** driveway	អម្រ៉ិង **11.** hammock		ម៉ាស៊ីនអារឈើ, រណារមានម៉ាស៊ីន	**25.** power saw
ហ្គារ៉ាស, យានដ្ឋាន	**2.** garage	ម៉ាស៊ីនកាត់ស្មៅ **12.** lawn mower		ស្រោមដៃពាក់ធ្វើការ	**26.** work gloves
អង់តែនទូរទស្សន៍	**3.** TV antenna	ប្រដាប់បាញ់ទឹកស្រោចស្មៅ **13.** sprinkler		ស្លាបព្រាច្រកដី	**27.** trowel
ដំបូល	**4.** roof	បំពង់ទឹក **14.** garden hose		កន្លែងដាក់ប្រដាប់ប្រដាឆ្សេងៗ	**28.** toolshed
រានហាល	**5.** deck	ស្មៅ **15.** grass		ម៉ាស៊ីនកាត់របងក្នុងលើ	**29.** hedge clippers
		ធុងស្រោចផ្កា **16.** watering can		រនាស់	**30.** rake
ផ្ទះពីរជាន់ (មានជណ្ដើរ)	**B. Colonial-style House**	រានហាលជាប់នឹងដី **17.** patio		ប៉ែល	**31.** shovel
		បំពង់បង្ហូរទឹក **18.** drainpipe		រទេះរុញកង់មួយ (សំរាប់ដឹកជញ្ជូន)	**32.** wheelbarrow
នហាល, ហោណាំង, ហាប់, ឈ្យ	**6.** porch	សំណាញ់ **19.** screen			
បង្អួច	**7.** window	ស្រោមដៃ **20.** mitt			
បង្ហ្រា (បង្អួច)	**8.** shutter	វែក, វែកដា **21.** spatula			
បំពង់ផ្សែង	**9.** chimney	ចង្ក្រានអាំងសាច់ **22.** grill			

បន្ទប់ទទួលភ្ញៀវ

ដង្ហាល់ពិដាន	**1.** ceiling fan	កៅអីទម្រេត	**16.** recliner
ពិដាន	**2.** ceiling	ប្រដាប់បញ្ជាអេឡិចត្រូនិច	**17.** remote control
ជញ្ជាំង	**3.** wall	ទីវី, ទេរវ, ទូរទស្សន៍	**18.** television
ក្រប	**4.** frame	ទូដាក់ការក្នុងបន្ទប់ទទួលភ្ញៀវ	**19.** wall unit
គំនូរ	**5.** painting	គ្រឿងស្ទេរេអូ	**20.** stereo system
ថូ	**6.** vase	អូប៉ាល៌រ	**21.** speaker
យ្យងដើងក្រានគ្រូ	**7.** mantel	ទូដាក់សៀវភៅ	**22.** bookcase
ដើងក្រានគ្រូ, កន្លែងដុតឧសក្នុងផ្ទះ	**8.** fireplace	វាំងននបង្អួច	**23.** drapes
ភ្លើង	**9.** fire	កូនខ្នើយ	**24.** cushion
ឧស	**10.** log	សូហ្វា	**25.** sofa
បង្កាន់ដៃ	**11.** banister	តុកាហ្វេ	**26.** coffee table
ជណ្ដើរ	**12.** staircase	ស្រោមចង្កៀង (ដើម្បីកុំឲ្យពន្លឺចាំងភ្នែក),	
កាំជណ្ដើរ	**13.** step	គម្របចង្កៀង	**27.** lampshade
តុ	**14.** desk	ចង្កៀង	**28.** lamp
ព្រំក្រាលពេញបន្ទប់	**15.** wall-to-wall carpeting	កូនតុ (ដាក់នៅចុងសូហ្វា)	**29.** end table

បន្ទប់ទទួលទានបាយ

ចាន	**1.** china		កម្រាលតុ	**16.** tablecloth
ទូដាក់ចាន	**2.** china closet		កៅអី	**17.** chair
ចង្កៀងមានអំពូលច្រើន, សង់ដីលេ្យ	**3.** chandelier		ប៉ាន់កាហ្វេ	**18.** coffeepot
ថូទឹក	**4.** pitcher		ប៉ាន់តែ	**19.** teapot
កែវស្រាទំពាំងបាយជូរ	**5.** wine glass		ពែង	**20.** cup
កែវទឹក	**6.** water glass		ទ្រនាប់ពែង	**21.** saucer
តុ	**7.** table		សមស្លាបព្រា	**22.** silverware
ស្លាបព្រា	**8.** spoon		ថូដាក់ស្ករ	**23.** sugar bowl
ប្រដាប់ដាក់ម្រេចរោយ	**9.** pepper shaker		ថូដាក់ក្រែម	**24.** creamer
ប្រដាប់ដាក់អំបិលរោយ	**10.** salt shaker		ចានដាក់សាឡាត់	**25.** salad bowl
ចានដាក់នំប៉័ងនិងប័រ	**11.** bread and butter plate		អណ្តាតភ្លើង	**26.** flame
សម	**12.** fork		ទៀន	**27.** candle
ចានទាប, ចានសំប៉ែត	**13.** plate		ជើងទ្រទៀន	**28.** candlestick
ក្រដាសជូតដៃ	**14.** napkin		តុដាក់ម្ហូប	**29.** buffet
កាំបិត	**15.** knife			

ម៉ាស៊ីនលាងចាន	**1.** dishwasher	ឆ្នាំង	**13.** pot	ប្រដាប់លុបញាមេ្យៅ	**25.** rolling pin
រាវចាន	**2.** dish drainer	ឆ្នាំងកាស្សីរ៉ូល	**14.** casserole dish	ជ្រៀ	**26.** cutting board
ប្រដាប់ចំហុយ	**3.** steamer	ក្រឡ ឬ ប្រដាប់ត្រចៀក	**15.** canister	កន្លែងរៀបចំម្ហូបនៅចង្ក្រានបាយ (ដូចតុ	
ប្រដាប់បើកកំប៉ុង	**4.** can opener	ប្រដាប់អាំងនំបុ័ង	**16.** toaster	តែធ្វើជាប់នៅនឹងជញ្ជាំង)	**27.** counter
ខ្លះ	**5.** frying pan	ចាសដាក់សាច់អាំង	**17.** roasting pan	កំសៀវដៅទឹក	**28.** teakettle
ប្រដាប់បើកដប	**6.** bottle opener	កន្សែងជូតចាន	**18.** dish towel	ក្បាលដើងក្រានដុតឧស្ម័ន (ហ្គាស់)	
ប្រដាប់សំរាបដាក់ឲ្យស្រស់ទឹក	**7.** colander	ទូទឹកកក	**19.** refrigerator	កំដៅធ្វើបបរអាហារ	**29.** burner
កូនឆ្នាំង	**8.** saucepan	ទូដាក់ម្ហូបកក, កន្លែងដាក់សាច់កក	**20.** freezer	ដើងចង្ក្រាន, ចង្ក្រាន	**30.** stove
គ្រប	**9.** lid	ចាសទឹកកក	**21.** ice tray	ប្រដាប់ធ្វើកាហ្វេ	**31.** coffeemaker
សាប៊ូលាងចាន	**10.** dishwashing	ទូដាក់សរ៉ាន់ (នៅចង្ក្រានបាយ)	**22.** cabinet	ឡ	**32.** oven
	liquid	ឡម៉ៃក្រូវេវ	**23.** microwave oven	កន្លែងអាំងសាច់	**33.** broiler
ប្រដាប់ដុសឆ្នាំង	**11.** scouring pad	ចានលាយគ្រឿង	**24.** mixing bowl	ប្រដាប់ទ្រាប់ដែកុំឲ្យក្តៅ	**34.** pot holder
ម៉ាស៊ីនកិន, ប្លិនឌ័រ	**12.** blender				

កិរិយាសព្ទនាក់ទងនឹងផ្ទះបាយ

កូរ	**1.** stir		កាត់	**9.** cut
ឈូស, កោស	**2.** grate		ហាន់	**10.** slice
បើក	**3.** open		ចិញ្ច្រាំ	**11.** chop
ចាក់	**4.** pour		ចំហុយ	**12.** steam
ចិតសំបក	**5.** peel		អាំង	**13.** broil
កាត់ ឬ ចៀរជាបន្តេៗ ឬ ដុំៗ	**6.** carve		ដុតក្នុងឡ	**14.** bake
បំបែក	**7.** break		ចៀន, បំពង	**15.** fry
វាយ	**8.** beat		ស្ងោរ	**16.** boil

បន្ទប់គេង

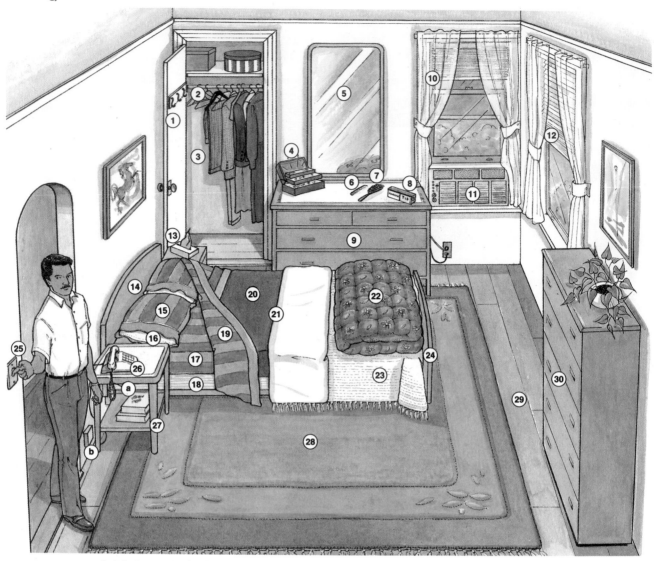

ទំពក់សំរាប់ព្យួរ	**1.** hook		ពូក	**17.** mattress
ប្រដាប់ព្យួរខោអាវ	**2.** hanger		រេស្ស៊័រពូក	**18.** box spring
កន្លែងព្យួរខោអាវ	**3.** closet		កម្រាលពូក (ធម្មតា)	**19.** (flat) sheet
ប្រអប់ដាក់គ្រឿងអលង្ការ	**4.** jewelry box		ភួយ	**20.** blanket
កញ្ចក់	**5.** mirror		គ្រែ	**21.** bed
ក្រាស	**6.** comb		ភួយញ៉ាត់សំឡី	**22.** comforter
ច្រាសសិតសក់	**7.** hairbrush		កម្រាលគ្របគ្រែ	**23.** bedspread
នាឡិការោទ៍	**8.** alarm clock		ក្តារចុងជើងគ្រែ	**24.** footboard
តុ	**9.** bureau		កុងតាក់	**25.** light switch
វាំងនន	**10.** curtain		តេឡេហ្វូន, ទូរស័ព្ទ	**26.** phone
ម៉ាស៊ីនត្រជាក់	**11.** air conditioner		ខ្សែ	**a.** cord
នរាំងបាំង	**12.** blinds		កន្លែងសិកខ្សែ	**b.** jack
ក្រដាសជូតមុខមាត់	**13.** tissues		កូនតុដាក់ជិតក្បាលគ្រែ	**27.** night table
ក្តារក្បាលគ្រែ ឬ អ្វីដែលប្រើជំនួស	**14.** headboard		ព្រំ	**28.** rug
ស្រោមខ្នើយ	**15.** pillowcase		ក្តារក្រាល, កម្រាល	**29.** floor
ខ្នើយ	**16.** pillow		ទូមានថត	**30.** chest of drawers

របាំងពន្លឺ	**1.** shade	កន្ទបសំពត់	**13.** cloth diaper	ផ្ទះបាយឡុកបាយឡុ
គ្រឿងព្យួរលើគ្រែឲ្យកូនង៉ាមើល	**2.** mobile	រទេះញញួនកូនង៉ែត	**14.** stroller	អគ្រីនគតខ្យេ
កូនខ្លាឃ្មុំញាត់សំឡី	**3.** teddy bear	ប្រដាប់សំរាប់ឲ្យដឹងថាមានភ្លើងឆេះផ្ទះ	**15.** smoke detector	កូនសត្វញាត់សំឡី
ព្រែកូនង៉ែត	**4.** crib	កៅអីដីកងោក	**16.** rocking chair	
ពូកហាំងកុំឲ្យទង្គិចនឹងព្រែ	**5.** bumper	ដប	**17.** bottle	តុក្កតា, កូនក្រមុំ
ឡៃលាបស្បែកកូនង៉ែត	**6.** baby lotion	ក្បាលដោះ	**18.** nipple	តុងដាក់គ្រឿងក្មេងលេង
ម្សៅលាបកូនង៉ែត	**7.** baby powder	ខោអាវរាជាប់គ្នាឲ្យបដើមសំរាប់កូនង៉ា	**19.** stretchie	ទ្រុងដាក់ឲ្យកូនង៉ាអង្គុយលេង
ក្រដាសសើមៗសំរាប់	**8.** baby wipes	សម្រេក	**20.** bib	រូបដែលគេកាត់ជាផ្នែក
សំអាតកូនង៉ាពេលដូរកន្ទប		ប្រដាប់អង្រួនឲ្យកូនង៉ាស្ងាប់	**21.** rattle	តួចៗសំរាប់យកមក
តុដូរកន្ទប	**9.** changing table	ក្បាលដោះបៀមលេង	**22.** pacifier	ផ្គុំគ្នាឲ្យចេញជារូបដូចដើមវិញ
សំឡីត្បារត្រចៀក	**10.** cotton swab	រទេះរៀនដើរ	**23.** walker	បុក, ដុំឫជ្រុងសំរាប់ឲ្យ
ម្ជុលខ្លាស់	**11.** safety pin	ទោង	**24.** swing	ក្មេងដាក់បន្លុកគ្នាលេង
កន្ទបប្រើរហើយបោះចោល	**12.** disposable diaper			ប្រដាប់ក្មេងជុះនោម

25. doll house		ផ្ទះបាយឡុកបាយឡុ
26. cradle		អគ្រីនគតខ្យេ
27. stuffed	animal	កូនសត្វញាត់សំឡី
28. doll		តុក្កតា, កូនក្រមុំ
29. toy chest		តុងដាក់គ្រឿងក្មេងលេង
30. playpen		ទ្រុងដាក់ឲ្យកូនង៉ាអង្គុយលេង
31. puzzle		
32. block		
33. potty		

បន្ទប់ទឹក

ដែកព្យួររាំងនន	**1.** curtain rod	ក្បាលម៉ាស៊ីនទឹកក្ដៅ	**17.** hot water faucet
ក្រវិលរាំងនន	**2.** curtain rings	ក្បាលម៉ាស៊ីនទឹកត្រជាក់	**18.** cold water faucet
មួកពាក់ងូតទឹក	**3.** shower cap	កន្លែងលាងដៃ ចាន ។ល។	**19.** sink
ក្បាលផ្កាឈូក (ងូតទឹក)	**4.** shower head	ច្រាសដុសក្រចក	**20.** nailbrush
រាំងននប៉ាំងកំឡុងទឹកសាត	**5.** shower curtain	ច្រាសដុសធ្មេញ	**21.** toothbrush
ចានសាប៊ូ	**6.** soap dish	ក្រណាត់លាងមុខមាត់	**22.** washcloth
អេប៉ុង	**7.** sponge	កន្សែងជូតខ្លួនតូច	**23.** hand towel
សំពុ, ថ្នាំកក់សក់	**8.** shampoo	កន្សែងជូតខ្លួន (ធំៗ)	**24.** bath towel
កន្លែងបង្ហូរទឹក	**9.** drain	កន្លែងព្យួរកន្សែង	**25.** towel rack
ឆ្នុក	**10.** stopper	ម៉ាស៊ីនបាញ់សក់ឲ្យស្ងួត	**26.** hair dryer
អាងងូតទឹក	**11.** bathtub	ឥដ្ឋក្បឿងស្តើងៗ	**27.** tile
ក្រណាត់ជូតជើង	**12.** bath mat	កញ្ចើរដាក់ខោអាវប្រឡាក់	**28.** hamper
ធុងសំរាម	**13.** wastepaper basket	បង្គន់	**29.** toilet
ទូដាក់ថ្នាំពេទ្យ	**14.** medicine chest	ក្រដាសបង្គន់	**30.** toilet paper
សាប៊ូ	**15.** soap	ច្រាសដុសលាងបង្គន់	**31.** toilet brush
ថ្នាំដុសធ្មេញ	**16.** toothpaste	ជញ្ជីង	**32.** scale

បន្ទប់ដាក់ប្រដាប់ប្រើប្រាស់ផ្សេងៗ

ជណ្ដើរ	**1.** stepladder	អេប៉ុងសំរាប់ផ្លាស់	**11.** (mop) refill	អំពូល	**22.** lightbulb
អំបោសស្លាបមាន់	**2.** feather duster	ឆ្នាំងអ៊ុត	**12.** iron	ក្រដាសជូតខែ	**23.** paper towels
ពិល	**3.** flashlight	ក្ដារសំរាប់អ៊ុតខោអាវ	**13.** ironing board	ម៉ាស៊ីនហាលខោអាវ	**24.** dryer
ក្រណាត់សំរាប់ជូតធូលី	**4.** rags	ប្រដាប់សំរាប់បង្ហូរស្អុះ	**14.** plunger	ម្សៅបោកខោអាវ	**25.** laundry detergent
កុងតាក់សំរាប់ផ្ដាច់ទាំងមូល	**5.** circuit breaker	ធុងទឹក	**15.** bucket	ថ្នាំសំរាប់បោកខោអាវឱ្យបួស្ខាក់ខ្លាំង	**26.** bleach
ប្រដាប់ជូតផ្ទះ	**6.** (sponge) mop	ម៉ាស៊ីនបោសផ្ទះ	**16.** vacuum cleaner	ថ្នាំដាក់ឱ្យខោអាវទន់	**27.** fabric softener
(ធ្វើពីអេប៉ុងមានដង)		របស់សំរាប់ប្រើជាមួយគ្រឿងអ៊ីមួយ	**17.** attachments	ខោអាវប្រឡាក់ត្រូវបោក	**28.** laundry
អំបោស	**7.** broom	បំពង់ទឹក	**18.** pipe	កញ្ច្រែងដាក់ខោអាវយកទៅបោក	**29.** laundry basket
ប្រដាប់សំរាប់ច្រកសំរាម	**8.** dustpan	ខ្សែហាលខោអាវ	**19.** clothesline	ម៉ាស៊ីនបោកខោអាវ	**30.** washing machine
ម្សៅ ឬ ទឹកសំរាប់ដុសលាង	**9.** cleanser	ដង្កៀបហាលខោអាវ	**20.** clothespins	ធុងដាក់សំរាម	**31.** garbage can
ថ្នាំលាងបង្អួច	**10.** window cleaner	ម្សៅបាញ់ខោអាវអ៊ុតដើម្បីឱ្យរាំង	**21.** spray starch	អន្ទាក់ដាក់កណ្ដុរ	**32.** mousetrap

បន្ទប់ជាង

ម៉ែត្រជាងឈើ	**1.** carpenter's rule	ដែកខ្វង	**9.** brace	ពូទៅ	**17.** hatchet
ដែកគាប	**2.** C-clamp	ក្លេ	**10.** wrench	រណារអារដែក	**18.** hacksaw
រណារខ្សែភ្លើងផ្តេចត្រង់ចុះទៅក្រោម	**3.** jigsaw	អន្លុងក្បាលស្មា	**11.** mallet	ដង្កាប់	**19.** pliers
ឈើ	**4.** wood	ក្លេធំ (ម៉្រាង)	**12.** monkey wrench	រណារខ្សែភ្លើង	**20.** circular saw
ខ្សែភ្លើងសំរាប់បន្តឲ្យវែង	**5.** extension cord	ញញួរ	**13.** hammer	(មានផ្លែជាវាសមូល)	
កន្លែងញាត់ខ្សែភ្លើង	**6.** outlet	ប្រដាប់កោស	**14.** scraper	ម៉ែត្រទាញចេញទាញចូល	**21.** tape measure
ក្បាលភ្ជាប់ខ្សែដី	**7.** grounding plug	ក្តារព្យួរប្រដាប់ប្រដាជាន	**15.** pegboard	តុជាន	**22.** workbench
រណារ	**8.** saw	ទំពក់	**16.** hook	ប្រអប់សំរាប់ដាក់ប្រដាប់ប្រដាជាន	**23.** toolbox

បន្ទប់ជាង

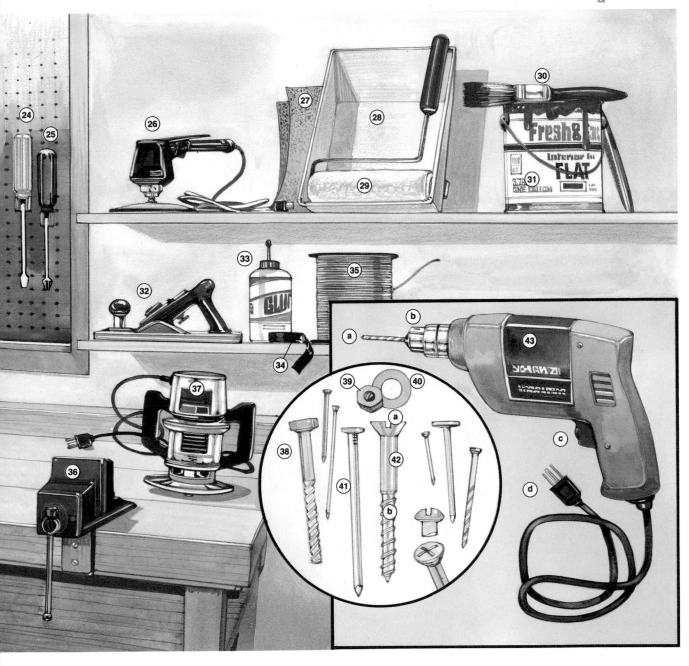

ទួណឺវីស	**24.** screwdriver	ការ	**33.** glue	វិស	**42.** screw
ទួណឺវីសក្បាលជ្រុង	**25.** Phillips screwdriver	ថេបវ៉ៃខ្សែភ្លើង	**34.** electrical tape	ក្បាលស្គ្រូ	**a.** head
ម៉ាស៊ីនខាត់	**26.** power sander	ខ្សែភ្លើង	**35.** wire	ស្គ្រូ	**b.** thread
ក្រដាសខាត់	**27.** sandpaper	ដង្កៀប	**36.** vise	ដែកខួងខ្សែភ្លើង	**43.** electric drill
ចានដាក់ថ្នាំលាប	**28.** pan	ម៉ាស៊ីនចោល	**37.** router	ផ្លែ	**a.** bit
ប្រដាប់លាបថ្នាំ	**29.** roller	ប៊ូឡុង, ខ្ចៅស្គ្រូ	**38.** bolt	ក្បាលសំរាប់មូលភ្ជាប់ផ្លែដែកខួង	
ច្រាស, ជក់	**30.** paintbrush	ក្បាលខ្ចៅស្គ្រូ	**39.** nut	ទៅនឹងគ្រឿងដែកខួង	**b.** shank
ថ្នាំលាប	**31.** paint	កាសទ្រាប់	**40.** washer	កុងតាក់	**c.** switch
ដែកឈូស	**32.** wood plane	ដែកគោល	**41.** nail	ប្រដាប់សិក	**d.** plug

កិរិយាសព្ទនាក់ទងនឹងកិច្ចការក្នុងផ្ទះនិងការជួសជុល

បត់	**1.** fold	ផ្លុត	**9.** dry
ដុស	**2.** scrub	ជួសជុល	**10.** repair
ខាត់	**3.** polish	អ៊ិត	**11.** iron
រឹត	**4.** tighten	ដាក់ប្រេង	**12.** oil
ជូត	**5.** wipe	ផ្លាស់ (កម្រាល)	**13.** change (the sheets)
ព្យួរ	**6.** hang	បូមនឹងម៉ាស៊ីនបោសសំអាតផ្ទះ	**14.** vacuum
បោស	**7.** sweep	ជូត ឬ បោសធូលី	**15.** dust
រៀប (គ្រែ)	**8.** make (the bed)	លាង	**16.** wash

ការពេទ្យបាលរោគនិងការបែនាំធ្មេញ

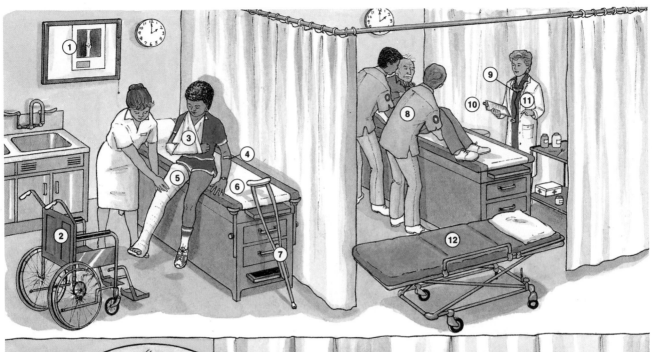

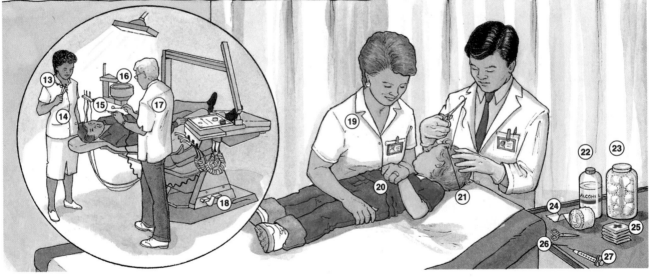

រូបថតអិច្ស៊រ៉េ	**1.** X ray	ប្រដាប់ស្តុងស្តាប់សួតនិងបេះដូង	**9.** stethoscope	ឆ្មោន់	**18.** pedal
កៅអីមានកង់សំរាប់មនុស្សពិការ		តារាងកត់ពត៌មានអ្នកជម្ងឺ	**10.** chart	គិលានុបដ្ឋាយិកា	**19.** nurse
ដើរមិនរួច	**2.** wheelchair	គ្រូពេទ្យ, វេជ្ជបណ្ឌិត	**11.** doctor	អ្នកជម្ងឺ	**20.** patient
ប្រដាប់ចងស្លាយ ឬ ចងបន្លោង	**3.** sling	គ្រែសែងអ្នកជម្ងឺ	**12.** stretcher	ថ្នេរ	**21.** stitches
បាន់ដេត, ប្រដាប់បិទរបួស	**4.** Band-Aid	ប្រដាប់ (សំរាប់ធ្វើអ្វីមួយ)	**13.** instruments	អាល់កុល	**22.** alcohol
រណោបម្នាងសិលា (សំរាប់រំឭង		ជំនួយពេទ្យធ្មេញ	**14.** oral hygienist	សំឡី	**23.** cotton balls
បាក់កុំឲ្យរាក់បែក)	**5.** cast	ប្រដាប់ខួង	**15.** drill	បង់សំរាប់បំងសិម៉ង	**24.** (gauze) bandage
តុពិនិត្យអ្នកជម្ងឺ	**6.** examining table	បាសៀង	**16.** basin	ក្រណាត់សំរាប់ជូត (ស្តើងៗ)	**25.** gauze pads
ឈើច្នាប	**7.** crutch	កន្លែងសំរាប់ស្តោរទឹកមាត់		មុល	**26.** needle
ជំនួយពេទ្យ	**8.** attendant	គ្រូពេទ្យធ្មេញ	**17.** dentist	សីរ៉ាំង	**27.** syringe

ជម្ងឺនិងរបួស

កន្ទួលរាល	**1.** rash		ផ្តាសាយ	**11.** cold
គ្រុន	**2.** fever		ឈឺក	**12.** sore throat
សត្វល្អិតខាំ	**3.** insect bite		បន្ទះឈើសង្កត់មើលបំពង់ក	**a.** tongue depressor
ស្រុំ(រំ)វិស្សាញ	**4.** chills		គ្រេច, ថ្ចោះ	**13.** sprain
ជាំ(ប្រឡុង)ភ្នែក	**5.** black eye		បង់បួបន្ទះសំពត់បាំងសឹម៉ង់យឹត	**a.** stretch bandage
ឈឺក្បាល	**6.** headache		ក្លាយ	**14.** infection
ឈឺពោះ	**7.** stomachache		ឆ្អឹងបាក់	**15.** broken bone
ឈឺចង្កេះ	**8.** backache		មុត	**16.** cut
ឈឺធ្មេញ	**9.** toothache		ជាំ	**17.** bruise
ឡើងឈាម	**10.** high blood pressure		រលាកភ្លើង	**18.** burn

ការព្យាបាលនិងថ្នាំព្យាបាលរោគ

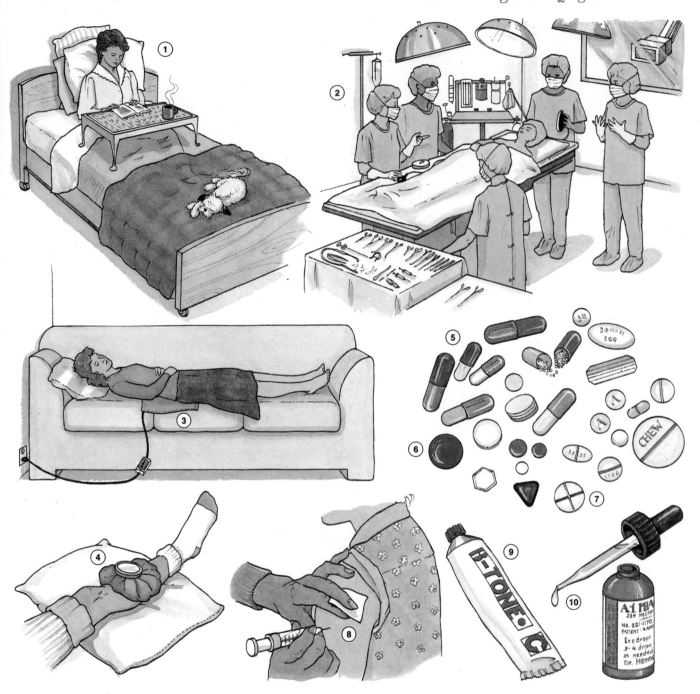

ការដេកសំរាកពេលមានជម្ងឺ	**1.** bed rest	ថ្នាំព្យាបាលរោគ	**Medicine**
ការវះកាត់	**2.** surgery	គ្រាប់ (ថ្នាំវាងមូលទ្រវែង)	**5.** capsule
ប្រដាប់កំដៅខ្លួន	**3.** heating pad	គ្រាប់ (ថ្នាំមូលសំប៉ែត)	**6.** tablet
ប្រដាប់ដាក់ទឹកកកស្អ	**4.** ice pack	គ្រាប់ (ថ្នាំគ្រាប់)	**7.** pill
		ការចាក់ថ្នាំ	**8.** injection
		ថ្នាំជាប្រេង ឬ ក្រមួន	**9.** ointment
		ថ្នាំដាក់ភ្នែក	**10.** eye drops

ការលត់ភ្លើង(នេះផ្លុះ) និង ជួយសង្គ្រោះ

ជណ្ដើរ	**1.** ladder	អ្នកលត់ភ្លើង	**10.** fire fighter
ឡានទឹក (លត់ភ្លើងនេះផ្លុះ)	**2.** fire engine	ឧបករណ៍ស្ទូនសំរាប់លត់ភ្លើង	**11.** fire extinguisher
ឡានដឹកគ្រឿងប្រដាប់លត់ភ្លើងនេះផ្លុះ	**3.** fire truck	មួកដែក	**12.** helmet
កន្លែងរត់ចេញទៅក្រៅពេលភ្លើងនេះផ្លុះ	**4.** fire escape	អាវរបស់អ្នកលត់ភ្លើងពាក់ពីក្រៅ	
ភ្លើងនេះ	**5.** fire	សំរាប់ការពារខ្លួន	**13.** coat
ឡានពេទ្យ	**6.** ambulance	ពូទៅ	**14.** ax
គ្រូពេទ្យជំនួយ	**7.** paramedic	ផ្សែង	**15.** smoke
បំពង់ទឹក (ធ្វើអំពីសំពត់ ឬ កៅស៊ូ)	**8.** hose	ទឹក	**16.** water
ក្បាលម៉ាស៊ីនទឹកលត់ភ្លើង	**9.** fire hydrant	ក្បាលបំពង់ទឹកលត់ភ្លើង	**17.** nozzle

បទឧក្រិដ្ឋនិងទណ្ឌកម្ម

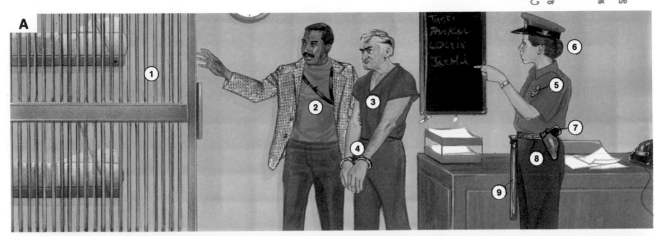

ប៉ូស្តិ៍ប៉ូលីស, ស្ថានីយតម្រួត	A. Police Station	អន្ទង (របស់ចៅក្រម)	12. gavel
គុក	1. jail	សាក្សី	13. witness
អ្នកស្ើុបអង្កេត	2. detective	ស្មៀន	14. court reporter
មនុស្សដែលគេសង្ស័យ	3. suspect	កំណត់ហេតុ	15. transcript
ខ្នាះដៃ	4. handcuffs	តុចៅក្រម	16. bench
ផ្លាកសំគាល់ខ្លួន	5. badge	សុភាចារបុរស	17. prosecuting attorney
ភ្នាក់ងារប៉ូលីស	6. police officer	កន្លែងសាក្សីអង្គុយ	18. witness stand
កាំភ្លើង	7. gun	តម្រួតសាលាកាត់ក្តី	19. court officer
ប្រដាប់ស្ៀតកាំភ្លើង	8. holster	កន្លែងគណៈវិនិច្ឆ័យអង្គុយ	20. jury box
ដំបង	9. nightstick	គណៈវិនិច្ឆ័យ	21. jury
		ស្មាក្តីចុងចោទ	22. defense attorney
សាលាកាត់ក្តី	B. Court	ចុងចោទ	23. defendant
ចៅក្រម	10. judge	(ស្នាម) ផ្និតម្រាមដៃ	24. fingerprints
អាវចៅក្រម	11. robes		

ផ្ទីក្រុង

អាគារការិយាល័យ	1. office building
បន្ទប់សំរាប់ចូល ឬ ចេញពីអគារ	2. lobby
ជ្រុង	3. corner
កន្លែងដើរឆ្លងថ្នល់	4. crosswalk
ហាងលក់សារ៉ាន់គ្រប់មុខ	5. department store
កន្លែងលក់នំ (ផុត)	6. bakery
ទេឡេហ្គុន, ទូរស័ព្ទសាធារណៈ	7. public telephone
ផ្លាកឈ្មោះផ្លូវ	8. street sign
ប្រៃសណីយស្ថាន, ប៉ុស្តិ៍	9. post office
តម្រួតចរាចរ, តម្រួតផ្លូវថ្នល់	10. traffic cop
កន្លែងផ្លូវកាត់គ្នា	11. intersection
អ្នកដើរ	12. pedestrian
កន្លែងរថយន្តឈប់ឈរ(ប៊ីស)ឈប់	13. bus stop
កៅអី	14. bench
ធុងដាក់សំរាម	15. trash basket
ស្ថានីយរទះភ្លើងក្រោមដី	16. subway station

ជណ្ដើរយោង	**17.** elevator	ទីសម្រាប់មនុស្សដើរនៅសងខាងថ្នល់	**25.** sidewalk
ហាងលក់សៀវភៅ, បណ្ណាគារ	**18.** bookstore	ចិញ្ចើមថ្នល់	**26.** curb
កន្លែងចតឡាន	**19.** parking garage	រទេះរុញកូនង៉ា	**27.** baby carriage
ប៉ាតិញ៉ូម៉ីទ័រ	**20.** parking meter	ផ្សារលក់បន្លែនិងផ្លែឈើ	**28.** fruit and vegetable market
ភ្លើងចរាចរ	**21.** traffic light	ភ្លើងបំភ្លឺថ្នល់	**29.** streetlight
ឱសថស្ថាន, ហាងលក់ថ្នាំពេទ្យ	**22.** drugstore	ទូបលក់សារពត៌មាន	**30.** newsstand
ផ្ទះល្វែង	**23.** apartment house	ផ្លូវ, ថ្នល់, វិថី	**31.** street
លេខអាគារ	**24.** building number	ប្រហោងសំរាប់ចុះទៅធ្វើការក្រោមដី	**32.** manhole

ប្រៃសណីយ៍នៃសហរដ្ឋអាមេរិក

ការចែកសំបុត្រ A. Delivering Mail

- ប្រអប់សំបុត្រ **1.** mailbox
- របស់ផ្ញើតាមប៉ុស្តិ៍ **2.** mail
- អ្នកចែកសំបុត្រ **3.** letter carrier
- ថង់សំបុត្រ **4.** mailbag
- រថយន្តប្រៃសណីយ៍ **5.** mail truck
- ប្រអប់សំបុត្រ(តាមថ្នល់) **6.** U.S. mailbox
- សំបុត្រ **7.** letter
- អាស្រ័យអ្នកផ្ញើ, អាស័យដ្ឋានអ្នកផ្ញើ **8.** return address
- ត្រាប៉ុស្តិ៍ **9.** postmark
- តែម **10.** stamp
- អាស្រ័យ, អាស័យដ្ឋាន **11.** address
- ហ្ស៊ីបកូដ, លេខតំបន់ប្រៃសណីយ **12.** zip code

ប្រៃសណីយស្ថាន, ប៉ុស្តិ៍ B. The Post Office

- កន្លែងស៊កសំបុត្រផ្ញើ **13.** mail slot
- ភ្នាក់ងារប្រៃសណីយ **14.** postal worker
- កន្លែងលក់តែម **15.** window

របស់ផ្សេងៗផ្ញើតាមប៉ុស្តិ៍ C. Types of Mail

- ស្រោមសំបុត្រ (ផ្ញើតាមអាកាស) **16.** (airmail) envelope
- កាតប៉ុស្តិ៍ស្តាល់ **17.** postcard
- ម៉ុនណេអ័រឌ័រ **18.** money order
- កញ្ចប់ផ្ញើតាមប៉ុស្តិ៍ **19.** package
- ខ្សែ **20.** string
- ប្លាកសរសេរអាស័យដ្ឋាន **21.** label
- បង់ស្អិត, ថេប **22.** tape
- (កញ្ចប់) ផ្ញើថ្នាក់លឿនបំផុត **23.** Express Mail (package)

បណ្ណាល័យសាធារណៈ

ខ្មែរ	English	ខ្មែរ	English	ខ្មែរ	English
អ្នកធ្វើការក្នុងបណ្ណាល័យ	**1.** library clerk	អ្នកនិពន្ធ	**8.** author	ផែនដី	**19.** globe
(ជាតិ សេសអ្នកគ្គុចតាច)		ឈ្មោះសៀវភៅ	**9.** title	សៀវភៅផែនទី	**20.** atlas
កន្លែងយកសៀវភៅចេញ,	**2.** checkout desk	ប្រធាន, ជំពូក	**10.** subject	កន្លែងសំរាប់ស្រាវជ្រាវរកសៀវភៅ	
កន្លែងខ្ចីសៀវភៅ		ជួរ	**11.** row	និងឯកសារផ្សេងៗ	**21.** reference section
កាតបណ្ណាល័យ,	**3.** library card	ក្រដាសរកសៀវភៅ	**12.** call slip	តុពត៌មាន	**22.** information desk
ប័ណ្ណបណ្ណាល័យ		ម៉ៃក្រូហ្វីល	**13.** microfilm	អ្នកបណ្ណាល័យ(សំរាប់ជួយស្រាវជ្រាវ	
(សំរាប់ខ្ចីសៀវភៅ)		ប្រដាប់មើលម៉ៃក្រូហ្វីល	**14.** microfilm reader	រកសៀវភៅនិងឯកសារផ្សេងៗ)	**23.** (reference) librarian
កន្លែងដាក់កាតសៀវភៅ	**4.** card catalog	ផ្នែកសៀវភៅមានលេខថ្មីៗគ្នា	**15.** periodicals section	វចនានុក្រម	**24.** dictionary
ថត	**5.** drawer	ទស្សនាវដ្តី	**16.** magazine	សារានុក្រម	**25.** encyclopedia
កាតសៀវភៅ	**6.** call card	ធ្នើរ	**17.** rack	ថ្នាក់ដាក់សៀវភៅ	**26.** shelf
លេខសៀវភៅ	**7.** call number	ម៉ាស៊ីនថតចម្លង, ម៉ាស៊ីនហ្ស៊ីរ៉ុក	**18.** photocopy machine		

A កងប្រដាប់អាវុធ

យាននិងបរិក្ខារផ្សេងៗ	**A. Vehicles and Equipment**	កងថ្មើរជើង	**15.** Army
យន្តហោះប្រយុទ្ធ	**1.** fighter plane	ទាហានជើងគោក	**16.** soldier
យន្តហោះទម្លាក់គ្រាប់បែក	**2.** bomber	កងម៉ារីន	**17.** Marines
គ្រាប់បែក	**3.** bomb	ទាហានម៉ារីន	**18.** marine
នាវាដឹកយន្តហោះចំបាំង	**4.** aircraft carrier	កងអាកាស	**19.** Air Force
នាវាចំបាំង	**5.** battleship	ទាហានកងអាកាស	**20.** airman
ឆ័ត្រយោង	**6.** parachute		
នាវាមុជទឹក	**7.** submarine	អាវុធនិងគ្រាប់រំសេវ	**C. Weapons and Ammunition**
កែវយ័ត្តនាវាមុជទឹកសំរាប់មើលពីក្រោមទឹក	**8.** periscope	កាំភ្លើងវែង	**21.** rifle
ឡានហ្ស៊ីប	**9.** jeep	គ្រៃ	**22.** trigger
រថក្រោះ	**10.** tank	បំពង់, មាត់គ្រែ	**23.** barrel
កាណុង	**11.** cannon	ចំពុះទុង	**24.** bayonet
របាំងដែកសំរាប់ការពារអ្នកប្រើកាំភ្លើង	**12.** gun turret	កាំភ្លើងយន្ត	**25.** machine gun
		គ្រាប់កាំភ្លើង	**26.** bullet
បុគ្គលិក	**B. Personnel**	ឡុតគ្រាប់កាំភ្លើង	**27.** shell
កងនាវាចរ	**13.** Navy	ម័រទេ, កាំភ្លើងក្បាល	**28.** mortar
ទាហានជើងទឹក	**14.** sailor	គ្រាប់បែកដៃ	**29.** hand grenade

របយន្តដឹកនាំផ្សារវ៉ាន់

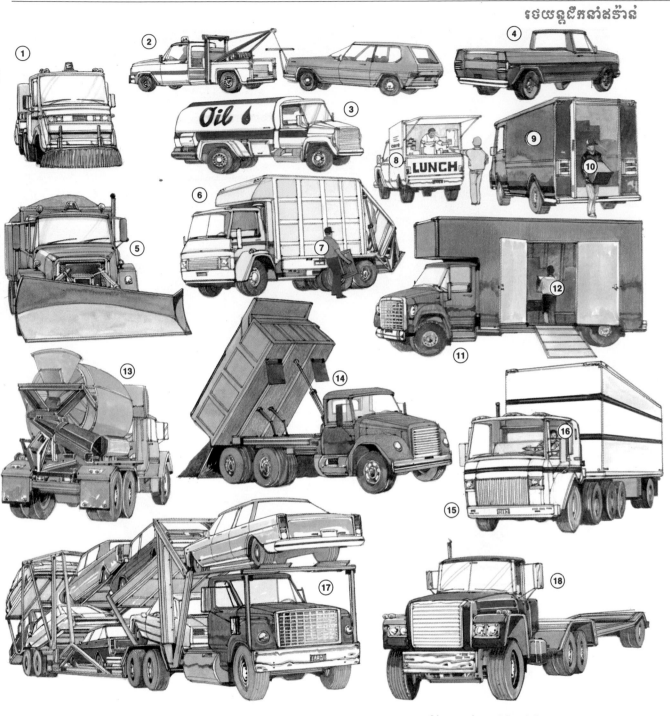

របយន្តបោសសំអាតផ្លូវ	1. street cleaner
ឡានសូច	2. tow truck
ឡានដឹកប្រេងសាំង	3. fuel truck
ឡានពិចកីប	4. pickup truck
ឡានឈូសទឹកកក (តាមផ្លូវ ។ល។)	5. snow plow
ឡានដឹកសំរាម	6. garbage truck
អ្នកយកសំរាម (ដឹកយកទៅចោល)	7. sanitation worker
ឡានលក់ម្ហូប	8. lunch truck
ឡានថ្រងឌុនឌុច	9. panel truck
អ្នកយកឥវ៉ាន់មកឲ្យដល់ផ្ទះ	10. delivery person
ឡានដឹកឥវ៉ាន់ប្តូរផ្ទះ	11. moving van
អ្នករកស៊ីដឹកឥវ៉ាន់ប្តូរផ្ទះ	12. mover
ឡានលាយស៊ីម៉ងត៍	13. cement truck
ឡានដឹកដី	14. dump truck
ឡានសំរាប់ទាញសណ្ដោង	15. tractor trailer
អ្នកបើកបររបយន្តធំៗ	16. truck driver
ឡានដឹករបយន្ត	17. transporter
ឡានគ្មានឌុនទៅពីក្រោយ	18. flatbed

របយន្ត

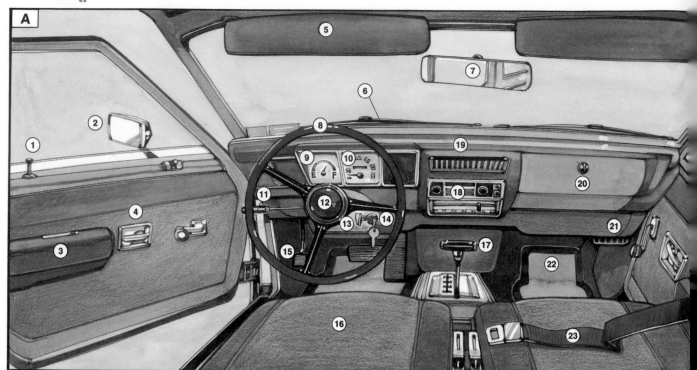

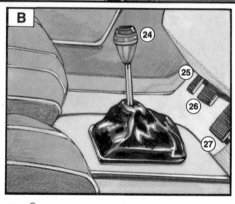

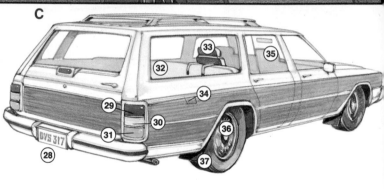

ប្រកប់លេខស្វ័យប្រវត្តិ	**A. Automatic Transmission**	ដងចង្កូត	**13.** column	អំប្រាយ៉ាស, ឈ្មាន់ដាក់លេខ	**25.** clutch
សោទ្វារ	**1.** door lock	កន្លែងបញ្ចេះម៉ាស៊ីន	**14.** ignition	ប្រាំង	**26.** brake
កញ្ចក់នៅចំហៀង	**2.** side mirror	ប្រាំងដៃ	**15.** emergency brake	ហ្គាហ្គ	**27.** accelerator
ប្រដាប់គងដៃ	**3.** armrest	កៅអីដាច់ពីគ្នា	**16.** bucket seat		
គន្លឹះទាញទ្វាររថ	**4.** door handle	ប្រដាប់ដាក់លេខ	**17.** gearshift	ឡ្មានស្គាស្រុងវ៉ាហ្គ	**C. Station Wagon**
ប្រដាប់បាំងកុំឱ្យថ្ងៃចាំង	**5.** visor	វិទ្យុ	**18.** radio	ផ្ទាកលេខឡ្មាន	**28.** license plate
ប្រដាប់ជូតទឹកភ្លៀង	**6.** windshield wiper	ប៉ាណូនៅមុខអ្នកបើក	**19.** dashboard	ភ្លើងប្រាំង	**29.** brake light
កញ្ចក់មើលទៅខាងក្រោយ	**7.** rearview mirror	កន្លែងដាក់ស្រោមដៃ	**20.** glove compartment	ភ្លើងថយក្រោយ	**30.** backup light
ដែចង្កូត	**8.** steering wheel	កន្លែងសំរាប់ខ្យល់ចូល	**21.** vent	ភ្លើងខាងក្រោយ	**31.** taillight
ប្រដាប់វាស់ប្រេងសាំង	**9.** gas gauge	ទ្រនាប់, កម្រាល	**22.** mat	កៅអីខាងក្រោយ	**32.** backseat
ប្រដាប់វាស់ល្បឿន	**10.** speedometer	ខ្សែក្រវ៉ាត់	**23.** seat belt	កៅអីកូនង៉ែត	**33.** child's seat
ប្រដាប់សំរាប់បិទបើកភ្លើងបត់	**11.** turn signal lever			ធុងសាំង	**34.** gas tank
ស៊ីផ្ទែ	**12.** horn	ប្រកប់លេខប្រើដៃ	**B. Manual Transmission**	បង្កើតក្បាល	**35.** headrest
		ប្រដាប់ដូរលេខ	**24.** stick shift	គម្របកង់	**36.** hubcap
				កង់	**37.** tire

D

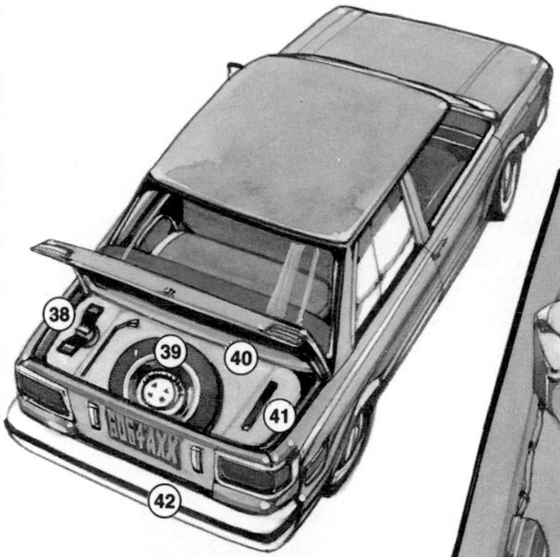

F

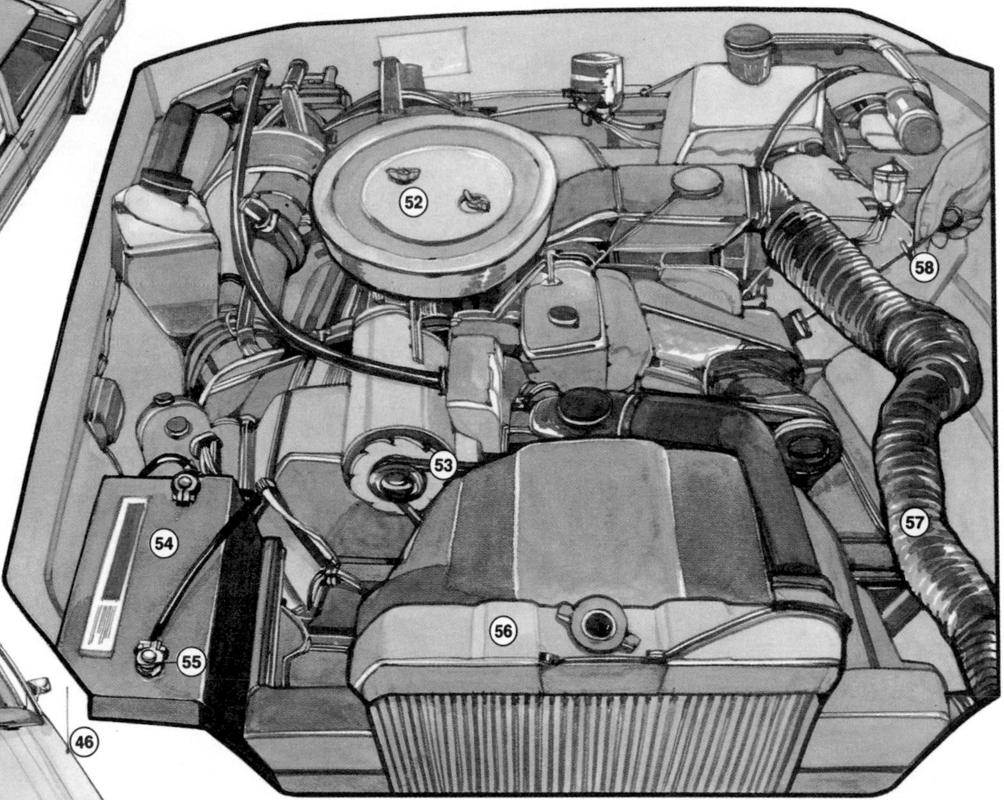

E

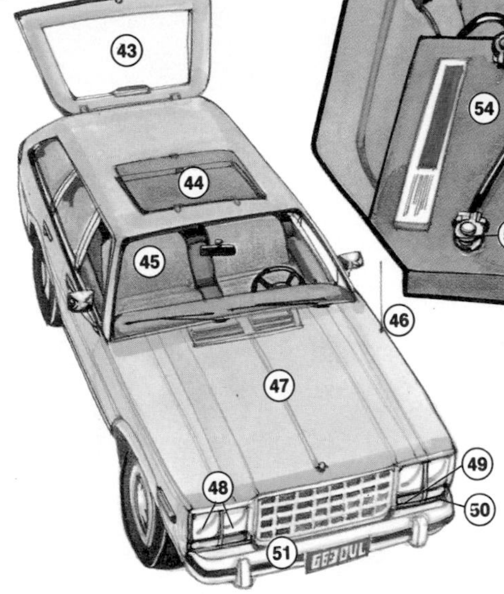

ឡានធម្មតា (ទ្វារពីរ) D. (Two-door) Sedan

ដែកគ្រីប **38.** jack
កង់សឺគួរ **39.** spare tire
កន្លែងដាក់ឥវ៉ាន់ **40.** trunk
ភ្លើងសំរាប់ពេលអាសន្ន **41.** flare
ប៉ារ៉ាសុកខាងក្រោយ **42.** rear bumper

ឡានកន្ទុយកាត់ទ្វារបួន E. Four-door Hatchback

ទ្វារខាងក្រោយបើកឡើងលើ **43.** hatchback
បង្អួចដំបូល **44.** sunroof
កញ្ចក់ខាងមុខ **45.** windshield
អង់តែន **46.** antenna
គម្របម៉ាស៊ីន **47.** hood
ភ្លើងមុខ, ហ្វា **48.** headlights
ភ្លើងចត **49.** parking lights
ភ្លើងបត់ **50.** turn signal (lights)
ប៉ារ៉ាសុកខាងមុខ **51.** front bumper

ម៉ាស៊ីន F. Engine

តម្រងខ្យល់ **52.** air filter
ខ្សែជង្គាល់ **53.** fan belt
ធុងអាគុយ **54.** battery
កន្លែងបន្តខ្សែភ្លើងភ្ជាប់នឹងធុងអាគុយ **55.** terminal
រ៉ាឌីយ៉ាទ័រ **56.** radiator
បំពង់ទឹក **57.** hose
ប្រដាប់ស្ទង់ប្រេងម៉ាស៊ីន **58.** dipstick

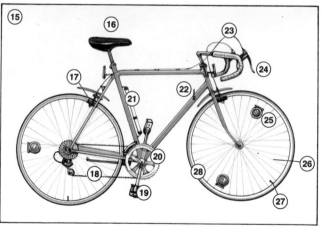

កង់សំរាប់ដាក់ឲ្យក្មេងរៀនជិះកង់	**1.** training wheels	តួកង់ប្រុស	**11.** boy's frame	ខ្សែ	**23.** cable
ដៃកង់ប្រណាំង	**2.** (racing) handlebars	ដៃធម្មតា	**12.** touring handlebars	ប្រាំងដៃ	**24.** hand brake
តួកង់ស្រី	**3.** girl's frame	សោ	**13.** lock	ប្រដាប់ចាំងភ្លើង	**25.** reflector
កង់	**4.** wheel	កន្លែងបញ្ឈរកង់ចត	**14.** bike stand	កាំ	**26.** spoke
ស៊ីផ្លេ	**5.** horn	កង់, ទោចក្រយាន	**15.** bicycle	វ៉ាល់	**27.** valve
កង់៣បី	**6.** tricycle	កែប	**16.** seat	កៅស៊ូ	**28.** tire
មួក (សំរាប់ពាក់ជិះកង់ ឬ ម៉ូតូ)	**7.** helmet	ប្រាំង, ច្រាំង	**17.** brake	រ៉ែស្ស៊័រ	**29.** motor scooter
កង់សំរាប់ជិះលេងនៅកន្លែងដែល		ច្រវាក់	**18.** chain	ម៉ូតូ, ទោចក្រយានយន្ត	**30.** motorcycle
គ្មានផ្លូវស្រួលបួល	**8.** dirt bike	ឈ្នាន់	**19.** pedal	រ៉ែស្ស៊័រ	**31.** shock absorbers
ចេនល់	**9.** kickstand	ចាស (មានធ្មេញ)	**20.** sprocket	ម៉ាស៊ីន	**32.** engine
គ្របភក់	**10.** fender	ស្នប់	**21.** pump	បំពង់ផ្សែង	**33.** exhaust pipe
		ប្រដាប់ដូរលេខ	**22.** gear changer		

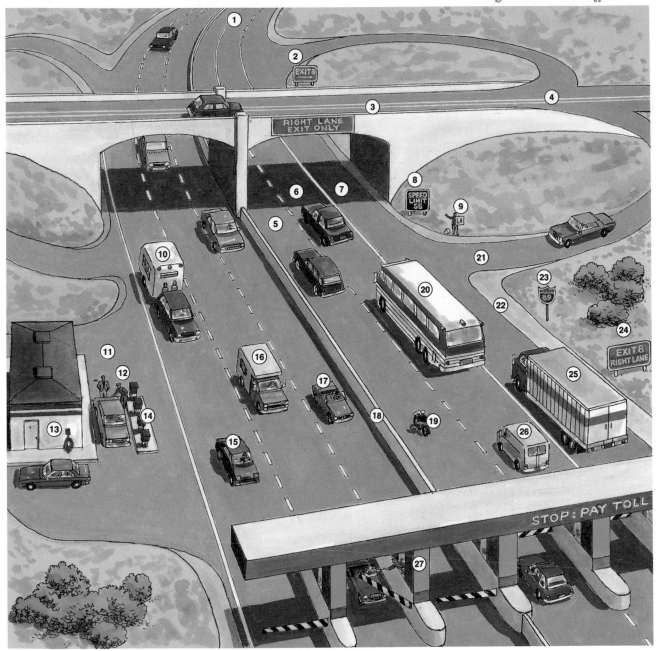

ខ្មែរ	English		ខ្មែរ	English		ខ្មែរ	English
យន្តបថឆ្លងរដ្ឋ	**1.** interstate highway		គ្រឿង	**10.** trailer		ម៉ូតូ, ទោចក្រយានយន្ត	**19.** motorcycle
ផ្លូវចេញ	**2.** exit ramp		កន្លែងចូលចាក់សាំង	**11.** service area		ប៊ីស, ឡានឈ្នួល	**20.** bus
ផ្លូវកាត់ពីលើ	**3.** overpass		អ្នកធ្វើការនៅកន្លែងចាក់សាំង	**12.** attendant		ផ្លូវចូលទៅផ្លូវធំ	**21.** entrance ramp
កន្លែងយន្តបថពីរកាត់ប្រសព្វគ្នា	**4.** cloverleaf		ប្រដាប់បូមខ្យល់ឡាន	**13.** air pump		ជាយផ្លូវ	**22.** shoulder
ទ្យេនខាងឆ្វេង	**5.** left lane		ម៉ាស៊ីនបូមសាំង	**14.** gas pump		ផ្លាកប្រាប់ព័ត៌មានអ្នកបើកបរ	**23.** road sign
ទ្យេនកណ្តាល	**6.** center lane		រថយន្តធម្មតា	**15.** passenger car		ផ្លាកប្រាប់ផ្លូវចេញ	**24.** exit sign
ទ្យេនខាងស្តាំ	**7.** right lane		ឡានសំរាប់ទៅកំប៉េ	**16.** camper		ឡានដឹកទំនិញ	**25.** truck
ផ្លាកប្រាប់ល្បឿនដែលអនុញ្ញាតឲ្យបើក	**8.** speed limit sign		ឡានស្ព័រ	**17.** sports car		វ៉ាន, ឡានទ្រុងតូច	**26.** van
អ្នកសុំឡានគេដោយឥតសារ	**9.** hitchhiker		របាំងចែកផ្លូវ	**18.** center divider		កន្លែងយកលុយថ្លៃផ្លូវ ។ល។	**27.** tollbooth

យានជំនិះសាធារណៈ

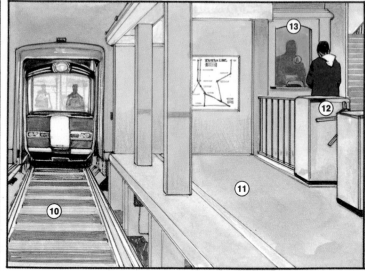

បិស, ឡ្ឡានឈ្នួល	**A. Bus**	សិបវេ៍, ម៉េត្រូ	**B. Subway**
ខ្សែទាញឲ្យឡ្លានឈប់	**1.** cord	អ្នកបើកសីុបវេ៍	**7.** conductor
កន្លែងអង្គុយ	**2.** seat	ប្រដាប់សំរាប់អ្នកដិះឈរបោះ	**8.** strap
អ្នកបើកបិស	**3.** bus driver	វ៉ាហ៊ុង, ទូរទះភ្លើង	**9.** car
ក្រដាសដិះបិសបន្ត	**4.** transfer	ផ្លូវរែក	**10.** track
ប្រអប់ដាក់លុយបង់ថ្លៃបិស	**5.** fare box	កន្លែងអ្នកដិះឈរចាំរថភ្លើង	**11.** platform
អ្នកដិះ	**6.** rider	នៅវែងសំរាប់ឲ្យមនុស្សចេញចូលម្នាក់ម្តង	**12.** turnstile
		កន្លែងទិញកាស (សំរាប់ដិះម៉េត្រូ)	**13.** token booth

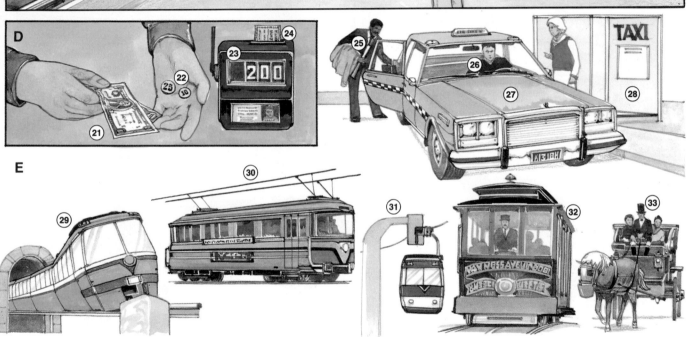

រទេះភ្លើង	**C.**	**Train**
រទេះភ្លើងដឹកមនុស្សទៅមកពីកន្លែងធ្វើការ	**14.**	commuter train
អ្នកបើករទេះភ្លើង	**15.**	engineer
សំបុត្រ	**16.**	ticket
អ្នកធ្វើដំណើរទៅមកពីកន្លែងធ្វើការ	**17.**	commuter
កន្លែងរទេះភ្លើងឈប់, ស្ថានីយរទេះភ្លើង	**18.**	station
កន្លែងលក់សំបុត្រ	**19.**	ticket window
តារាងប្រាប់ម៉ោងរទេះភ្លើងចេញ ឬ មកដល់	**20.**	timetable
តាក់ស៊ី	**D.**	**Taxi**
ថ្លៃឈ្នួល	**21.**	fare
ទិប, លុយទឹកតែ	**22.**	tip
ម៉ាស៊ីនប្រាប់ថ្លៃឈ្នួល	**23.**	meter
រស៊ីត, បង្កាន់ដៃ	**24.**	receipt
អ្នកជិះ	**25.**	passenger
អ្នកបើកតាក់ស៊ី	**26.**	cab driver
ឡានតាក់ស៊ី	**27.**	taxicab
កន្លែងតាក់ស៊ីឈប់	**28.**	taxi stand
គ្រឿងសំរាប់ជិះធ្វើដំណើរផ្សេងៗទៀត	**E.**	**Other Forms of Transportation**
រទេះភ្លើងបើកលើផ្លូវដែកតែមួយ	**29.**	monorail
រទេះភ្លើងរត់តាមផ្លូវ	**30.**	streetcar
រទេះភ្លើងរត់លើផ្លូវខ្សែដុតពីលើ	**31.**	aerial tramway
រទេះភ្លើងរត់ដោយខ្សែទាញពីក្រោម	**32.**	cable car
រទេះសេះ	**33.**	horse-drawn carriage

ការធ្វើដំណើរតាមយន្តហោះ

កន្លែងយកកន្ទ្រាវ៉ាន់នៅប្រឡប់អោយគេដាក់ក្នុងយន្តហោះ	**Airport Check-In**	សន្តិសុខ	**Security**	អ្នកបើកប្រដៃកុងរថ	**16.** copilot
ហិបខោអាវ	**1.** garment bag	តម្រួតសន្តិសុខ	**9.** security guard	អ្នកមើលខាងម៉ាស៊ីន	**17.** flight engineer
ហិបយួរឡើងយន្តហោះ	**2.** carry-on bag	ប្រដាប់ឆែករកលោហធាតុ	**10.** metal detector	សំបុត្រអនុញ្ញាតឲ្យឡើងជិះ	**18.** boarding pass
អ្នកធ្វើដំណើរ	**3.** traveler	ម៉ាស៊ីនឆ្លុះមើលឥវ៉ាន់	**11.** X-ray screener	បន្ទប់អ្នកជិះ	**19.** cabin
សំបុត្រ	**4.** ticket	ប្រដាប់ទាញឥវ៉ាន់មកខ្លួនឯង	**12.** conveyor belt	អ្នកបំរើក្នុងយន្តហោះ	**20.** flight attendant
អ្នកជញ្ជូនឥវ៉ាន់យកកលម្បល	**5.** porter			កន្លែងដាក់ឥវ៉ាន់	**21.** luggage compartment
ប្រដាប់ដាក់ឥវ៉ាន់រុញ	**6.** dolly	ការឡើងជិះយន្តហោះ	**Boarding**		
វ៉ាលិស	**7.** suitcase	កន្លែងអ្នកបើកបរ	**13.** cockpit	តុដាក់ចានបរិភោគបាយ	**22.** tray table
ឥវ៉ាន់ (របស់អ្នកធ្វើដំណើរ)	**8.** baggage	ទ្វិតចិនឹងគ្រឿងស្ទង់ផ្សេងៗ	**14.** instruments	ច្រកដើរទៅមក	**23.** aisle
		អ្នកបើកកប៉ាល់ហោះ	**15.** pilot		

យន្តហោះ, អាកាសយាន

A

B

យន្តហោះផ្សេងៗ	**A. Aircraft Types**	កប៉ាល់ហោះឡើង	**B. Takeoff**
បាឡុងហោះដោយសារកំដៅ	**1.** hot air balloon	ម៉ាស៊ីនរេអាក់ស្យុង, ម៉ាស៊ីនប្រេអ៊ុត	**11.** jet engine
អេលិកុបតែរ, ឧទ្ធម្ភាគចក្រ	**2.** helicopter	កន្លែងដាក់ឥវ៉ាន់	**12.** cargo area
ដង្កាល់	**a.** rotor	ទ្វារចូលទៅកន្លែងដាក់ឥវ៉ាន់	**13.** cargo door
កប៉ាល់ហោះប្រេុតឯកជន	**3.** private jet	តួយន្តហោះ	**14.** fuselage
កប៉ាល់ហោះឥតម៉ាស៊ីន	**4.** glider	គ្រឿងទ្រកប៉ាល់ហោះឲ្យខ្លួនពីដី	**15.** landing gear
បាឡុងហោះមានម៉ាស៊ីន	**5.** blimp	អាគារសំរាប់អ្នកដំណើរសំចតនៅមុនពេលឡើង	
ខ្លែងមានមនុស្សគោងជិះ	**6.** hang glider	ឬ ចុះពីកប៉ាល់ហោះ	**16.** terminal building
យន្តហោះដង្កាល់	**7.** propeller plane	កន្លែងកប៉ាល់ហោះចូលចត ឬ ចូលជួសជុល	**17.** hangar
ចុងខាងមុខ (កប៉ាល់ហោះ)	**8.** nose	ប្រេុត, កប៉ាល់ហោះរេអាក់ស្យុ	**18.** (jet) plane
ស្លាប	**9.** wing	ផ្លូវកប៉ាល់ហោះឡើងចុះ	**19.** runway
កន្ទុយ	**10.** tail	អាគារអ្នកឲ្យបញ្ជាទៅកប៉ាល់ហោះ	**20.** control tower

នៅកំពង់ផែ

កប៉ាល់នេសាទត្រី **1.** fishing boat
អ្នកនេសាទត្រី **2.** fisherman
ផែ **3.** pier
ម៉ាស៊ីនលើកឥវ៉ាន់ធ្ងន់ៗ **4.** forklift
ក្បាល (កប៉ាល់) **5.** bow
ប្រដាប់ស្ទូច **6.** crane
ឡាំងធំៗផ្ទុកឥវ៉ាន់ **7.** container
កន្លែងផ្ទុកឥវ៉ាន់ក្នុងនាវា **8.** hold
នាវាដឹកនាំឡាំងផ្ទុកឥវ៉ាន់ធំៗ **9.** (container) ship
បន្ទុក, ឥវ៉ាន់ដែលនាវាផ្ទុក **10.** cargo
កន្សៃ (នាវា) **11.** stern
ទូកផ្ទុករបស់ផ្សេងៗ **12.** barge
នាវាសណ្តោង **13.** tugboat
សើនបញ្ចាំងភ្លើង (សំរាប់បង្ហាញផ្លូវនាវា) **14.** lighthouse
នាវាផ្ទុកវត្ថុរាវ **15.** tanker
ពោង (បង្ហាញផ្លូវនាវា) **16.** buoy
នាវាចម្លង, សាឡាង **17.** ferry
បំពង់ផ្សែង **18.** smokestack
ទូកតូចៗសំរាប់ប្រើពេលកប៉ាល់លិច **19.** lifeboat
ច្រកតាមកៀននាវា **20.** gangway
បង្អួចនាវា **21.** porthole
ផ្ទៃករាបស្មើនៅលើនាវា **22.** deck
ប្រដាប់ខារ **23.** windlass
យុថ្កា **24.** anchor
ពួរ (សំរាប់ចងនាវា) **25.** line
បង្គោលចងនាវា **26.** bollard
នាវាសមុទ្រដឹកអ្នកដំណើរ **27.** ocean liner
ផែ **28.** dock
អាគារសំរាប់អ្នកដំណើរជ្រកមុនពេលចុះ ឬ ក្រោយពេលឡើងពីនាវា **29.** terminal

ប្រដាប់ពាក់កុំឱ្យលង់ទឹក	**1.** life jacket	ម៉ាស៊ីនអុីវ៉ីរ៉ូ	**12.** outboard motor
កាណូ (ទូកអុំ�រ៉ាងក្បាលនិងកន្ទ្យែរសំប៉ែត)	**2.** canoe	កាណូត	**13.** motorboat
ច្រវា	**3.** paddle	អ្នកជិះបន្ទះក្ដាមានក្ដោង	**14.** windsurfer
ទូកក្ដោង	**4.** sailboat	បន្ទះក្ដារមានក្ដោង	**15.** sailboard
ចង្កូត	**5.** rudder	នាវាជិះលេងមានកន្លែងរស់នៅដូចក្នុងផ្ទះ	**16.** cabin cruiser
បន្ទះក្ដារលិចទៅក្រោមទំកណ្ដាលទូក		កាយ៉ាក់ (ទូកអុំរ៉ាងតូចហើយបិទជិតត្រង់ចង្កេះអ្នកអុំ)	**17.** kayak
ដើម្បីកុំឱ្យយោង ឬ រសាត់	**6.** centerboard	ទូកយ៉ាងតូចគ្មានម៉ាស៊ីន	**18.** dinghy
សារ៉	**7.** boom	ប្រដាប់ចងទូកកុំឱ្យរសាត់	**19.** mooring
ឌងក្ដោង	**8.** mast	ក្ដូនកៅស៊ូ	**20.** inflatable raft
ក្ដោង	**9.** sail	ដែកសំរាប់សិកច្រវាអុំ	**21.** oarlock
អ្នកលេងស្គីលើទឹក	**10.** water-skier	ចែវ, ច្រវា	**22.** oar
ខ្សែរសណ្ដោង	**11.** towrope	ទូកអុំ	**23.** rowboat

រុក្ខជាតិស្មូចផ្

	Flowers			****
ផ្កា, បុប្ផ			ហ្គាឌីនិញ្ញា, នូនស្រី	**14.** gardenia
ទូលីប	**1.** tulip		ព័យសេតស្យា	**15.** poinsettia
ដើម, មែក	**a.** stem		វីយ៉ូឡេ	**16.** violet
បាំងសេ	**2.** pansy		ចិតទ័រឆប	**17.** buttercup
លីលី	**3.** lily		ក្ឫឡាប	**18.** rose
គ្រីស្សង់តែម	**4.** (chrysanthe) mum		ផ្កាក្រពុំ	**a.** bud
ដេហ្ស៊ី	**5.** daisy		ស្រទាប់, ត្របក	**b.** petal
ម៉ារីហ្គោល	**6.** marigold		បន្លា	**c.** thorn
ប៉េទុននិញ្ញា	**7.** petunia		ផ្កាឈូករតន៍	**19.** sunflower
ដាហ្វូឌីល	**8.** daffodil			
ម៉ើម	**a.** bulb		ស្មៅនិងធញ្ញជាតិ	**Grasses and Grains**
ក្រុកស	**9.** crocus		អំពៅ	**20.** sugarcane
ហៃយ៉ាសុីន	**10.** hyacinth		ស្រូវ	**21.** rice
អៃរិះ	**11.** iris		ស្រូវសាលី	**22.** wheat
អគីដេ	**12.** orchid		ស្រូវអាវ៉ាន់	**23.** oats
ហ្ស៊ីននិញ្ញា	**13.** zinnia		ពោត	**24.** corn

រុក្ខជាតិនិងរុក្ខ

ដើមឈើ	**Trees**	ស្រល់	**34.** pine	រុក្ខជាតិផ្សេងៗទៀត	**Other Plants**
ឈើក្រហម	**25.** redwood	ស្លឹកស្រល់	**a.** needle	រុក្ខជាតិសំរាប់ដាំក្នុងផ្ទះ	**39.** house plants
រុក្ខជាតិជំពូក ដូង, ស្លា, ត្នោត ។ល។	**26.** palm	ផ្លែស្រល់	**b.** cone	ដំបងយក្ស	**40.** cactus
អ៊ីកាលិបទុស	**27.** eucalyptus	ដើមឈើ	**35.** tree	គុម្ពោត	**41.** bushes
ដកវ៉ូត	**28.** dogwood	មែក	**a.** branch	វល្លិ៍	**42.** vine
ម៉ាក់ណូល្យ៉ា	**29.** magnolia	ដើម	**b.** trunk		
ផប់ឡើ	**30.** poplar	សំបក	**c.** bark	រុក្ខជាតិមានពិស	**Poisonous Plants**
វិលឡូវ, សូល	**31.** willow	ឫស	**d.** root		
ប៊ីរច៍	**32.** birch	អែលម៍	**36.** elm	អុករមាស់	**43.** poison oak
សែន	**33.** oak	ស្លឹក	**a.** leaf	ស៊ូម៉ាក់រមាស់	**44.** poison sumac
មែក (តូចៗ)	**a.** twig	ហ្ស៊ល្លី	**37.** holly	អៃវីរមាស់	**45.** poison ivy
ផ្លែសែន	**b.** acorn	ម៉េប៉ុល	**38.** maple		

សត្វជំពួកទាប (សត្វមិនធានវិទ្យទ្បន័នៅឡេីយ)

ខ្ចៅ, ខ្យង	**1.** snail		ព្រោន	**8.** shrimp
ស្ចក	**a.** shell		ក្ដាម	**9.** crab
ពុកមាត់	**b.** antenna		ស្ពាទ្យប, លាសមុទ្រធំៗមួយរ៉ាង	**10.** scallop
ខ្យងស្ងិត, អារ	**2.** oyster		ជន្ទែន	**11.** worm
ចំពុះទា	**3.** mussel		ជំពុលទឹក, ខ្ទឹមសមុទ្រ	**12.** jellyfish
ខ្យង (ឥតស្ចក)	**4.** slug		ដៃ, ប្រមៃាយ	**a.** tentacle
ត្រីយ៉ីហ៉ី	**5.** squid		បង្កងសមុទ្រ	**13.** lobster
ព្យ៉ីវ	**6.** octopus		ដង្ខ្បៀប	**a.** claw
ក្រចាប់សមុទ្រ	**7.** starfish			

សត្វល្អិត

ដង្កូវមេអំបៅ	**1.** caterpillar		ករណ្តៀរ	**11.** termite
សំបុកនាង ឬ សត្វល្អិតផ្សេងៗទៀត	**2.** cocoon		ស្រមោច, អង្គ្រង, សង្ហារ	**12.** ant
មេអំបៅ	**3.** butterfly		មូស	**13.** mosquito
កន្លុយ	**4.** dragonfly		អណ្ដើកមាស	**14.** ladybug
ស្លាប	**a.** wing		សំណាញ់	**15.** web
ចង្រិត	**5.** cricket		ពីងពាង	**16.** spider
កណ្ដូប	**6.** grasshopper		អំពិលអំពែក	**17.** firefly
កណ្ដូបសេះ	**7.** mantis		រុយ	**18.** fly
ខ្យប	**8.** scorpion		ឃ្មុំ	**19.** bee
ទិច	**a.** sting		ឪម៉ាល់	**20.** wasp
កន្លាត	**9.** cockroach		សត្វល្អិតមប្រាំងដូចមេអំបៅ	**21.** moth
បីតិល	**10.** beetle		សត្វឪកក្ខែប ។ល។	**22.** centipede

សត្វស្លាប

ព្រាប	**1.** pigeon	ចាបស្រុក	**10.** sparrow	កូនមាន់	**22.** chick
ស្លាប	**a. wing**	កាឌីណាល់	**11.** cardinal	មាន់	**23.** chicken
ហាំមិញប៊ីដ (សត្វស្លាបមួយប្រភេទ)	**2.** hummingbird	អូទ្រិស	**12.** ostrich	ទុង	**24.** pelican
ក្អែក	**3.** crow	ពង	**13.** egg	ចំពុះ	**a. bill**
ចំពុះ	**a. beak**	កាណារី	**14.** canary	ទា	**25.** duck
រិពេ	**4.** sea gull	សេក (តូចៗ)	**15.** parakeet	ក្ងាន	**26.** goose
សត្វឥន្ទ្រី	**5.** eagle	សេក (ធំៗ)	**16.** parrot	ប៉ិនឌ្វិន	**27.** penguin
ទិទុយ	**6.** owl	ត្រសេះ	**17.** woodpecker	ហង្ស	**28.** swan
ស្ទាំង	**7.** hawk	ក្ងោក	**18.** peacock	ហ្វាមិញហ្គោ	**29.** flamingo
ស្លាប	**a. feather**	ហ្វីហ្សង់	**19.** pheasant	សត្វស្លាបមួយប្រភេទចក្រុក	**30.** stork
បិៈហ្គេ	**8.** blue jay	មាន់បារាំង	**20.** turkey	សំបុក	**31.** nest
រ៉ូប៊ីន	**9.** robin	មាន់ឈ្មោល	**21.** rooster	រ៉ុតរ៉ិនន័រ	**32.** roadrunner

ត្រី និង ឧរង្គសត្វ

ត្រី	**A. Fish**		ប្រប៉ែល	**6.** stingray		អណ្ដើក	**12.** turtle
សេះសមុទ្រ	**1.** sea horse		ត្រីអណ្ដាតឆ្កែ	**7.** flounder		អ៊ី្គាន់ណា	**13.** iguana
ត្រៅ (ត្រីម្យ៉ាង)	**2.** trout					សាឡាម៉ង់	**14.** salamander
ត្រីសមុទ្រម្យ៉ាងមានមាត់ស្រួចវែងលម	**3.** swordfish		**ថយលិក និង ឧរង្គសត្វ**	**B. Amphibians**		សត្វជំពុកបង្គយ	**15.** lizard
កន្ទុយ	**a.** tail			**and Reptiles**		កូនកុក	**16.** tadpole
ព្រុយ	**b.** fin		ក្រពើ	**8.** alligator		កង្កែប	**17.** frog
ស្រកី	**c.** gill		ពស់	**9.** (garter) snake		អណ្ដើក	**18.** tortoise
ត្រីខ្លឹង, អន្ទង់	**4.** eel		(ពតមានពិសម្យ៉ាងមាននៅទ្វីបអាមេរិកខាងជើង)			(រស់នៅលើគោក)	
ឆ្នាម	**5.** shark		ពស់កណ្ដៀង	**10.** rattlesnake		ស្បែក	**a.** shell
			ពស់វែក	**11.** cobra			

ថនិកសត្វ ១

ថនិកសត្វមានថង់,
គ្មានធ្មេញ ឬចេះហើរ

កៅឡ្បា	**Pouched, Toothless, or Flying Mammals**
	1. koala
សត្វពាស្រលម្យ៉ាងនៅទ្វីបអាមេរិក	**2.** armadillo
កង់ហ្គូរ	**3.** kangaroo
កន្ទុយ	**a.** tail
ជើងក្រោយ	**b.** hind legs
ថង់	**c.** pouch
ជើងមុខ	**d.** forelegs
ប្រជៀវ	**4.** bat
សត្វស៊ីស្រមោច	**5.** anteater

ទេច្ធេតី, សត្វកកេរ

	Rodents
លីបម៉ង់ (សត្វម្យ៉ាងដូចកំប្រុកតែតូចជាង)	**6.** chipmunk
កណ្ដុរប្រែ	**7.** rat
ហ្គោហ្ទ័រ (សត្វម្យ៉ាងដូចកណ្ដុរប្រែតែធំជាង)	**8.** gopher

កណ្ដុរប្រម៉េះ	**9.** mouse
កំប្រុក	**10.** squirrel
សត្វប្រម៉ា	**11.** porcupine
កាំ	**a.** quill
បីវ័រ	**12.** beaver
ទន្សាយ	**13.** rabbit

សត្វមានក្រចកផ្ទាៗ

	Hoofed Mammals
ដំរីទឹក	**14.** hippopotamus
ឡ្យាម៉ា	**15.** llama
រមាស	**16.** rhinoceros
កុយរមាស	**a.** horn
ដំរី	**17.** elephant
ប្រមោយ	**a.** trunk
ភ្លុក	**b.** tusk
ហ្សេប, សេះបង្កង់	**18.** zebra

ប៊ីហ្សុង	**19.** bison		សត្វហ្ស៊ីរ៉ាហ្វ, សត្តុកវែង	**29.** giraffe
កូនសេះ	**20.** pony		ជ្រូក	**30.** hog
សេះ	**21.** horse		កូនគោ	**31.** calf
សក់កសេះ	**a.** mane		គោញី	**32.** cow
កូនសេះ ឬ លា (អាយុតិចជាងមួយឆ្នាំ)	**22.** foal		អូដ្ឋ	**33.** camel
លា	**23.** donkey		ថ្ពក	**a.** hump
កូនចៀម	**24.** lamb		គោឈ្មោល	**34.** bull
ចៀម	**25.** sheep		មូហ្ស	**35.** moose
ឈ្លូស, ក្តាន់, ប្រើស	**26.** deer		ស្នែង	**a.** antler
កូនឈ្លូស	**27.** fawn		ក្រចក(សេះ, គោៗលៗ)	**b.** hoof
ពពែ	**28.** goat			

ថនិកសត្វ ២

ខ្លារខិន	**1.** leopard	**ថនិកសត្វរស់នៅក្នុងទឹក**	**Aquatic Mammals**
ខ្លាធំ	**2.** tiger	ត្រីបាឡែន	**9.** whale
ក្រញ៉ាំជើង	**a.** c l a w	ភេ	**10.** otter
តោ, សិង្ហ	**3.** lion	លោមមច្ឆា	**11.** walrus
ឆ្មា	**4.** cat	(សត្វ) ហុក	**12.** seal
កូនឆ្មា	**5.** kitten	ព្រុយហុកខាងមុខ (ដូចដៃ)	**a.** flipper
កញ្ជ្រោង	**6.** fox	ដូហ្វាំង	**13.** dolphin
រ៉ាគូន, សំពោច	**7.** raccoon		
ស្កុង	**8.** skunk		

វានរជាតិ	**Primates**		ឆ្កែ	**Dogs**
ស្វា	**14.** monkey		ឆ្កែម្យ៉ាងតូចល្មមស្លឹកត្រចៀកធ្លាក់ទាប	
ទោច	**15.** gibbon		មានរោមទន់ហើយរួញ	**24.** spaniel
ស្វាធំ	**16.** chimpanzee		ឆ្កែម្យ៉ាងតូចហើយរោសរហ្យស	**25.** terrier
ស្វាធំ,ហ្គ៊រវិឡ	**17.** gorilla		ឆ្កែម្យ៉ាងគេចិញ្ចឹមសំរាប់ឲ្យពាំសត្វ	
ស្វាក្រហម, អរ័ង់អ៊ុតង់	**18.** orangutan		ដែលគេបាញ់ធ្លាក់យកមកឲ្យ	**26.** retriever
ស្វាអណ្ដូត	**19.** baboon		កូនឆ្កែ	**27.** puppy
			ឆ្កែបៃបេរ្យ	**28.** shepherd
ខ្លាឃ្មុំ	**Bears**			
បំងឌា, ខ្លាឃ្មុំស្រុកចិន	**20.** panda		ឆ្កែចចក	**29.** wolf
ខ្លាឃ្មុំខ្មៅ	**21.** black bear		ក្រញ៉ាំជើង	**a.** p a w
ខ្លាឃ្មុំស	**22.** polar bear		សត្វស្វាន	**30.** hyena
ខ្លាឃ្មុំក្ដោត	**23.** grizzly bear			

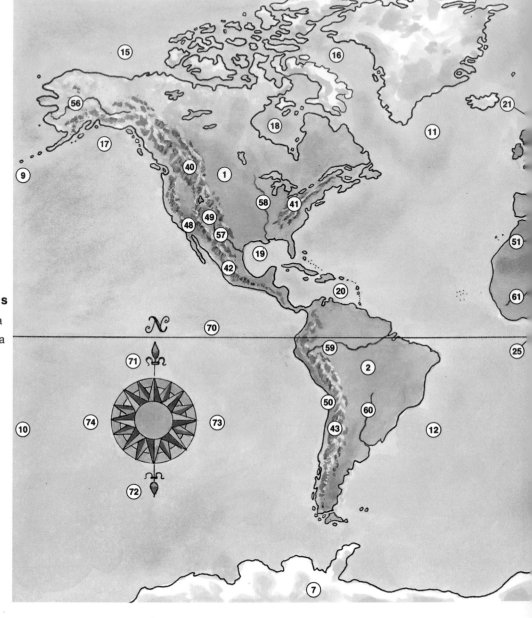

ធ្លឹប **Continents**

ទ្វីបអាមេរិកខាងជើង **1. North America**
ទ្វីបអាមេរិកខាងត្បូង **2. South America**
ទ្វីបអឺរ៉ុប **3. Europe**
ទ្វីបអាហ្វ្រិក **4. Africa**
ទ្វីបអាស៊ី **5. Asia**
ទ្វីបអូស្ត្រាលី **6. Australia**
ទ្វីបអង់តាកទិក **7. Antarctica**

មហាសមុទ្រ **Oceans**

មហាសមុទ្រ **8. Arctic**
ទឹកកកខាងជើង

មហាសមុទ្រ **9. North Pacific**
ប៉ាស៊ីហ្វិកខាងជើង

មហាសមុទ្រ **10. South Pacific**
ប៉ាស៊ីហ្វិកខាងត្បូង

មហាសមុទ្រ **11. North Atlantic**
អាត្លង់ទិកខាងជើង

មហាសមុទ្រ **12. South Atlantic**
អាត្លង់ទិកខាងត្បូង

មហាសមុទ្រឥណ្ឌា **13. Indian**

មហាសមុទ្រ **14. Antartic**
អង់តាកទិក

សមុទ្រ, **Seas,**

ឈូងសមុទ្រ **Gulfs,**

និងឆកសមុទ្រ **and Bays**

សមុទ្របៀហ្វរ **15. Beaufort Sea**

ឆកសមុទ្របាហ្វិន	**16.** Baffin Bay	សមុទ្រកាស់ស្ពាន	**27.** Caspian Sea
ឈូងសមុទ្រអាឡាស្កា	**17.** Gulf of Alaska	ឈូងសមុទ្របែលស៊ីក	**28.** Persian Gulf
ឆកសមុទ្រហុតសុន	**18.** Hudson Bay	សមុទ្រក្រហម	**29.** Red Sea
ឈូងសមុទ្រមិចស៊ិកកូ	**19.** Gulf of Mexico	សមុទ្រអារ៉ាប់	**30.** Arabian Sea
សមុទ្រការ៉ៃប	**20.** Caribbean Sea	សមុទ្រកា៉រ	**31.** Kara Sea
សមុទ្រខាងជើង (នៅខាងជើងទ្វីបអឺរ៉ុប)	**21.** North Sea	ឆកសមុទ្រចិនហ្គាល	**32.** Bay of Bengal
សមុទ្របាល់ទិត	**22.** Baltic Sea	សមុទ្រឡាប់តុហ្វ	**33.** Laptev Sea
សមុទ្របារ៉ិន	**23.** Barents Sea	សមុទ្របៃរិង	**34.** Bering Sea
សមុទ្រមេឌីតេរ៉ាណេ	**24.** Mediterranean Sea	សមុទ្រអុខុតស្ក៍	**35.** Sea of Okhotsk
ឈូងសមុទ្រហ្គីណេ	**25.** Gulf of Guinea	សមុទ្រជ៉ីពុន	**36.** Sea of Japan
សមុទ្រខ្មៅ	**26.** Black Sea	សមុទ្រលៀង	**37.** Yellow Sea

ទន្លេ ឬ ស្ទឹង		Rivers
ទន្លេយូកុន	៥6.	Yukon
ទន្លេរីយោក្រង់ដេ	57.	Rio Grande
ទន្លេមីស៊ីស៊ីពី	58.	Mississippi
ទន្លេអាម៉ាហ្សូន	59.	Amazon
ទន្លេប៉ារ៉ាណា	60.	Paraná
ទន្លេនីហ្សេរ	61.	Niger
ទន្លេកុងហ្គោ	62.	Congo
ទន្លេនីល	63.	Nile
ទន្លេអុប	64.	Ob
ទន្លេយេនីសេ	65.	Yenisey
ទន្លេឡេណា	66.	Lena
ទន្លេហ្គង់	67.	Ganges
ទន្លេហួង ឬ ហ្វាង	68.	Huang
ទន្លេយ៉ង់សេ	69.	Yangtze
អេក្វាទ័រ, ភូមិឆ្ឡ្យរេខា	70.	equator
ទិសខាងជើង	71.	north
ទិសខាងត្បូង	72.	south
ទិសខាងកើត	73.	east
ទិសខាងលិច	74.	west

សមុទ្រចិនខាងកើត	38.	East China Sea
សមុទ្រចិនខាងត្បូង	39.	South China Sea

ជួរ ឬ ជណ្តើ		Mountain Ranges
ជួរភ្នំរ៉ក់គី	40.	Rocky Mountains
ជួរភ្នំអាប៉ាឡាស្យ៉ាង	41.	Appalachian Mountains
ជួរភ្នំស្យេរ៉ាម៉ាដ្រេ	42.	Sierra Madre
ជួរភ្នំអង់ឌែប្រ	43.	Andes
ជួរភ្នំអាល់ព៍	44.	Alps
ជួរភ្នំកូកាស្យ៍	45.	Caucasus
ជួរភ្នំអ៊ុរ៉ល់	46.	Urals

ជួរភ្នំហេមពាន្ត	47.	Himalayas

សមុទ្រខ្សាច់		Deserts
សមុទ្រខ្សាច់ម៉ូហាវី	48.	Mojave
សមុទ្រខ្សាច់ប៉េនតិត	49.	Painted
សមុទ្រខ្សាច់អាតាកាម៉ា	50.	Atacama
សមុទ្រខ្សាច់សាហារ៉ា	51.	Sahara
សមុទ្រខ្សាច់រ៉ឹបអាល់ខាលី	52.	Rub' al Khali
សមុទ្រខ្សាច់តាក្លាម៉ាកាន់	53.	Takla Makan
សមុទ្រខ្សាច់ហ្គោប៊ី	54.	Gobi
សមុទ្រខ្សាច់ក្រេតសាន់ឌី	55.	Great Sandy

សហរដ្ឋអាមេរិក, ស្រុកអាមេរិក

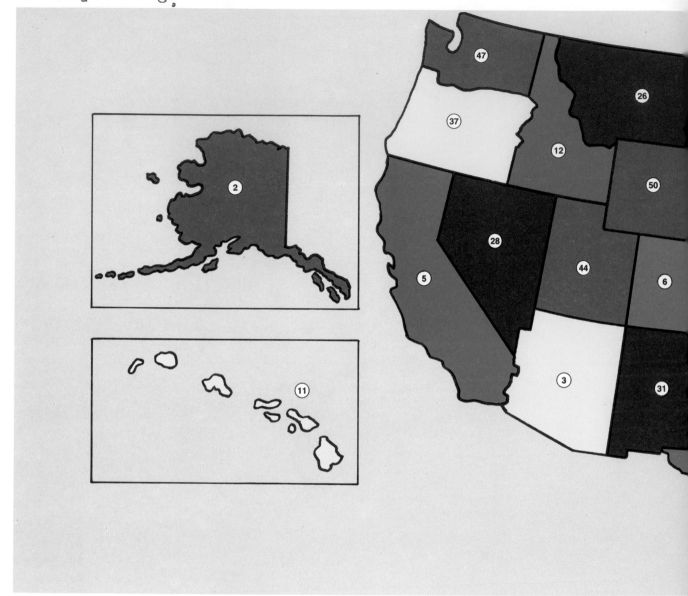

អាឡាបាម៉ា	**1.** Alabama		អ៊ិនឌ្យាណា	**14.** Indiana
អាឡាស្កា	**2.** Alaska		អៃយ៉ូវ៉ា	**15.** Iowa
អារីហ្សូណា	**3.** Arizona		កង់សាស់, កាន់ហ្សាស់	**16.** Kansas
អារកាន់សាស់	**4.** Arkansas		កិនទឹកគី	**17.** Kentucky
កាលីហ្ស៊័រនិញ៉ា, កាលីហ្ស៊័រនី	**5.** California		ល្វីហ្ស៊ីស៊ីយ៉ាណា	**18.** Louisiana
កូឡូរ៉ាដូ	**6.** Colorado		ម៉េន	**19.** Maine
កុនណិចទឹកិត	**7.** Connecticut		ម៉េរីឡ្យាន់	**20.** Maryland
ដែឡ្យាវ៉ែរ	**8.** Delaware		ម៉ាស្សាឈូសេត	**21.** Massachusetts
ហ្វ្លរិដា, ហ្វ្លរិដ	**9.** Florida		មិស៊ុហ្គិន	**22.** Michigan
ហ្ស៊កហ្ស៊ីយ៉ា	**10.** Georgia		មិណេសូតា	**23.** Minnesota
ហាវៃ	**11.** Hawaii		មិស៊ុស៊ីពី	**24.** Mississippi
អៃដាហូ	**12.** Idaho		មិហ្ស៊ូរី	**25.** Missouri
អ៊ីលីណយ	**13.** Illinois		ម៉ុនថាណា	**26.** Montana

សហរដ្ឋអាមេរិក

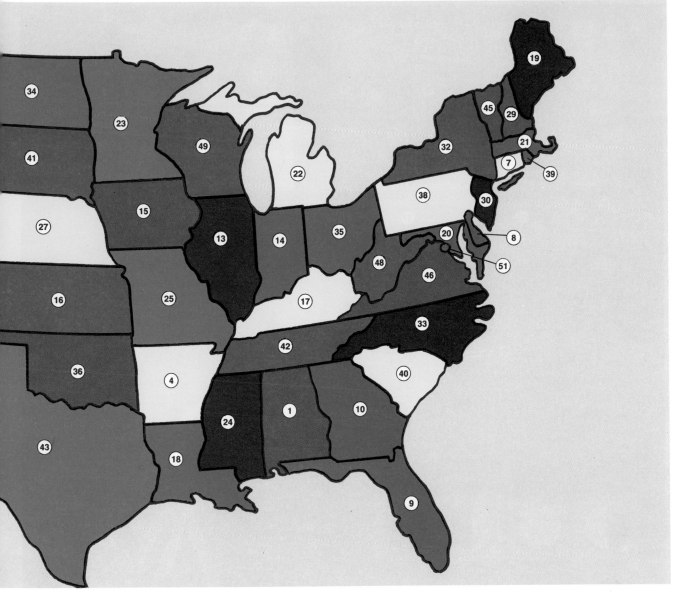

ណេប្រាស្កា	**27.** Nebraska	សៅការ៉ូខ្សៃណា	**40.** South Carolina
ណេវ៉ាដា	**28.** Nevada	សៅដាកូតា	**41.** South Dakota
នូហាំស៊ីរ	**29.** New Hampshire	តិណ្ណីស៊ី	**42.** Tennessee
នូជឺហ្សេ	**30.** New Jersey	តិចហ្សាស់, តិចសាស់	**43.** Texas
នូម៉េចហ្ស៊ិក	**31.** New Mexico	យូថា	**44.** Utah
នូយ៉ក, ញ៉ូវយ៉ក, ញ៉ូវយ៉ក	**32.** New York	វ៉ឺម៉ន, វ៉ែម៉ន	**45.** Vermont
ន័រការ៉ូខ្សៃណា	**33.** North Carolina	វៀហ្ស៊ីនញ៉ា, វៀហ្ស៊ី	**46.** Virginia
ន័រដាកូតា	**34.** North Dakota	វ៉ាស៊ីនតោន	**47.** Washington
អូហៃយ៉ូ	**35.** Ohio	វ៉ែសវៀហ្ស៊ីនញ៉ា	**48.** West Virginia
អូក្លាហូម៉ា	**36.** Oklahoma	វិសុនស៊ិន	**49.** Wisconsin
អរេហ្គិន	**37.** Oregon	វ៉ៃយ៉ូមិញ	**50.** Wyoming
ប៉ិនស៊ីវ៉ានី	**38.** Pennsylvania			
រ៉ូដអៃឡ្យាន់, រ៉ូដអៃឡ្យិន	**39.** Rhode Island	ឌ្រិស្ទ្រិច(អូហ្វ)ក្លូឡុមប៊ីយ៉ា	**51.** District of Columbia

សាកលលោក

អវកាស	A. Outer Space	ផ្កាយព្រះគ្រោះ	The Planets	គន្លងទន់រង់, វង្គវិល, អីរ៉ូបិត	21. orbit
ហ្គាឡាក់ស៊ី	1. galaxy	មើគ្យួរី	11. Mercury	កែវយឺត	22. telescope
ផ្កាយដុះកន្ទុយ	2. comet	វីនុស	12. Venus		
ក្រុមផ្កាយ (ខ្យៃផ្ចំ)	3. (Big Dipper) constellation	ព្រះធរណី, ផែនដី	13. Earth	ទិញនៅមកនៃព្រះចន្ទ	C. Phases
ផ្កាយ, តារា	4. star	ម៉ាស់	14. Mars	ដំណើររបៀបប្ប្លួនៅ	of the
អាកាសបាតុភូត	5. meteor	ហ្ស៊ុពីតែរ៍	15. Jupiter		Moon
		សាទន	16. Saturn	ព្រះចន្ទខ្នើត	23. first quarter
ប្រព័ន្ធព្រះអាទិត្យ	B. The Solar System	រង្វង់ជុំវិញ	a. ring	ខែពេញវង់, ព្រះចន្ទពេញបូរមី	24. full moon
ចន្ទគ្រាស	6. lunar eclipse	អ៊ុរ៉ានុស	17. Uranus	ព្រះចន្ទរនាច	25. last quarter
ថ្ងៃ, ព្រះអាទិត្យ	7. Sun	ណិបទូន	18. Neptune	ខែងងឹតសូន្យ	26. new moon
ព្រះធរណី, ផែនដី	8. Earth	ភ្លុ	19. Pluto		
លោកខែ, ព្រះចន្ទ	9. Moon				
សូរគ្រាស	10. solar eclipse	អាស្តេរ៉យ៍	20. asteroid		

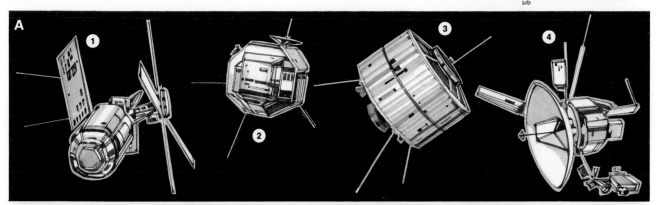

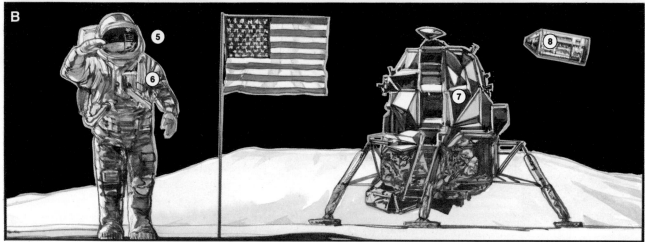

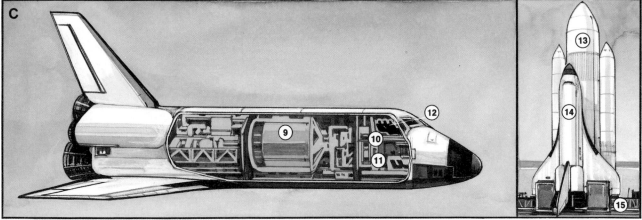

អវកាសយាន	**A. Spacecraft**	ការចុះលើលោកខែ	**B. Landing on the Moon**	កន្លែងសំរាប់អ្នកបើកបរ
ស្ថានីយអវកាស	**1.** space station			កន្លែងដេកសម្រាក
សាតែលលិតគមនាគមន៍	**2.** communication satellite	អ្នកអវកាស	**5.** astronaut	យានិក (មនុស្សទាំង
សាតែលលិតសំរាប់ សង្កេតមើលធាតុអាកាស	**3.** weather satellite	ខោអាវអ្នកអវកាស	**6.** space suit	អស់នៅក្នុងអវកាសយាន)
ឧបករណ៍ស្ទង់អវកាស	**4.** space probe	ឧបករណ៍ចុះលើលោកខែ	**7.** lunar module	កាំជ្រួច, រ៉ុកែត
		អវកាសយានបញ្ជាការ	**8.** command module	យានចម្លងសុតគីល
				កន្លែងបាញ់បង្ហោះ

10. flight deck
11. living quarters
12. crew
13. rocket
14. space shuttle
15. launchpad

យានចម្លងសុតគីល	**C. The Space Shuttle**
កន្លែងផ្ទុកឥវ៉ាន់	**9.** cargo bay

បន្ទប់រៀន

ទង់ជ័យ	**1.** flag	សៀវភៅសរសេរវិណ្ឌដែកល្វស	**15.** spiral notebook
នាឡិកា	**2.** clock	តុ	**16.** desk
អូប៉ាលើរ	**3.** loudspeaker	កាវ	**17.** glue
គ្រូបង្រៀន	**4.** teacher	ជក់	**18.** brush
ក្តារខៀន	**5.** chalkboard	កូនសិស្ស, និស្សិត	**19.** student
កន្លែងដាក់ឥវ៉ាន់	**6.** locker	ប្រដាប់ចិតសម្រចខ្មៅដៃ	**20.** pencil sharpener
ក្តារបិទប្រកាស	**7.** bulletin board	ជ័រលុប	**21.** pencil eraser
កុំព្យូទ័រ	**8.** computer	ប៊ិច	**22.** ballpoint pen
កន្លែងដាក់ដីស	**9.** chalk tray	បន្ទាត់	**23.** ruler
ដីស	**10.** chalk	ខ្មៅដៃ	**24.** pencil
ប្រដាប់សំរាប់លុប	**11.** eraser	ដែកគោលចុច	**25.** thumbtack
ច្រកនៅចិន្លោះបន្ទប់រៀនសំរាប់ទៅមក	**12.** hall	សៀវភៅមៀល	**26.** (text)book
ក្រដាស	**13.** (loose-leaf) paper	ប្រដាប់បញ្ចាំងរូបពីលើអ្នកមើល	**27.** overhead projector
ក្របសៀវភៅសរសេរមានកង	**14.** ring binder		

កិរិយាសព្ទនៅក្នុងសាលារៀន

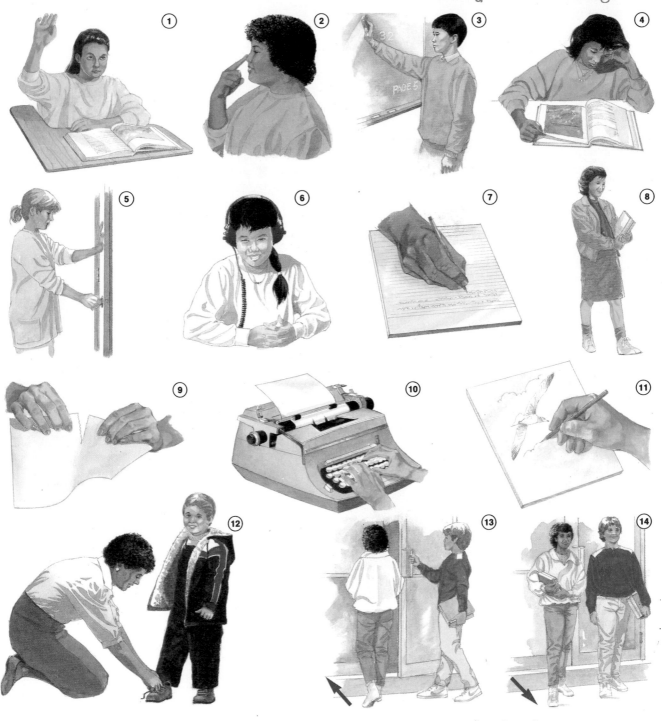

លើក (ដៃ)	**1.** raise (one's hand)	ដើរ	**8.** walk
ស្ទាប	**2.** touch	ហែក	**9.** tear
លុប	**3.** erase	វាយដាក់ទីឌ្យូ, វាយម៉ាស៊ីន	**10.** type
មើល, អាន	**4.** read	គូរ	**11.** draw
បិទ	**5.** close	ចង	**12.** tie
ស្ដាប់	**6.** listen	ចេញ	**13.** leave
សរសេរ	**7.** write	ចូល	**14.** enter

កន្លែងពិសោធន៍វិទ្យាសាស្ត្រ

ប្រិស្ម៍	**1.** prism	ឧបករណ៍កំណត់ម៉ោង	**13.** timer	កែវមានកម្រិតចំណុះ	**25.** graduated
ផប	**2.** flask	បំពង់កែវសំរាប់បូមវត្ថុរាវ	**14.** pipette		cylinder
ចានចិញ្ចើមមេរោគ	**3.** petri dish	កែវពង្រីក	**15.** magnifying glass	ប្រដាប់បន្តក់ថ្នាំ	**26.** medicine
ជញ្ជីង	**4.** scale	ក្រដាសតម្រង	**16.** filter paper		dropper
កូនជញ្ជីង	**5.** weights	ជីវឡារ៉ាវ	**17.** funnel	មេដែក	**27.** magnet
បណ្ដាញដែកល្បោស	**6.** wire mesh screen	បំពង់កៅស៊ូ, ទុយយោ	**18.** rubber tubing	ដង្កៀប, ដង្ខាប់	**28.** forceps
ដង្កៀប	**7.** clamp	ប្រដាប់សំរាប់ទ្រកែវពិសោធន៍ពេលដុតភ្លើងពីក្រោម	**19.** ring stand	ដង្កៀប	**29.** tongs
ប្រដាប់សំរាប់ដាក់តម្រៀប	**8.** rack	ប្រដាប់សំរាប់ដុតហ្គាសកំដៅ	**20.** Bunsen burner	អតិសុខុមទស្សន៍	**30.** microscope
កែវពិសោធន៍	**9.** test tube	អណ្ដាតភ្លើង	**21.** flame	បន្ទះកែវ	**31.** slide
ឆ្នុក	**10.** stopper	ទែម៉ូម៉ែត្រ	**22.** thermometer	ចន្ទាស	**32.** tweezers
ក្រដាសគូរក្រាហ្វិក	**11.** graph paper	កែវមានមាត់ធំហើយមានចង្អូរចាក់	**23.** beaker	ប្រដាប់សំរាប់វះកាត់	**33.** dissection kit
វ៉ែនតាការពារភ្នែក	**12.** safety glasses	តុ (សំរាប់ធ្វើការពិសោធន៍)	**24.** bench	កៅអី (គ្មានស្ពឹផ្អែក)	**34.** stool

គណិតសាស្ត្រ

A

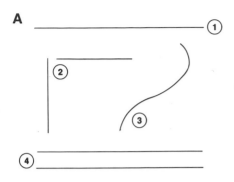

B

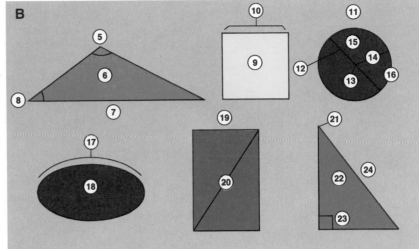

C

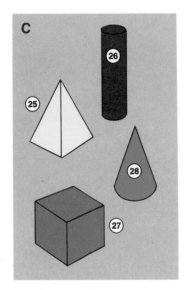

D

E

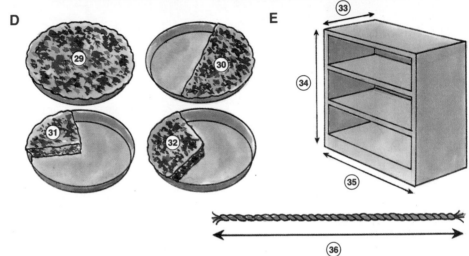

បន្ទាត់	**A. Lines**
បន្ទាត់ត្រង់	**1.** straight line
បន្ទាត់កាត់គ្នា ៩០ ដីក្រេ	**2.** perpendicular lines
បន្ទាត់កោង	**3.** curve
បន្ទាត់ស្រប	**4.** parallel lines

ផ្ទៃរេខាគណិត	**B. Geometrical Figures**
មុមធំជាង ៩០ ដីក្រេ	**5.** obtuse angle
ត្រីកោណ	**6.** triangle
បាត	**7.** base
មុមតូចជាង ៩០ ដីក្រេ	**8.** acute angle
ចតុរ័ស្សកែងស្មើ, ឬបន្ទ្រង់ស្មើ	**9.** square
ជ្រុង	**10.** side
រង្វង់មូល	**11.** circle
វិជ្ជុមាត្រ	**12.** diameter

ចំណុចកណ្ដាល	**13.** center
កាំ	**14.** radius
ផ្នែក (នៃរង្វង់មូល)	**15.** section
ធ្នូ (នៃរង្វង់មូល)	**16.** arc
វណ្ឌមណ្ឌល	**17.** circumference
រង្វង់ពងក្រពើ	**18.** oval
ចតុរ័ស្ស, ឬបន្ទ្រង់ទ្រវែង	**19.** rectangle
វិជ្ជុកោណ	**20.** diagonal
កំពូល	**21.** apex
ត្រីកោណមានមុម ៩០ ដីក្រេមួយ	**22.** right triangle
មុមមានកម្រិត ៩០ ដីក្រេ	**23.** right angle
អ៊ីប៉ូតេនុស្យ៍	**24.** hypotenuse

ផ្ទៃរេខាគណិតចំណុះ	**C. Solid Figures**
សាជីជ្រុង	**25.** pyramid

ស៊ីឡាំង, រង្វាការ	**26.** cylinder
គូប, គុប, ឆឡៀង្ស	**27.** cube
កោណ	**28.** cone

ប្រភាគ	**D. Fractions**
ចំនួនគត់	**29.** whole
កន្លះ	**30.** a half (1/2)
មួយភាគបួន	**31.** a quarter (1/4)
មួយភាគបី	**32.** a third (1/3)

ខ្នាត់ខ្នាល់	**E. Measurement**
ជម្រៅ	**33.** depth
កំពស់	**34.** height
ទទឹង	**35.** width
បណ្ដោយ	**36.** length

ថាមពល

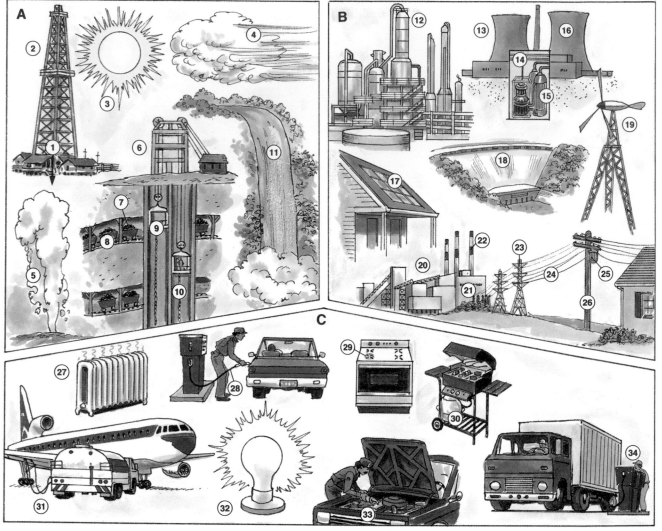

ប្រភពថាមពល	A.	Sources of Power	រ៉េអាក់ទ័រនុយក្លេអ៊ែរ	13.	nuclear reactor	ការប្រើប្រាស់ហើយ	C.	Uses and
			សួល	14.	core	និងផលិតផលផ្សេងៗ		Products
អណ្ដូងប្រេងកាត	1.	oil well	បំពង់អ៊ុយរ៉ានីញ៉ម	15.	uranium rods	កំដៅ	27.	heat
សំណង់ខ្ពស់នៅមាត់អណ្ដូងប្រេងកាត	2.	derrick	អាគារសំរាប់ធ្វើឱ្យត្រជាក់	16.	cooling tower	ប្រេងសាំង	28.	gas(oline)
ថ្ងៃ, ព្រះអាទិត្យ	3.	sun	គ្រឿងស្រូបយកថាមពលព្រះអាទិត្យ	17.	solar collector	ហ្គាស់	29.	natural gas
ខ្យល់	4.	wind	ទំនប់ទឹក	18.	dam	ប្រូប៊ែន, ប្រេងកាតឧស្ម័ន	30.	propane gas
កន្លែងចំហាយទឹកបាញ់ចេញពីក្នុងដី	5.	geyser	ដង្ហាល់	19.	windmill	ប្រេងសាំងសំរាប់	31.	jet fuel
រ៉ែផ្លូវថ្ម	6.	coal mine	ស្ថានីយអគ្គិសនី, ម៉ាស៊ីនភ្លើង	20.	power station	កប៉ាល់ហោះរ៉េអាក់សួន		
ផ្លូវថ្ម	7.	coal	ហ្សេណេរ៉ាទ័រ,	21.	electrical generator	អគ្គិសនី	32.	electricity
ឆុងដឹកពញ្ចានផ្លូវថ្ម	8.	shuttle car	ឧបករណ៍បង្កើតអគ្គិសនី			ប្រេងសាំងស៊ីន	33.	motor oil
ទ្រុងដឹកកម្មករចុះឡើង	9.	elevator	បំពង់ផ្សែង	22.	smokestack	ប្រេងឌីយេហ្សែល	34.	diesel fuel
ប្រហោងជណ្ដើរយោងឡើងចុះ	10.	shaft	បង្គោលខ្សែភ្លើងធំ	23.	transmission towers			
ទឹកធ្លាក់	11.	waterfall	ខ្សែភ្លើង	24.	power lines			
			ត្រង់ស្វ័រម៉ាទ័រ	25.	transformer			
ការបង្កើតថាមពល	B.	Generation of Power	បង្គោលខ្សែភ្លើងតូច (ធម្មតាយកដើមឈើ ទាំងមូលមួយដើមមកធ្វើ)	26.	utility pole			
កន្លែងសួរប្រេងកាត	12.	refinery						

ការធ្វើស្រែចំការនិងចិញ្ចឹមសត្វ

កន្លែងចិញ្ចឹមគោយកទឹកដោះ	**A. Dairy Farm**		មេគោយកទឹកដោះ	**11.** dairy cow		ជួរ	**18.** row
ចំការលើផ្ទៃ	**1.** orchard					ចន្លោង, ទិងមោងបន្លាចសត្វ	**19.** scarecrow
ឈើផ្ទៃ	**2.** fruit tree	ចំការដាំស្រូវសាលី	**B. Wheat**				
ផ្ទះរបស់អ្នកស្រែចំការ	**3.** farmhouse		Farm		កន្លែងចិញ្ចឹមសត្វ	**C. Ranch**
ជង្រុក	**4.** silo	បសុសត្វ	**12.** livestock		(ហ្វូង) គោ	**20.** (herd of) cattle
ក្រោលគោនិងកន្លែងដាក់ឥវ៉ាន់	**5.** barn	(ដុំ) ចំបើង	**13.** (bale of) hay	ខោបាយ, គង្វាលគោប្រុស	**21.** cowboy
វាលស្មៅ (សំរាប់សត្វស៊ី)	**6.** pasture	ចន្លាយ, ដែកនាយ	**14.** pitchfork	គង្វាលគោស្រី	**22.** cowgirl
អ្នកស្រែចំការ	**7.** farmer	ត្រាក់ទ័រ	**15.** tractor	សេះ	**23.** horses
ទីធ្លា (នៅផ្ទះប្រែលគោ)	**8.** barnyard	ស្រែ, ចំការ (ដាំស្រូវសាលី)	**16.** (wheat) field	ក្រោល	**24.** corral
របង	**9.** fence	ម៉ាស៊ីនច្រូតកាត់	**17.** combine	ធុងដាក់ចំណីឲ្យសត្វ	**25.** trough
ចៀម	**10.** sheep					

ការសង់សំណង់

កន្លែងសង់សំណង់	A. Construction Site
បង្គង ឬ ផ្ដោង	1. rafters
គ្រឿងប្រក់	2. shingle
ប្រដាប់ស្ទង់ឲ្យដឹងថាស្មើឬមិនស្មើ	3. level
មួកដែក	4. hard hat
ជាងសង់ផ្ទះ	5. builder
ប្លង់ផ្ទះ	6. blueprints
រន្ធា	7. scaffolding
ជណ្ដើរ	8. ladder
កាំជណ្ដើរ	9. rung
ស៊ីម៉ង់	10. cement

គ្រឹះ	11. foundation
ឥដ្ឋ	12. bricks
ចបត្រសេះ	13. pickax
កម្មករសង់ផ្ទះ	14. construction worker
ប៉ែល	15. shovel
បន្ទះឈើ	16. board
ជាងបន្ទខ្សែភ្លើង	17. linesman
ប្រដាប់សំរាប់ស្ងួយទៅទីខ្ពស់	18. cherry picker

កិច្ចការតាមផ្លូវថ្នល់	B. Road Work
សាជីដាក់ចែកផ្លូវ (បណ្ណោះអាសន្ន)	19. cone

ទង់	20. flag
ប្រដាប់ដាក់ឃាំង ម៉ាស៊ីនខួងផ្ទះ (ប្រើកម្លាំងខ្យល់, ធម្មតាគេច្រើនប្រើសំរាប់វាយដីគាស់ផ្ទែគ្រាលផ្លូវ)	21. barricade
22. jackhammer
រទេះរុញ (សំរាប់ដឹកដញ្ចូនដី, ឥដ្ឋជាដើម)	23. wheelbarrow
របាំងចែកផ្លូវវង្វល់ជាពីរ	24. center divider
ឡានលាយស៊ីម៉ង់	25. cement mixer
ត្រាក់ទ័រមានប្រដាប់កាយដីនៅពីក្រោយ	26. backhoe
ម៉ាស៊ីនឈូសដី, ត្រាក់ទ័រឈូសដី	27. bulldozer

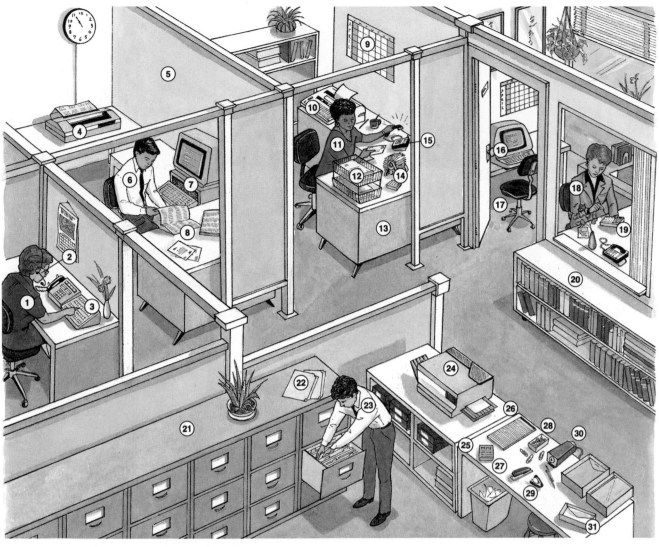

អ្នកបេរាទ័រ, អ្នកផ្លើយតេឡេហ្វូន	**1.**	switchboard operator
ប្រដាប់ពាក់ស្តាប់	**2.**	headset
ឧបករណ៍បន្តតេឡេហ្វូនពីមួយទៅមួយទៀត	**3.**	switchboard
ម៉ាស៊ីនវាយ (ចេញជា) អក្សរ	**4.**	printer
បន្ទប់បូនជ្រុងតូចៗ	**5.**	cubicle
អ្នកវាយអង្គុលីលេខ	**6.**	typist
ម៉ាស៊ីនសរសេរ	**7.**	word processor
ក្រដាសចេញពីម៉ាស៊ីនវាយអក្សរ	**8.**	printout
ប្រក្រតិទិន	**9.**	calendar
អង្គុលីលេខ	**10.**	typewriter
ស្មៀន, លេខាធិការ	**11.**	secretary
ប្រអប់ដាក់សំបុត្រ ឬ ក្រដាសចូល ឬមកដល់	**12.**	in-box
តុ	**13.**	desk
រ៉ូឡូដិច (ប្រអប់សំរាប់ឥត្តឈ្មោះក្រុមហ៊ុន	**14.**	rolodex
ឬ មនុស្សដែលគេចង់ទាក់ទងនៅថ្ងៃក្រោយ		
តេឡេហ្វូន	**15.**	telephone
កុំព្យូទ័រ	**16.**	computer
កៅអីសំរាប់អង្គុយវាយដាក់ទិព្វ	**17.**	typing chair
អ្នកមើលខុសត្រូវ, អ្នកគ្រប់គ្រា	**18.**	manager
ម៉ាស៊ីនគិតលេខ	**19.**	calculator
ទូដាក់សៀវភៅ	**20.**	bookcase
ទូដាក់បញ្ជី	**21.**	file cabinet
ក្របសំរាប់ដាក់សំណុំរឿង, បញ្ជី ឬ ក្រដាសផ្សេងៗ	**22.**	file folder
អ្នករៀបចំបញ្ជី	**23.**	file clerk
ម៉ាស៊ីនថតចំលងបុត្រ	**24.**	photocopier
ក្រដាសកត់ពាក្យបណ្ដាំ (ធម្មតាតាមតេឡេហ្វូន)	**25.**	message pad
ក្រដាសសរសេរធុនធំ	**26.**	(legal) pad
ប្រដាប់កិប	**27.**	stapler
ដែកខ្លាស់	**28.**	paper clips
ប្រដាប់ដោះដែកកិប	**29.**	staple remover
ប្រដាប់ចិតសុ៊ចខ្មៅដៃ	**30.**	pencil sharpener
ស្រោមសំបុត្រ	**31.**	envelope

មុខរបរ ១: នៅតាមផ្លូវក្នុងផ្សារផ្លូវនៃស.រ.អ.

និស្សិតការី	**1.** pharmacist		អ្នកធ្វើនំ (នំប៉័ង ។ល។)	**8.** baker
ជាងជួសជុលឡាន	**2.** mechanic		អ្នកលក់វ៉ែនតា	**9.** optician
ជាងកាត់សក់	**3.** barber		ជាងធ្វើសក់	**10.** hairdresser
ភ្នាក់ងារខាងការធ្វើដំណើរ	**4.** travel agent		អ្នកលក់ផ្កា	**11.** florist
ជាងជួសជុល	**5.** repairperson		អ្នកលក់គ្រឿងអលង្ការ	**12.** jeweller
ជាងកាត់ដេរ	**6.** tailor		អ្នកលក់សាច់	**13.** butcher
អ្នកលក់បន្លែផ្លែឈើ	**7.** greengrocer			

ការជួសជុលនិងការថែទាំ	A. Repair and Maintenance
ជាងបំពង់ទឹក	1. plumber
ជាងឈើ	2. carpenter
អ្នកថែទាំសួនច្បារ	3. gardener
ជាងផ្ដើរសោ	4. locksmith
អ្នករកស៊ីលក់ផ្ទះ ឬ ដី	5. real estate agent
ជាងខ្សែភ្លើង	6. electrician
អ្នកលាបថ្នាំ (ផ្ទះ)	7. painter

បរិចារកិច្ចតាមផ្ទះ	B. Household Services
អ្នកសំអាតរៀបចំផ្ទះ (ថ្មគេ)	8. housekeeper
អ្នកបោសជូត	9. janitor
អ្នកយកឥវ៉ាន់មកច្ប្យដល់ផ្ទះ	10. delivery boy
អ្នកយាមទ្វារ	11. doorman

កិច្ចការក្នុងរោងចក្រ	C. Factory Work
កម្មកររោងចក្រ	12. shopworker
មេក្រុមកម្មករ	13. foreman

មុខរបរ ៣

គ្រឿងផ្សាយពត៌មាននិងសិល្បៈ៖	**A. Media and Arts**
អ្នកផ្សាយផ្នែកធាតុអាកាស	**1.** weather forecaster
អ្នកផ្សាយពត៌មាន	**2.** newscaster
សិល្បករ	**3.** artist
អ្នកថតរូប	**4.** photographer
ម៉ូដែល	**5.** model
អ្នកផ្នែកប្រឌិតសំលៀកបំពាក់ទំនើប	**6.** fashion designer
អ្នកនិពន្ធ	**7.** writer
និម្មាបនិក	**8.** architect
អ្នកចាក់ភ្លេង	**9.** disc jockey (DJ)
អ្នកថតទូរទស្សន៍	**10.** cameraperson
អ្នកយកពត៌មាន (កាសែត, ទូរទស្សន៍ ។ល។)	**11.** reporter

អ្នកលក់ | **12.** salesperson

កិច្ចការធនាគារ	**B. Banking**
បុគ្គលិកផ្នាក់ខ្ពស់	**13.** officer
អ្នកការ៉ាប់សន្តិសុខ	**14.** security guard
អ្នកបើក ឬ ទទួលប្រាក់	**15.** teller

អ្នកធ្វើការខាងពាណិជ្ជកម្ម	**C. Business Workers**
អ្នកសរសេរប្រូក្រាមកុំព្យូទ័រ	**16.** computer programmer
អ្នកទទួលភ្ញៀវ	**17.** receptionist
គណនេយ្យករ, អ្នកកាន់បញ្ជីប្រាក់ចេញចូល	**18.** accountant
អ្នកនាំសារ	**19.** messenger

សួនល់វែមានៅជិតៗផ្ទះ

សួនសត្វ	**1.** zoo		ធុងសំរាម	**11.** trash can
រោងលេងភ្លេង	**2.** band shell		ប្រដាប់រអិលលេខ	**12.** slide
អ្នកលក់ដូរ	**3.** vendor		កន្លែងដាក់ដីខ្សាច់ឲ្យក្មេងលេង	**13.** sandbox
រទេះរុញ	**4.** hand truck		ប្រដាប់បាច ឬ បាញ់ទឹក	**14.** sprinkler
ម៉ូរីហ្គោវៀន	**5.** merry-go-round		កន្លែងក្មេងលេង	**15.** playground
អ្នកជិះសេះ	**6.** horseback rider		ទោង	**16.** swings
ផ្លូវជិះសេះ	**7.** bridle path		ប្រដាប់ក្មេងលេងមានកាំឡើងចុះ	
ស្រះ (សំរាប់ទា)	**8.** (duck) pond		ផ្ទៃអ្វីលើសំរាប់ឲ្យក្មេងឡើងលេខ	**17.** jungle gym
ផ្លូវសំរាប់រត់ហាត់ប្រាណ	**9.** jogging path		ក្ដារ(ជិះលេខ)បះចុះបះឡើង	**18.** seesaw
កៅអីអង្គុយលេខ	**10.** bench		ក្បាលម៉ាស៊ីនទឹកសំរាប់ផឹក	**19.** water fountain

សកម្មភាពក្រៅផ្ទះ

ខ្លង់រាប	**1.** plateau		ថង់នេសាទត្រី	**9.** fishing net
អ្នកដើរលេងតាមព្រៃ	**2.** hikers		ខោកៅស៊ូពាក់លុយទឹក	**10.** waders
ជ្រោះជ្រៅ	**3.** canyon		ថ្ម	**11.** rocks
ភ្នំទាបៗ	**4.** hill			
តម្រួតឧទ្យាន	**5.** park ranger		**កន្លែងធ្វើពិចនិច**	**Picnic Area**
			ប្រដាប់អាំងសាច់	**12.** grill
ការនេសាទត្រី	**Fishing**		កញ្ចើសំរាប់ដាក់គ្រឿងពិចនិច	**13.** picnic basket
អូរ, ធ្លរទឹក	**6.** stream		ថែរម៉ូស	**14.** thermos
ដងសន្ទច	**7.** fishing rod		តុពិចនិច	**15.** picnic table
ខ្សែសន្ទច	**8.** fishing line			

	Rafting
ក្បូន	**16.** raft
កន្លែងទឹកហូរភ្លូចខ្លាំង	**17.** rapids
ទឹកធ្លាក់	**18.** waterfall

ជិះក្បូនលេង

	Mountain Climbing
ភ្នំ	**19.** mountain
កំពូល	**20.** peak
ច្រាំងចោត គ្រឿងចងប្រដាប់ប្រទិនសំរាប់	**21.** cliff
យោងទាញ ឫ ភ្ជាប់និងអ្វីទៀត	**22.** harness
ខ្សែ	**23.** rope

កីឡាឡើងភ្នំ

	Camping
តង់	**24.** tent
ចង្ក្រាន	**25.** camp stove
១បសំពត់	**26.** sleeping bag
ប្រដាប់ប្រដាផ្សេងៗ	**27.** gear
សំពាយមានឆ្អឹង	**28.** frame backpack
ចង្កៀង	**29.** lantern
ស្មឹង	**30.** stake
ភ្លក់ភ្លើងក៍បើ	**31.** campfire
ឧស	**32.** woods

កំបេ៉

នៅមាត់សមុទ្រ

រានដើរកំសាន្ត (តាមមាត់សមុទ្រ)	**1.**	boardwalk	ភ្នំខ្សាច់	**12.**	sand dunes
តូបលក់គ្រឿងផឹក:	**2.**	refreshment stand	ហ្វ្រិសប៊ី	**13.**	Frisbee™
ម៉ូតែល	**3.**	motel	វ៉ែនតាពាក់កុំឲ្យចាំងភ្នែក, វ៉ែនតាខ្មៅ	**14.**	sunglasses
អ្នកជិះកង់	**4.**	biker	កន្សែងសំរាប់ក្រាលអង្គុយមាត់សមុទ្រ	**15.**	beach towel
កញ្ចែ	**5.**	whistle	ធុង	**16.**	pail
តម្រួតមើលមនុស្សហែលទឹក	**6.**	lifeguard	បៀល	**17.**	shovel
កែវយឹត	**7.**	binoculars	ខោអាវង្កូតទឹក, ខោអាវស្ទ្រៀតពាក់លេងទឹក	**18.**	bathing suit
កៅអីតម្រួតមើលមនុស្សហែលទឹក	**8.**	lifeguard chair	អ្នកដេកហាលថ្ងៃកំសាន្ត	**19.**	sunbather
ពោង	**9.**	life preserver	កៅអីអង្គុយទម្រេតលេង	**20.**	beach chair
ទូកសំរាប់ប្រើនៅពេលមានអាសន្ន	**10.**	lifeboat	ឆត្រ (ផំៗសំរាប់ប្រើនៅពេលទៅ លេងមាត់សមុទ្រ ។ល។)	**21.**	beach umbrella
បាល់សំរាប់លេងនៅមាត់សមុទ្រ	**11.**	beach ball			

ខ្លែង	**22.** kite	ប្រាសាទធ្វើអំពីខ្សាច់	**32.** sandcastle
អ្នករត់	**23.** runners	ខោស្ទៀតហែលទឹក	**33.** bathing trunks
រលក	**24.** wave	បំពង់ដកដង្ហើមក្នុងទឹក	**34.** snorkel
ការជិះលេងលើរលក	**25.** surfboard	កែវពាក់មុជទឹក	**35.** mask
ពូកកៅស៊ូ(ផ្លុំខ្យល់)	**26.** air mattress	កៅស៊ូពាក់ហែលទឹក (ពាក់នៅចុងជើង)	**36.** flippers
ការសំរាប់ពោះហែល	**27.** kickboard	ធុងដាក់ខ្យល់	**37.** scuba tank
អ្នកហែលទឹក	**28.** swimmer	ខោអាវកៅស៊ូពាក់ចុះទឹក	**38.** wet suit
ពោះវៀនកង់ឡាន	**29.** tube	ថ្នាំលាបស្បែកហាលថ្ងៃ	**39.** suntan lotion
ទឹក	**30.** water	សំបកលាស ឬ ខ្យង ។ល។	**40.** shell
ដីខ្សាច់	**31.** sand	ធុងទឹកកក	**41.** cooler

ភីឡា(ជា)ក្រុម

បេហ្ស៊ីបល		**Baseball**
អាជ្ញាកណ្តាល (កីឡា)	**1.**	umpire
អ្នកចាប់	**2.**	catcher
របាំងមុខអ្នកចាប់	**3.**	catcher's mask
ស្រោមដៃអ្នកចាប់	**4.**	catcher's mitt
ដំបងវាយបាល់	**5.**	bat
មួកអ្នកវាយបាល់	**6.**	batting helmet
អ្នកវាយបាល់	**7.**	batter
ក្រុមបេហ្ស៊ីបលកុមារ		**Little League Baseball**
កុមារអ្នកលេងបេហ្ស៊ីបល	**8.**	Little Leaguer
ឯកសណ្ឋាន	**9.**	uniform
ភីឡាបាល់ទន់		**Softball**
បាល់ទន់	**10.**	softball
មួក	**11.**	cap
ស្រោមដៃ	**12.**	glove
ភីឡាហ្វុតបល		**Football**
បាល់ (រាងមូលទ្រវែង)	**13.**	football
មួក	**14.**	helmet
ភីឡាឡាក្រស		**Lacrosse**
របាំងមុខ	**15.**	face guard
កន្ត្រងឡាក្រស	**16.**	lacrosse stick
ភីឡាហុកគី		**Ice Hockey**
កូនគោល	**17.**	puck
ដំបង (វាយកូនគោល)	**18.**	hockey stick
ភីឡាបាស្កេតបល ឬ បាល់បោះ		**Basketball**
ក្តារបាំញ	**19.**	backboard
កព្ញោង	**20.**	basket
បាល់ (សំរាប់លេងបាស់ស្កេតបល)	**21.**	basketball
ភីឡាវ៉ុលនៃ្លបល ឬ បាល់ទះ		**Volleyball**
បាល់ (សំរាប់លេងបាល់ទះ)	**22.**	volleyball
សំណាញ់	**23.**	net
ភីឡាបាល់ទាត់		**Soccer**
ឆ្មាំទី, អ្នកចាំទី	**24.**	goalie
ទី	**25.**	goal
បាល់ (សំរាប់លេងបាល់ទាត់)	**26.**	soccer ball

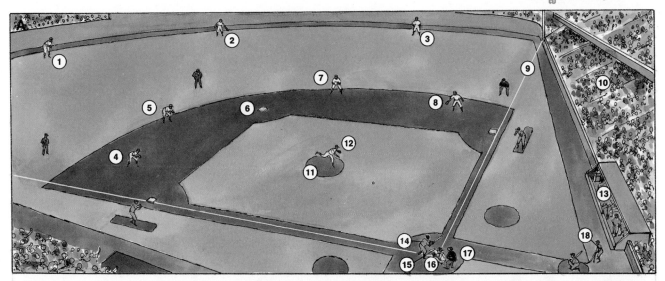

ឆ្នាលេងបេហ្ស៊ីប័ល	**A.**	**Baseball Diamond**	កន្លែងអ្នកអង្គុយមើល	**10.**	stands	អ្នកហ្វឹកហ្វឺន	**21.**	coach

ឆ្នាលេងបេហ្ស៊ីប័ល

A . Baseball Diamond

អ្នកចាប់ (បាល់) ខាងក្រោយខាងឆ្វេង
1 . left fielder

អ្នកចាប់ (បាល់) ខាងក្រោយខាងស្តាំ
2 . center fielder

អ្នកចាប់ (បាល់) ខាងក្រោយខាងកណ្តាល
3 . right fielder

អ្នកចាំបេហ្ស៊ីទី៣
4 . third baseman

អ្នកចាប់ចន្លោះបេហ្ស៊ី ទី២ និង ទី៣
5 . shortstop

បេហ្ស៊ី
6 . base

អ្នកចាំបេហ្ស៊ីទី២
7 . second baseman

អ្នកចាំបេហ្ស៊ីទី១
8 . first baseman

បន្ទាត់បាល់ចេញក្រៅ
9 . foul line

កន្លែងអ្នកអង្គុយមើល
10. stands

កន្លែងអ្នកចោលបាល់
11. pitcher's mound

អ្នកចោលបាល់
12. pitcher

កន្លែងសំរាប់អ្នកលេងអង្គុយ
13. dugout

អ្នកវាយបាល់
14. batter

កម្រាលដើមទី
15. home plate

អ្នកចាប់បាល់
16. catcher

អាជ្ញាកណ្តាល
17. umpire

អ្នកកាន់កាប់ដំបង
18. batboy

ឆ្នាកីឡាហ្វុតប័ល

B . Football Field

កន្លែងដាក់ពិន្ទុបង្ហាញ (នៅពេលកំពុងលេង)
19. scoreboard

ក្រុមស្ត្រីអ្នកស្រែកលើកទឹកចិត្ត
20. cheerleaders

អ្នកហ្វឹកហ្វឺន
21. coach

អាជ្ញាកណ្តាល
22. referee

ចុងទី
23. end zone

អ្នកទទួលបាល់
24. split end

អ្នកចាប់ជ្រោកផ្លូវខាងឆ្វេង
25. left tackle

អ្នកការពារខាងឆ្វេង
26. left guard

អ្នកនៅកណ្តាល
27. center

អ្នកការពារខាងស្តាំ
28. right guard

អ្នកចាប់ជ្រោកផ្លូវខាងស្តាំ
29. right tackle

អ្នកឆែវនិងអ្នកចាប់ជ្រោកផ្លូវខាងស្តាំ
30. tight end

អ្នកនៅរាម
31. flanker

អ្នកចោលបាល់
32. quarterback

អ្នកនៅក្រោយមធ្យម
33. halfback

អ្នកនៅក្រោយបំផុត
34. fullback

បង្គោលទី
35. goalpost

ភិឡ្បាមានអ្នកប្រកួតតែម្នាក់

តែននីស	**Tennis**		ស្បែកជើងលេងប៉ាតាំង	26. skate	
បាល់តែននិស	1. tennis ball		បន្ទះដែកស្បែកជើងលេងប៉ាតាំង	27. blade	
រ៉ាកែត	2. racket		**ភិឡ្បាបាល់ទាយ**	**Racquetball**	
ភិឡ្បាបូលលិញ	**Bowling**		វ៉ែនតាការពារភ្នែក	28. safety goggles	
ចង្អូរ	3. gutter		រ៉ាកែត	29. racquet	
កន្លែងបោះបាល់	4. lane		បាល់(សំរាប់លេង)ភិឡ្បាបាល់វាយ	30. racquetball	
បង្គោល (ភិឡ្បាបូលលិញ)	5. pin		**ការរត់ប្រណាំង**	**Track and Field**	
បាល់(សំរាប់លេង)បូលលិញ	6. bowling ball		អ្នករត់	31. runner	
ភិឡ្បាហ្គុលហ្គ	**Golf**		ផ្លូវរត់	32. track	
បាល់(សំរាប់លេង)ហ្គុលហ្គ	7. golf ball		**ស្គីកាត់តំបន់ដែលគ្មានផ្លូវស្រួលមូល**	**Cross-Country Skiing**	
រន្ធ	8. hole		ស្គី	33. skis	
ដំបងលេងហ្គុលហ្គ (ម្រ៉ាង)	9. putter		ឈើរុញ	34. pole	
អ្នកលេងហ្គុលហ្គ	10. golfer		អ្នកលេងស្គី	35. skier	
ភិឡ្បាហាន់ប័ល	**Handball**				
ស្រោមដៃ	11. glove				
បាល់សំរាប់លេងហាន់ប័ល	12. handball				
កន្លែងលេងហាន់ប័ល ។ល។	13. court				
ភិឡ្បាប្រដាល់	**Boxing**				
ប្រដាប់ពាក់ការពារក្បាល	14. head protector				
ស្រោមដៃ	15. glove				
អាជ្ញាកណ្ដាល	16. referee				
សេវៀន	17. ring				
ពីងប៉ុង	**Ping-Pong**				
រ៉ាកែត	18. paddle				
ពីងប៉ុង	19. ping-pong ball				
ភិឡ្បាប្រណាំងសេះ	**Horse Racing**				
កែប	20. saddle				
អ្នកជិះ	21. jockey				
បង្ហៀរ	22. reins				
ភិឡ្បាកាយសម្ព័ន	**Gymnastics**				
អ្នកកីឡ្បាកាយសម្ព័ន	23. gymnast				
ឈើសំរប់ថ្លឹងដើរ ឫ លោត	24. balance beam				
ប៉័តាំង	**Ice Skating**				
កន្លែងលេងប៉ាតាំង	25. rink				

កន្លែងនិងវាលលេខកីឡា

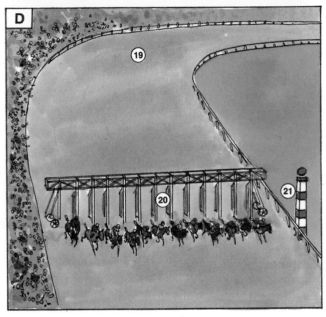

កន្លែងលេខតេននីស	**A. Tennis Court**
ជ្រុងសំរាប់បាល់សេរវិសធ្លាក់	**1.** service court
សំណាញ់	**2.** net
បន្ទាត់វាយសេរវិស	**3.** service line
បន្ទាត់ក្រោយបំផុត	**4.** baseline

វាលលេខហ្គុលហ្វ៍	**B. Golf Course**
ដំបងវាយ	**5.** clubs
កន្លែងដែលគេមិនថែទាំកាត់ស្មៅ	**6.** rough
សំពាយអ្នកលេងហ្គុលហ្វ៍	**7.** golf bag
រទេះអ្នកលេងហ្គុលហ្វ៍	**8.** golf cart

ទង់	**9.** flag
វាលស្មៅតម្រឹមយ៉ាងស្មាតនៅជុំវិញរន្ធ	
ដែលគេត្រូវវាយបាល់បញ្ចូល	**10.** green
ខ្សាច់សំរាប់ផ្តើមឧបសគ្គ	**11.** sand trap
ទីវាល (សំរាប់លេងហ្គុលហ្វ៍)	**12.** fairway
លេីដំកល់បាល់	**13.** tee

ទីៗវាលសំរាប់លេខស្គី	**C. Ski Slope**
លេីសំរាប់រុញ	**14.** pole
ស្បែកជេីងលេខស្គី	**15.** ski boot

គ្រឿងចងស្បែកជេីងភ្ជាប់ទៅនឹងស្គី	**16.** binding
ស្គី	**17.** ski
ម៉ាស៊ីនយោងអ្នកលេខស្គីទៅទីខ្ពស់	**18.** ski lift

វាលបររសេះ	**D. Race Track**
ផ្នែកត្រង់នៃផ្លូវប្រណាំងសេះ	**19.** stretch
(ធម្មតានៅមុខអាគារអ្នកអង្គុយមេីល)	
ទ្វារចាប់ផ្តើមការប្រណាំងសេះ	**20.** starting gate
ខ្សែផ្តាច់ព្រាត់, ខ្សែបញ្ចប់ការប្រណាំង	**21.** finish line

កិរិយាសព្ទនាក់ទងនឹងកីឡា

វាយ	**1.** hit	ហុចឱ្យ, បោះទៅឱ្យ	**5.** pass
វាយបាល់ចាប់ផ្ដើម ឬ នៅពេលបូររវែន	**2.** serve	រត់	**6.** run
ទាត់	**3.** kick	ធ្លាក់, ដួល	**7.** fall
ចាប់	**4.** catch	លោត	**8.** jump

កិរិយាសព្ទនាក់ទងនឹងកីឡា

លេងប៉ាតាំង	**9.** skate	ជិះ	**13.** ride
ចោល, បោះ	**10.** throw	លោតដាក្បាលចុះ	**14.** dive
លោត (ដូចជាបាល់ ។ល។)	**11.** bounce	បើក (ឡាន ។ល។)	**15.** drive
ជិះបន្ទះក្ដារលើរលក	**12.** surf	បាញ់	**16.** shoot

 គ្រឿងភ្លេង, គ្រឿងតូរ្យតន្រ្តី

គ្រឿងភ្លេងមានខ្សែ	Strings
ប៉្យាណូ	**1.** piano
គីបត, កន្លែងវាយ	**a.** keyboard
ក្រដាសភ្លេង	**2.** sheet music
យូកុលីលី, កូនហ្គីតា	**3.** ukulele
ម៉ង់ដូលីន	**4.** mandolin
បង់ហ្សូ	**5.** banjo
ពិណ (ប្រទេសអឺរ៉ុប)	**6.** harp
វីយ៉ូឡុង	**7.** violin
ឆាក, ប្រដាប់កូត	**a.** bow
វីយ៉ូឡា	**8.** viola
ឆែលឡូ	**9.** cello
(គ្រឿងតន្រ្តីម្យ៉ាងដូចវីយ៉ូឡុងតែធំជាង)	
បាស់	**10.** bass
ខ្សែ	**a.** string
ហ្គីតា	**11.** guitar
ក្រចក (សំរាប់ដេញហ្គីតា)	**a.** pick

គ្រឿងភ្លេងដែល មានអណ្ដាត	Woodwinds
ពិកូឡូ	**12.** piccolo
ប៉ុី	**13.** flute
បាស់ស៊ីន	**14.** bassoon
អូប	**15.** oboe
ក្លារីណេត	**16.** clarinet

គ្រឿងភ្លេង វាយ ឬ គោះ	Percussion
តំប៊ូរីន	**17.** tambourine
ឆាប (គ្រឿងភ្លេង)	**18.** cymbals
ស្គរ	**19.** drum
ចង្កឹះវាយស្គរ	**a.** drumsticks
ស្គរបបញ្ចូរ, កុងហ្គា	**20.** conga
ស្គរម្យ៉ាងរាងដូចខ្លះឆា	**21.** kettledrum
បុងហ្គោ	**22.** bongos

គ្រឿងភ្លេងផ្លុំ ផ្ទុំពីស្ពាន់	Brass
ត្រំប៊ូន	**23.** trombone
សាក់សូហ្គន	**24.** saxophone
ត្រែ, ត្រំប៉េត	**25.** trumpet
ត្រែបារាំង	**26.** French horn
ត្រែសម្លេងធំ	**27.** tuba

គ្រឿងភ្លេង ផ្សេងៗទៀត	Other Instruments
អាក័រដេអុង	**28.** accordion
អ៊ក់	**29.** organ
អាម៉ូនិកា, ហាម៉ូនិកា	**30.** harmonica
ស៊ីឡូហ្គន	**31.** xylophone

ពាក្យ	**A. The Ballet**		បន្ទប់អ្នកមើល	**11.** box seat		ថ្លុប្រស	**19.** actor
វាំងនន	**1.** curtain		កន្លែងអ្នកស្តាប់ ឬ មើលនៅមុខគេ	**12.** orchestra seating		ថ្លុស្រី	**20.** actress
តាប្ចូ,ទស្សនីយភាព	**2.** scenery		ជាន់ទី២ នៅក្នុងរោងមហោស្រព	**13.** mezzanine			
អ្នករាំ	**3.** dancer		ឡេ្យ៉ា, ជាន់ខាងលើ (ចាប់ពីជាន់ទី៣ឡើង)	**14.** balcony		**ក្រុមភ្លេងរ៉ុកកាន់រ៉ូល**	**C. Rock Group**
ភ្លើងបញ្ជាំង	**4.** spotlight		អ្នកស្តាប់ ឬ អ្នកមើល	**15.** audience		គ្រឿងភ្លេងអេឡិចត្រូនិច	**21.** synthesizer
ឆាក	**5.** stage		អ្នកនាំបង្ហាញកន្លែងអង្គុយ	**16.** usher		អ្នកលេងគីបត	**22.** keyboard player
វង់ភ្លេង, វង់តន្ត្រី	**6.** orchestra		ប្រូក្រាម, កម្មវិធី	**17.** programs		អ្នកលេងហ្គីតាបាស្ស	**23.** bass guitarist
វេទិកា	**7.** podium					អ្នកច្រៀង	**24.** singer
មេភ្លេង	**8.** conductor		**ឆាកកំប្លែងមានតន្ត្រី**			អ្នកលេងហ្គីតានាំមុខគេ	**25.** lead guitarist
ចន្ទ្រះ	**9.** baton					ហ្គីតាអេឡិចទ្រិច	**26.** electric guitar
អ្នកលេងភ្លេង	**10.** musician		ក្រុមអ្នកចម្រៀង	**B. Musical Comedy**		អ្នកវាយស្គរ	**27.** drummer
				18. chorus			

អេឡិចត្រូនិច និង ការថតរូប

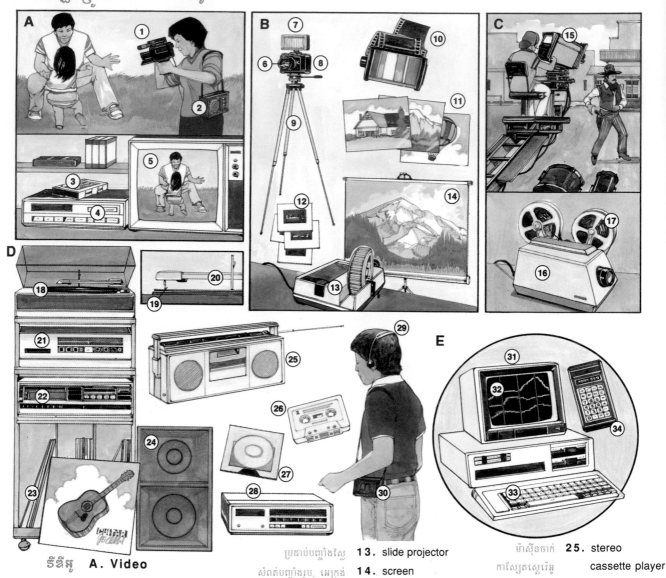

ទីឌីអូ	**A. Video**			ប្រដាប់បញ្ចាំងស្លៃ	**13.** slide projector	ម៉ាស៊ីនចាក់	**25.** stereo
ការម៉ោវីរ៉ាតពរវីឌីអូ	**1.** video camera			សំពត់បញ្ចាំងរូប, អេក្រង់	**14.** screen	ការស្សែតស្តេរេអូ	cassette player
ម៉ិនីកាំ (ម៉ាស៊ីនថតវីឌីអូ)	**2.** Minicam™			កុន	**C. Film**	ការស្សែត	**26.** cassette
ខ្សែអាត់ពរវីឌីអូ	**3.** videocassette (tape)			ម៉ាស៊ីនថតកុន	**15.** movie camera	ស៊ីឌី	**27.** compact
ម៉ាស៊ីនថតវីឌីអូ	**4.** VCR			ម៉ាស៊ីនបញ្ចាំងកុន	**16.** projector		disc (CD)
	(videocassette recorder)			(ដុំ) ហ្វិល	**17.** (reel of) film	ម៉ាស៊ីនចាក់ស៊ីឌី	**28.** compact
តេវេ, ទីវី, ទូរទស្សន៍	**5.** television						disc player
				ក្រៀវរ៉ូងអេឡិចត្រូនិច	**D. Audio**	ប្រដាប់ពាក់ស្តាប់	**29.** headphones
ការថតរូប	**B. Photography**			សំរាប់ស្តាប់		វិគម៉ាន់ស៊ូនី	**30.** Sony Walkman
កែវ	**6.** lens			ម៉ាស៊ីនច្រៀង	**18.** turntable		
ហ្វ្លាស	**7.** flash			មួល	**19.** cartridge needle	ភ្ជុំព្យូធ័រ	**E. Computers**
ការម៉េរ៉ា, ម៉ាស៊ីនថតរូប	**8.** camera			ដៃ (ម៉ាស៊ីនច្រៀង)	**20.** arm	កុំព្យូទ័រឯកត្តជន(ពីស៊ី)	**31.** personal
ជើង (ការម៉េរ៉ា)	**9.** tripod			វិទ្យុទទួលសម្លេង	**21.** receiver		computer (PC)
(ដុំ) ហ្វិល	**10.** (roll of) film			ម៉ាស៊ីនចាក់ការស្សែត	**22.** cassette deck	ម៉ូនីទ័រ	**32.** monitor
រូបថត	**11.** prints			ចាស់ម៉ាស៊ីន	**23.** records	គីបិត័(កុំព្យូទ័រ)	**33.** keyboard
ស្លៃ	**12.** slides			អូប៉ាល់័រ	**24.** speaker	ប្រដាប់គិតលេខ,	**34.** calculator
						កាល់គុលទ្បេទ័រ	

ដេរប៉ាក់	A. Sewing				
ម៉ាស៊ីនដេរ	1. sewing machine	ទ្បេវរកិប	13. snap	(អម្បោះ)ខ្សៀន	23. wool
(ហុង) អម្បោះ	2. (spool of) thread	ទំពក់និងដែកសំរាប់ថ្កក់	14. hook and eye	ដុំខ្សៀន ឬ អម្បោះ	24. skein
កូនខ្នើយដោតមូល	3. pincushion	ម៉ែត្រសំពត់	15. tape measure	មូលចាក់ទ្រីក	25. knitting needle
ក្រណាត់	4. material	ហ្ស៊ីបព័រ, ខ្សៀរូត	16. zipper	រូបប៉ាក់ (លើបន្ទះសំពត់គ្រាស់)	26. needlepoint
កន្ត្រៃកាត់កុំឱ្យរសាត់	5. pinking shears	កន្ត្រៃ	17. (pair of) scissors	រូបប៉ាក់ (លើសំពត់ធម្មតា)	27. embroidery
ផ្ទាំងគំរូ	6. pattern piece	មូល	18. needle	វត្ថុធ្វើឡើងដោយយក	28. crochet
គំរូ (ទាំងមូល)	7. pattern	ថ្នេរ	19. stitch	អម្បោះមកចាក់ថ្កក់	
រន្ធទ្បេវរ	8. buttonhole	មូលបារាំង	20. pin	មូលចាក់ថ្កក់	29. crochet hook
ទ្បេវរ	9. button	ស្នាប់ដេរ	21. thimble	ក្បាញ	30. weaving
ថ្នេរ	10. seam			អម្បោះ	31. yarn
ជាយ (សំពត់, អាវ ។ល។)	11. hem	កិច្ចការដេរប៉ាក់	B. Other	ការកាត់សំពត់ជាបន្ទះតូចៗបូនផ្សេង	
ក្រណាត់ចំដើង (ថ្នេរ)	12. hem binding	ផ្សេងៗទ្បេវត	Needlecrafts	ហើយដេរភ្ជាប់គ្នា	32. quilting
		ចាក់ទ្រីក	22. knitting		

ដេរប៉ាក់

ឯ, នៅ, ត្រង់ (បង្អួច)	**1.** at (the window)	នៅក្នុង (ថត)	**7.** in (the drawer)
លើ, នៅលើ (ឆ្មាខ្មៅ)	**2.** above (the black cat)	នៅក្រោម (តុ)	**8.** under (the desk)
ក្រោម, នៅក្រោម (ឆ្មាស)	**3.** below (the white cat)	នៅក្រោយ, នៅខាងក្រោយ (កៅអី)	**9.** behind (the chair)
នៅចន្លោះ (ខ្នើយ)	**4.** between (the pillows)	នៅលើ (តុ)	**10.** on top of (the table)
លើ (កំរាល)	**5.** on (the rug)	នៅជិត (ទីវី)	**11.** next to (the TV)
នៅមុខ (ក្រានភ្លើង)	**6.** in front of (the fireplace)		

កាត់, តាមកុង (សើនបញ្ជាំងភ្លើង)	**1.**	through (the lighthouse)
ជុំវិញ (សើនបញ្ជាំងភ្លើង)	**2.**	around (the lighthouse)
ចុះ, ចុះពី (ដីខ្ពស់)	**3.**	down (the hill)
ទៅ, ឆ្ពោះ (រន្ធ)	**4.**	toward (the hole)
ពី, ចេញពី (រន្ធ)	**5.**	away from (the hole)
កាត់, ឆ្លងកាត់ (ទឹក)	**6.**	across (the water)
ពី, ចេញពី(ទឹក)	**7.**	out of (the water)
លើ, ពីលើ (ស្ពាន)	**8.**	over (the bridge)
ទៅ, ឆ្ពោះទៅ (កន្លែងលេង)	**9.**	to (the course)
ពី, ចេញពី (កន្លែងលេង)	**10.**	from (the course)
ឡើង (ទួល)	**11.**	up (the hill)
ទៅក្នុង (រន្ធ)	**12.**	into (the hole)

បរិសិដ្ឋ

ឈ្មោះខែទាំងអស់ក្នុងមួយឆ្នាំ / Months of the Year

មករា	January	កក្កដា	July
កុម្ភៈ	February	សីហា	August
មីនា	March	កញ្ញា	September
មេសា	April	តុលា	October
ឧសភា	May	វិច្ឆិកា	November
មិថុនា	June	ធ្នូ	December

ឈ្មោះថ្ងៃទាំងអស់ក្នុងមួយអាទិត្យ / Days of the Week

ថ្ងៃអាទិត្យ	Sunday
ថ្ងៃចន្ទ	Monday
ថ្ងៃអង្គារ	Tuesday
ថ្ងៃពុធ	Wednesday
ថ្ងៃព្រហស្បតិ៍	Thursday
ថ្ងៃសុក្រ	Friday
ថ្ងៃសៅរ៍	Saturday

ពណ៌ Colors

red ក្រហម	green បៃតង
blue ខៀវ	pink ស៊ីជម្ពូ, ស៊ីឃ្យាប
yellow លឿង	purple ស្វាយ
white ស	brown ស៊ីកូឡា, ត្នោត
black ខ្មៅ	orange ស្វាយ ទុំ
gray ប្រផេះ	

លេខ / Numbers

០	សូន្យ	0 zero
១	មួយ	1 one
២	ពីរ	2 two
៣	បី	3 three
៤	បួន	4 four
៥	ប្រាំ	5 five
៦	ប្រាំមួយ	6 six
៧	ប្រាំពីរ	7 seven
៨	ប្រាំបី	8 eight
៩	ប្រាំបួន	9 nine
១០	ដប់	10 ten
១១	ដប់មួយ	11 eleven
១២	ដប់ពីរ	12 twelve
១៣	ដប់បី	13 thirteen
១៤	ដប់បួន	14 fourteen
១៥	ដប់ប្រាំ	15 fifteen
១៦	ដប់ប្រាំមួយ	16 sixteen
១៧	ដប់ប្រាំពីរ	17 seventeen
១៨	ដប់ប្រាំបី	18 eighteen
១៩	ដប់ប្រាំបួន	19 nineteen
២០	ម្ភៃ	20 twenty
២១	ម្ភៃមួយ	21 twenty-one
៣០	សាមសិប	30 thirty
៤០	សែសិប	40 forty
៥០	ហាសិប	50 fifty
៦០	ហុកសិប	60 sixty
៧០	ចិតសិប	70 seventy
៨០	ប៉ែតសិប	80 eighty
៩០	កៅសិប	90 ninety
១០០	មួយរយ	100 a/one hundred
៥០០	ប្រាំរយ	500 five hundred
៦២១	ប្រាំមួយរយម្ភៃមួយ	621 six hunrded (and) twenty-one
១.០០០	មួយពាន់	1,000 a/one thousand
១.០០០.០០០	មួយលាន	1,000,000 one million

Two numbers occur after words in the index: the first refers to the page where the word is illustrated and the second to the item number of the word on that page. For example, above [ə bŭv′] **102** 2 means that the word *above* is the item numbered 2 on page 102. If only a bold number appears, then that word is part of the unit title or a subtitle.

The index includes a pronunciation guide for all the words illustrated in the book. This guide uses symbols commonly found in dictionaries for native speakers. These symbols, unlike those used in transcription systems such as the International Phonetic Alphabet, tend to preserve spelling and so should help you to become more aware of the connections between written English and spoken English.

Consonants

[b] as in **back** [băk]	[k] as in **kite** [kīt]	[sh] as in **shell** [shĕl]
[ch] as in **cheek** [chēk]	[l] as in **leaf** [lēf]	[t] as in **tape** [tāp]
[d] as in **date** [dāt]	[m] as in **man** [măn]	[th] as in **three** [thrē]
[dh] as in **the** [dh]	[n] as in **neck** [nĕk]	[v] as in **vine** [vīn]
[f] as in **face** [fās]	[ng] as·in **ring** [rĭng]	[w] as in **waist** [wāst]
[g] as in **gas** [găs]	[p] as in **pack** [păk]	[y] as in **yam** [yăm]
[h] as in **half** [hăf]	[r] as in **rake** [rāk]	[z] as in **zoo** [zo͞o]
[j] as in **jack** [jăk]	[s] as in **sand** [sănd]	[zh] as in **measure** [mĕzh′ər]

Vowels

[ā] as in **bake** [bāk]	[ī] as in **lime** [līm]	[o͞o] as in **cool** [ko͞ol]
[ă] as in **back** [băk]	[ĭ] as in **lip** [lĭp]	[o͝o] as in **book** [bo͝ok]
[ä] as in **bar** [bär]	[ï] as in **beer** [bïr]	[ow] as in **cow** [kow]
[ē] as in **beat** [bēt]	[ō] as in **post** [pōst]	[oy] as in **boy** [boy]
[ĕ] as. in **bed** [bĕd]	[ŏ] as in **box** [bŏks]	[ŭ] as in **cut** [kŭt]
[ë] as in **bear** [bër]	[ö] as in **claw** [klö]	[ü] as in **curb** [kürb]
	or **for** [för]	[ə] as in **above** [ə bŭv′]

All pronunciation symbols used are alphabetical except for the schwa [ə], which is the most frequent vowel sound in English. If you use it appropriately in unstressed syllables, your pronunciation will sound more natural.

You should note that an umlaut ([¨]) calls attention to the special quality of vowels before [r]. (The sound [ö] can also represent a vowel not followed by [r] as in *claw*.) You should listen carefully to native speakers to discover how these vowels actually sound.

Stress

This guide also follows the system for marking stress used in many dictionaries for native speakers.
   (1) Stress is not marked if a word consisting of a single syllable occurs in isolation.
   (2) Where stress is marked, two levels are distinguished:
      a bold accent [**′**] is placed after each syllable with primary stress,
      a light accent [′] is placed after each syllable with secondary stress.

Syllable Boundaries

Syllable boundaries are indicated by a single space.

NOTE: The pronunciation used in this index is based on patterns of American English. There has been no attempt to represent all of the varieties of American English. Students should listen to native speakers to hear how the language actually sounds in a particular region.

above [ə bŭv/] **102** 2

abdomen [ăb/də mən] **4** 14

accelerator [ăk sĕl/ə rā/tər] **50** 27

accordion [ə kör/dē ən] **98** 28

accountant [ə kown/tənt] **86** 18

acorn [ā/körn] **61** 33b

acorn squash [ā/körn skwŏsh/] **7** 28

across [ə krös/] **103** 6

actor [ăk/tər] **99** 19

actress [ăk/trəs] **99** 20

acute angle [ə kyo͞ot/ ăng/gəl] **79** 8

address [ă/drĕs] **46** 11

adjectives [ăj/ĭk tĭvz] **24, 25**

aerial tramway [ër/ē əl trăm/wā] **55** 31

Africa [ă/frĭ kə] **70** 4

after-shave lotion [ăf/tər shāv lō/shən] **23** 21

ailments [āl/mənts] **40**

air conditioner [ër/kən dĭ/shə nər] **32** 11

air filter [ër/fĭl/tər] **51** 52

Air Force [ër/förs/] **48** 19

air mattress [ër/mă/trəs] **91** 26

air pump [ër/ pŭmp/] **53** 13

air travel [ër/ tră/vəl] **56**

aircraft [ër/krăft/] **57**

aircraft carrier [ër/krăft kăr/yər] **48** 4

aircraft types [ër/krăft tīps/] **57**

(airmail) envelope [ër/māl ĕn/və lōp] **46** 16

airman [ër/mən] **48** 20

airport check-in [ër/pört chĕk/ĭn] **56**

aisle [ī/əl] **14** 10, **56** 23

Alabama [ăl/ə bă/mə] **72** 1

alarm clock [ə lärm/ klŏk] **32** 8

Alaska [ə lăs/kə] **72** 2

alcohol [ăl/kə höl/] **39** 22

alligator [ăl/ə gā/tər] **65** 8

almond(s) [ö/mənd(z)] **9** 31

Alps [ălps] **70** 44

Amazon River [ă/mə zŏn rĭv/ər] **71** 59

ambulance [ăm/byə ləns] **42** 6

amphibians [ăm fĭ/bē ənz] **65**

ammunition [ăm/yə nĭsh/ən] **48**

anchor [ăng/kər] **58** 24

Andes [ăn/dēz] **71** 43

ankle [ăng/kəl] **5** 49

animals [ăn/ə məlz] **62-69**

ant [ănt] **63** 12

Antarctic Ocean [ănt ärk/ tĭk ō/ shən] **70** 14

Antarctica [ănt ärk/tĭ kə] **70** 7

anteater [ănt/ē/tər] **66** 5

antenna [ăn tĕn/ə] **51** 46, **62** 1b

antler [ănt/lər] **67** 35a

apartment house [ə pärt/mənt hows/] **45** 23

apex [ā/pĕks] **79** 21

Appalachian Mountains [ăp/ə lā/chē ən mown/ tənz] **71** 41

apple [ă/pəl] **8** 2

apricot [ăp/rə kŏt/] **9** 25

apron [ā/prən] **16** 6

aquatic mammals [ə kwŏ/tĭk·mă/məlz] **68**

Arabian Sea [ə rā/bē ən sē/] **70** 30

arc [ärk] **79** 16

architect [är/kə tĕkt/] **86** 8

Arctic [ärk/tĭk] **70** 8

Arizona [ăr/ə zō/nə] **72** 3

Arkansas [är/kən sö/] **72** 4

arm [ärm] **4** 6, **100** 20

armadillo [ăr/ mə dĭ/lō] **66** 2

armed forces [ärmd/ för/səz] **48**

armpit [ärm/pĭt/] **4** 10

armrest [ärm/rĕst/] **50** 3

Army [är/mē] **48** 15

around [ə rownd/] **103** 2

artery [är/tə rē] **5** 69

artichoke [är/tə chōk/] **6** 11

artist [är/təst] **86** 3

arts [ärts] **86**

ashtray [ăsh/trā/] **16** 29

Asia [ā/zhə] **70** 5

asparagus [ə spăr/ə gəs] **6** 18

asteroid [ăs/tə royd/] **74** 20

astronaut [ăs/trə nöt/] **75** 5

at [ăt] **102** 1

Atacama Desert [ăt/ə kŏ/mə dĕz/ərt] **71** 50

athletic supporter [ăth lĕ/tĭk sə pör/tər] **22** 4

atlas [ăt/ləs] **47** 20

attachments [ə tăch/mənts] **35** 17

attendant [ə tĕn/dənt] **39** 8, **53** 12

audience [ö/dē əns] **99** 15

audio [ö/dē ō/] **100**

aunt [ănt] **3** 6

Australia [ö strāl/yə] **70** 6

author [ö/thər] **47** 8

automatic transmission [ö/ tə măt/ĭk trănz mĭ/shən] **50**

avocado [ăv/ə kŏ/dō] **9** 33

away from [ə wā/ frŭm] **103** 5

axe [ăks] **42** 14

baboon [bă bo͞on/] **69** 19

baby [bā/bē] **2** 5

baby carriage [bā/bē kăr/ĭj] **45** 27

baby lotion [bā/bē lō/shən] **33** 6

baby powder [bā/bē pow/dər] **33** 7

baby wipes [bā/bē wīps/] **33** 8

baby's room [bā/bēz ro͞om/] **33**

back [băk] **4** 11, **23** 19

backache [băk/āk/] **40** 8

backboard [băk/börd/] **92** 19

backhoe [băk/hō/] **82** 26

backpack [băk/păk/] **19** 4

backseat [băk/sēt/] **50** 32

backyard [băk/yärd/] **27**

back-up light [băk/əp līt/] **50** 30

bacon [bā/kən] **10** 11, **18,** 33

badge [băj] **43** 5

Baffin Bay [băf/ən bā/] **70** 16

bag [băg] **12** 8, **15** 25, **21** 35

baggage [băg/ĭj] **56** 8

bake [bāk] **31** 14

baked beans [bākt/ bēnz/] **18** 3

baked goods [bākt go͞odz/] **14** 11

baked potato [bākt/ pə tā/tō] **18** 20

baker [bā/kər] **84** 8

bakery [bā/kə rē] **44** 6

balance beam [băl/əns bēm/] **94** 24

balcony [băl/kə nē] **99** 14

(bale of) hay [bāl/ əv hā/] **81** 13

ball [böl] **5** 52

ballet [bă lā/] **99**

ballfields [böl/fēldz/] **93**

ballpoint pen [böl/poynt pĕn/] **76** 22

Baltic Sea [böl/tĭk sē/] **70** 22

bananas [bə nă/nəz] **9** 20

Band-Aid [bănd/ ād/] **39** 4

band shell [bănd/ shĕl/] **87** 2

bandage [băn/dĭj] **39** 24

banister [băn/ə stər] **28** 11

banjo [băn/jō/] **98** 5

banking [băng/kĭng] **86**

bar [bär] **13** 18, **16** 24

bar stool [bär/stool/] **16** 25

barber [bär/bər] **84** 3

Barents Sea [băr/ənts sē/] **70** 23

barge [bärj] **58** 12

bark [bärk] **61** 35c

barn [bärn] **81** 5

barnyard [bärn/yärd/] **81** 8

barrel [băr/əl] **48** 23

barricade [băr/ə kād/] **82** 21

bartender [bär/tĕn/dər] **16** 21

base [bās] **79** 7, **93** 6

baseball [bās/böl/] **92**

baseball diamond [bās/böl dī/mənd] **93**

baseline [bās/līn/] **95** 4

basin [bā/sən] **39** 16

basket [băs/kət] **92** 20

basketball [băs/kət böl/] **92, 92** 21

bass [bās] **98** 10

bass guitarist [bās/gə tär/əst] **99** 23

bassoon [bă soon/] **98** 14

bat [băt] **66** 4, **92** 5

batboy [băt/boy/] **93** 18

bath mat [băth/ măt/] **34** 12

bath towel [băth/ tow/əl] **34** 24

bathing suit [bā/dhĭng soot/] **90** 18

bathing trunks [bā/ dhĭng trŭngks/] **91** 33

bathrobe [băth/ rōb] **22** 20

bathroom [băth/ room/] **34**

bathtub [băth/ tŭb/] **34** 11

baton [bə tŏn/] **99** 9

batter [băt/ ər] **92** 7, **93** 14

battery [băt/ə rē] **51** 54

batting helmet [băt/ĭng hĕl/mət] **92** 6

battleship [băt/ əl shĭp/] **48** 5

Bay of Bengal [bā/ əv bĕn göl/] **70** 32

bayonet [bā/ ə nĕt/] **48** 24

bays [bāz] **70**

beach [bēch] **90**

beach ball [bēch/ böl/] **90** 11

beach chair [bēch/ chër/] **90** 20

beach towel [bēch/ tow/ əl] **90** 15

beach umbrella [bēch/əm brĕl/ə] **90** 21

beads [bēdz] **23** 7

beak [bēk] **64** 3a

beaker [bē/kər] **78** 23

beard [bïrd] **4** 39

bears [bërz] **69**

beat [bēt] **31** 8

Beaufort Sea [bō/ fərt sē/] **70** 15

beaver [bē/vər] **66** 12

bed [bĕd] **32** 21

bed rest [bĕd/ rĕst/] **41** 1

bedroom [bĕd/room/] **32**

bedspread [bĕd/sprĕd/] **32** 23

bee [bē] **63** 19

beef [bēf] **10** 1

beef stew [bēf/ stoo/] **18** 14

beer [bïr] **16** 23

beet(s) [bēts] **7** 33

beetle [bē/təl] **63** 10

behind [bə hīnd/] **102** 9

below [bə lō/] **102** 3

belt [bĕlt] **20** 16

bench [bĕnch] **43** 16, **44** 14, **78** 24, **87** 10

beret [bə rā/] **19** 22

Bering Sea [bër/ĭng sē/] **70** 34

berries [bër/ēz] **8**

between [bə twēn/] **102** 4

beverages [bĕv/rə jəz] **14** 14

bib [bĭb] **33** 20

bicycle [bī/sĭ kəl] **52** 15

big [bĭg] **24** 8

(Big Dipper) constellation [bĭg/ dĭ/pər kŏn stə lā/shən] **74** 3

big toe [bĭg/ tō/] **5** 53

bike stand [bīk/ stănd/] **52** 14

biker [bī/kər] **90** 4

bikes [bīks] **52**

(bikini) panties [bə kē/ nē pănˊ tēz] **22** 11

bill [bĭl] **64** 24a

bin [bĭn] **15** 16

binding [bīn/ dĭng] **95** 16

binoculars [bə nŏk/ yə lərs] **90** 7

birch [bürch] **61** 32

birds [bürdz] **64**

biscuit [bĭs/ kət] **18** 27

bison [bī/sən] **67** 19

bit [bĭt] **37** 43a

black bear [blăk bër/] **69** 21

black bean(s) [blăk/ bēn(z)/] **6** 14

black eye [blăk/ ī/] **40** 5

Black Sea [blăk/ sē/] **70** 26

blackberries [blăk/ bër/ ēz] **8** 12

bladder [blă/ dər] **5** 72

blade [blād] **94** 27

blanket [blăng/ket] **32** 20

blazer [blā/zer] **20** 2

bleach [blēch] **35** 26

blender [blĕn/dər] **30** 12

blimp [blĭmp] **57** 5

blinds [blīndz] **32** 12

block [blŏk] **33** 32

blouse [blows] **21** 34

blue jay [bloo/ ja/] **64** 8

(blue) jeans [bloo/ jēnz/] **19** 6

blueberries [bloo/ bër/ēz] **8** 14

blueprints [bloo/ prĭnts/] **82** 6

blush [blŭsh] **23** 32

board [börd] **82** 16

boarding [bör/ dĭng] **56**

boarding pass [bör/ dĭng păs/] **56** 18

boardwalk [börd/wök/] **90** 1

body [bŏ/dē] **4**

boil [boyl] **31** 16

bollard [bŏl/ ərd] **58** 26

bolt [bōlt] **37** 38

bomb [bŏm] **48** 3

bomber [bŏm/ ər] **48** 2

bongos [bŏng/ gōz] **98** 22

book [book] **13** 17

(book of) matches [book/ əv mă/ chəz] **16** 28

bookcase [book/ kās] **28** 22, **83** 20

bookstore [book/ stör] **45** 18

boom [boom] **59** 7

booth [booth] **16** 9

boots [boots] **19** 21, **21** 32

bottle [bŏt/ əl] **12** 3, **33** 17

bottle opener [bŏt/ əl ō/ pə nər] **30** 6

bounce [bowns] **97** 11

bow [bō] **98** 7a

bow [bow] **58** 5

bowl [bōl] **13** 23

bowling [bōl/ĭng] **94**

bowling ball [bōl/ĭng böl/] **94** 6

box [bŏks] **13** 12

box seat [bŏks/ sēt/] **99** 11

box spring [bŏks/ sprĭng/] **32** 18

boxer shorts [bŏk/ sər shörts/] **22** 2

boxing [bŏk/ sĭng] **94**

boy's frame [boyz/ frām/] **52** 11

bra(ssiere) [brŏ]/[brə zïr/] **22** 13

brace [brās] **36** 9

bracelet [brās/ lət] **23** 9

brain [brān] **5** 57

brake [brāk] **50** 26, **52** 17

brake light [brāk/ līt/] **50** 29

branch [brănch] **61** 35a

brass [brăs] **98**

bread [brĕd] **14** 12

bread and butter plate
    [brĕd/ ənd bŭt/ ər plāt/] **29** 11

break [brāk] **31** 7

breast [brĕst] **11** 21

bricks [brĭks] **82** 12

bridle path [brīd/ əl păth/] **87** 7

briefcase [brēf/ kās/] **21** 37

briefs [brēfs] **22** 12

broccoli [brŏk/ ə lē] **6** 2

broil [broyl] **31** 13

broiler [broy/ lər] **30** 33

broken bone [brō/ kən bōn/] **40** 15

broom [broõm] **35** 7

brother [brŭdh/ ər] **3** 9

brother-in-law [brŭdh/ ər ən lö/] **3** 11

bruise [broõz] **40** 17

brush [brŭsh] **76** 18

brussels sprouts [brŭs/ əl sprowts/] **6** 4

bucket [bŭk/ ət] **35** 15

bucket seat [bŭk/ ət sēt/] **50** 16

buckle [bŭk/ əl] **20** 17

bud [bŭd] **60** 18a

buffet [bə fā/] **29** 29

builder [bĭl/ dər] **82** 5

building number [bĭl/ dĭng nŭm/ bər]
    45 24

bulb [bŭlb] **60** 8a

bull [boõl] **67** 34

bulldozer [boõl/ dō/ zər] **82** 27

bullet [boõl/ ĭt] **48** 26

bulletin board [boõl/ ĭ tən börd/] **76** 7

bumper [bŭm/ pər] **33** 5

bun [bŭn] **18** 7

bunch [bŭnch] **8** 1

Bunsen burner [bŭn/ sən bür/ nər]
    78 20

buoy [boõ/ ē]/[boy] **58** 16

bureau [byoõr/ ō] **32** 9

burn [bürn] **17** 14, **40** 18

burner [bür/ nər] **30** 29

bus [bŭs] **53** 20, **54**

bus driver [bŭs/ drī/ vər] **54** 3

bus stop [bŭs/ stŏp/] **44** 13

busboy [bŭs/ boy/] **16** 3

bushes [boõsh/ əz] **61** 41

business workers [biz/ nəs wür/ kərz] **86**

butcher [boõ/ chər] **84** 13

butter [bŭt/ ər] **18** 18

buttercup [bŭt/ ər kŭp/] **60** 17

butterfly [bŭt/ ər flī/] **63** 3

buttocks [bŭt/ əks] **4** 15

button [bŭt/ ən] **20** 3, **101** 9

buttonhole [bŭt/ ən hōl/] **101** 8

C-clamp [sē/ klămp/] **36** 2

cab driver [kăb/ drī/ vər] **55** 26

cabbage [kăb/ ĭj] **6** 3

cabin [kăb/ ĭn] **56** 19

cabin cruiser [kăb/ ĭn kroõ/ zər] **59** 16

cabinet [kăb/ ə nət] **30** 22

cable [kā/ bəl] **52** 23

cable car [kā/ bəl kär/] **55** 32

cactus [kăk/ təs] **61** 40

calculator [kăl/ kyə lā/ tər] **83** 19,
    100 34

calendar [căl/ ən dər] **83** 9

calf [kăf] **4** 20, **67** 31

California [kăl/ ə för/ nyə] **72** 5

call card [köl/ kärd/] **47** 6

call number [köl/ nŭm/ bər] **47** 6

call slip [köl/ slĭp/] **47** 12

camel [kăm/ əl] **67** 33

camera [kăm/ ər ə] **100** 8

cameraperson [kăm/ ər ə pür/ sən] **86** 10

camisole [kăm/ ə sōl/] **22** 9

camp stove [kămp/ stōv/] **89** 25

camper [kăm/ pər] **53** 16

campfire [kămp/ fīr/] **89** 31

camping [kăm/ pĭng] **89**

can [kăn] **12** 10

can opener [kăn/ ō/ pə nər] **30** 4

canary [kə nër/ ē] **64** 14

candle [kăn/ dəl] **29** 27

candlestick [kăn/ dəl stĭk/] **29** 28

canister [kăn/ ə stər] **30** 15

canned goods [kănd/ goõdz/] **14** 13

cannon [kăn/ ən] **48** 11

canoe [kə noõ/] **59** 2

cantaloupe [kăn/ tə lōp/] **9** 36

canyon [kăn/ yən] **88** 3

cap [kăp] **19** 2, **21** 43, **92** 11

capsule [kăp/ səl] **41** 5

car [kär] **54** 9

card catalog [kärd/ kăt/ ə lög] **47** 4

cardigan [kär/ dĭ gən] **21** 26

cardinal [kärd/ nəl] **64** 11

cargo [kär/ gō] **58** 10

cargo area [kär/ gō ër/ ē ə] **57** 12

cargo bay [kär/ gō bā/] **75** 9

cargo door [kär/ gō dör/] **57** 13

Caribbean Sea [kăr/ ə bē / ən sē /]
    70 20

carpenter [kär/ pən tər] **85** 2

carpenter's rule [kär/ pən tərz roõl/]
    36 1

carrot(s) [kăr/ ət(s)] **7** 32

carry [kăr/ ē] **26** 16

carry-on bag [kăr/ ē ŏn băg/] **56** 2

cars [kärz] **50-51**

carton [kär/ tən] **12** 1

cartridge needle [kär/ trĭj nē/ dəl]
    100 19

carve [kärv] **31** 6

cash register [kăsh/ rĕ/ jə stər] **15** 21

cashew(s) [kăsh/ oõ(z)] **9** 27

cashier [kă shïr/] **15** 22

Caspian Sea [kăs/ pē ən sē/] **70** 27

casserole dish [kăs/ ə rōl dĭsh/] **30** 14

cassette [kə sĕt/] **100** 26

cassette deck [kə sĕt/ dĕk/] **100** 22

cast [kăst] **39** 5

cat [kăt] **68** 4

catch [kăch] **96** 4

catcher [kăch/ ər] **92** 2, **93** 16

catcher's mask [kăch/ ərz măsk/] **92** 3

catcher's mitt [kăch/ ərz mĭt/] **92** 4

caterpillar [kăt/ ər pĭl/ ər] **63** 1

cattle [kăt/ əl] **81** 20

Caucasus [kö/ kə səs] **71** 45

cauliflower [kŏl′ ə flow′ ər] **6** 1

ceiling [sē′lǐng] **28** 2

ceiling fan [sē′lǐng făn′] **28** 1

celery [sĕl′ ə rē] **6** 10

cello [chĕl′o] **98** 9

cement [sə mĕnt′] **82** 10

cement mixer [sə mĕnt′ mǐk′ sər] **82** 25

cement truck [sə mĕnt′ trŭk′] **49** 13

center [sĕn′ tər] **79** 13, **93** 27

center divider [sĕn′ tər də vī′ dər] **53** 18, **82** 24

center fielder [sĕn′ tər fēl′ dər] **93** 2

center lane [sĕn′ tər lān′] **53** 6

centerboard [sĕn′ tər börd′] **59** 6

centipede [sĕn′ tə pēd′] **63** 22

chain [chān] **23** 5, **52** 18

chair [chër] **29** 17

chalk [chök] **76** 10

chalk tray [chök′ trā′] **76** 9

chalkboard [chök′ börd′] **76** 5

chandelier [shăn′ də lïr′] **29** 3

change (the sheets) [chānj′ dhə shēts′] **38** 13

changing table [chān′ jǐng tā′ bəl] **33** 9

charcoal briquettes [chär′ kōl brǐ kĕts′] **27** 23

chart [chärt] **39** 10

check [chĕk] **15** 27, **16** 14

checked [chĕkt] **24** 18

checkout counter [chĕk′ owt kown′ tər] **15** 26

checkout desk [chĕk′ owt dĕsk′] **47** 2

cheerleaders [chïr′ lē′ dərz] **93** 20

cheek [chēk] **4** 35

cherries [chër′ ēz] **9** 19

cherry picker [chër′ ē pǐk′ ər] **82** 18

chest [chĕst] **4** 12

chest of drawers [chĕst′ əv drörz′] **32** 30

chestnut(s) [chĕs′ nŭt(s)] **9** 32

chick [chĭk] **64** 22

chicken [chĭk′ ən] **11** 24, **64** 23

child's seat [chīldz′ sēt′] **50** 33

children [chǐl′ drən] **2** 7

chills [chǐlz] **40** 4

chimney [chǐm′ nē] **27** 9

chimpanzee [chǐm păn′ zē] **69** 16

chin [chǐn] **4** 3

china [chī′ nə] **29** 1

china closet [chī′ nə klŏz′ ət] **29** 2

chipmunk [chǐp′ mŭnk] **66** 6

chop [chŏp] **26** 11, **31** 11

chops [chŏps] **10** 9, **10** 15

chorus [kör′ əs] **99** 18

(chrysanthe)mum [krə săn′ thə məm]/[mŭm] **60** 4

cigarette [sǐg′ ə rĕt′] **16** 31

circle [sür′ kəl] **79** 11

circuit breaker [sür′ kət brā′ kər] **35** 5

circular saw [sür′ kyə lər sö′] **36** 20

circumference [sür kŭm′ fə rəns] **79** 17

citrus fruits [sǐ′ trəs frōōts′] **8**

city [sǐt′ ē] **44-45**

clam(s) [klăm(z)] **11** 32

clamp [klămp] **78** 7

clarinet [klăr′ə nĕt′] **98** 16

clasp [klăsp] **23** 17

classroom [klăs′ rōōm′] **76**

claw [klö] **62** 13a, **68** 2a

clean [klēn] **24** 6, **26** 2

cleanser [klĕn′ zər] **35** 9

clear [klïr] **17** 6

cliff [klǐf] **89** 21

clip-on earring [klǐp′ ŏn ïr′ ǐng] **23** 15

clock [klŏk] **76** 2

close (v) [klōz] **77** 5

closed [klōzd] **24** 16

closet [klŏz′ ət] **32** 3

cloth diaper [klöth′ dī′ pər] **33** 13

clothes [klōz] **19-24**

clothesline [klōz′ līn′] **35** 19

clothespins [klōz′ pǐnz′] **35** 20

cloudy [klow′ dē] **25** 2

clove [klōv] **7** 25a

cloverleaf [klō′ vər lēf′] **53** 4

clubs [klŭbz] **95** 5

clutch [klŭch] **50** 25

coach [kōch] **93** 21

coal [kōl] **80** 7

coal mine [kōl′ mīn′] **80** 6

coaster [kō′ stər] **16** 27

coat [kōt] **19** 24, **42** 13

cob [kŏb] **6** 12a

cobra [kō′ brə] **65** 11

cockpit [kŏk′ pǐt′] **56** 13

cockroach [kŏk′ rōch′] **63** 9

cocktail lounge [kŏk′ tāl lownj′] **16**

cocktail waitress [kŏk′ tāl wā′ trəs] **16** 32

cocoon [kə kōōn′] **63** 2

coconut [kō′ kə nŭt′] **8** 3

coffee [kö′ fē] **18** 35

coffeemaker [kö′ fē mā′ kər] **30** 31

coffeepot [kö′ fē pŏt′] **29** 18

coffee table [kö′ fē tā′ bəl] **28** 26

coins [koynz] **13** 26

colander [kŏl′ ən dər] **30** 7

cold [kōld] **25** 10, **40** 11

cold water faucet [kōld′ wŏ tər fö′ sət] **34** 18

collar [kŏl′ ər] **20** 20

colonial-style house [kə lō′ nē əl stīl hows′] **27**

Colorado [kŏl′ ə rŏd′ ō] **72** 6

column [kŏl′ əm] **50** 13

comb [kōm] **32** 6

combine (n) [kŏm′ bīn] **81** 17

comet [kŏm′ ət] **74** 2

comforter [kŭm′ fər tər] **32** 22

command module [kə mănd′ mŏj′ ōōl] **75** 8

communication satellite [kə myōō′ nə kā shən săt′ ə līt] **75** 2

commuter [kə myōō′ tər] **55** 17

commuter train [kə myōō′ tər trān′] **55** 14

compact disc (CD) [kŏm′ păkt dǐsk′]/[sē′ dē′] **100** 27

compact disc player [kŏm′ păkt dǐsk′ plā′ ər] **100** 28

computer [kəm pyōō′ tər] **76** 8, **83** 16, **100**

computer programmer [kəm pyōō′ tər prō′ grăm ər] **86** 16

conductor [kən dŭk′ tər] **54** 7, **99** 8

cone [kōn] **61** 34b, **79** 28, **82** 19

conga [kŏng′ gə] **98** 20

Congo River [kŏng′ gō rǐv′ ər] **71** 62

Connecticut [kə nĕ′ tǐ kət] **72** 7

constellation [kŏn′ stə lā′ shən] **74** 3

construction [kən strŭk′ shən] **82**

(construction) boots [kən strŭk′ shən bōōts′] **21** 32

construction site [kən strŭk′ shən sīt′] **82**

construction worker
[kən strŭk′ shən wür′ kər] **82** 14

container [kən tā′nər] **12** 2, **58** 7

(container)ship [kən tā′ nər shĭp′] **58** 9

containers [kən tā′ nərz] **12**

continents [kŏn′ tə nənts] **70**

control tower [kən trōl′ tow′ər] **57** 20

conveyor belt [kən vā′ər bĕlt] **15** 23,
56 12

cook (n) [kook] **17** 4

cook (v) [kook] **17** 4

cookie [kook′ ē] **18** 22

cool [kool] **25** 9

cooler [koo′ lər] **91** 41

cooling tower [koo′ lĭng tow′ər] **80** 16

copilot [kō′pī lət] **56** 16

cord [körd] **32** 26a, **54** 1

(corduroy) pants [kör′ də roy pănts′]
21 27

core [kör] **8** 2b, **80** 14

cork [körk] **16** 18

corkscrew [körk′ skroo′] **16** 17

corn [körn] **6** 12, **60** 24

corner [kör′ nər] **44** 3

corral [kə răl′] **81** 24

cosmetics [kŏz mĕt′ ĭks] **23**

cotton balls [kŏt′ ən bölz′] **39** 23

cotton swab [kŏt′ ən swŏb′] **33** 10

counter [kown′ tər] **30** 27

court [kört] **43**, **94** 13

court officer [kört′ ö′ fə sər] **43** 19

court reporter [kört′ rə pör′ tər] **43** 14

cousin [kŭz′ən] **3** 7

cow [kow] **67** 32

cowboy [kow′ boy′] **81** 21

cowgirl [kow′ gürl′] **81** 22

crab(s) [kră b(z)] **11** 36, **62** 9

cradle [krā′ dəl] **33** 26

cranberries [krăn′ bër′ ēz] **8** 13

crane [krān] **58** 6

creamer [krē′ mər] **29** 24

crew [kroo] **75** 12

(crewneck) sweater
[kroo′ nĕk swĕt′ ər] **19** 7

crib [krĭb] **33** 4

criket [krĭk′ ət] **63** 5

crime [krīm] **43**

crochet [krō shā′] **101** 28

crochet hook [krō′ shā′ hook′] **101** 29

crocus [krō′ kəs] **60** 9

cross-country skiing
[krös′ kŭn trē skē′ ĭng] **94**

crosswalk [krös′ wök′] **44** 4

crow [krō] **64** 3

crutch [krŭch] **39** 7

cube [kyoob] **79** 27

cubicle [kyoo′ bə kəl] **83** 5

cucumber(s) [kyoo′ kŭm bər(z)] **7** 20

cuff links [kŭf′ lĭnks′] **23** 12

cup [kŭp] **13** 19, **29** 20

curb [kürb] **45** 26

curtain [kür′ tən] **32** 10, **99** 1

curtain rings [kür′ tən rĭngz′] **34** 2

curtain rod [kür′ tən röd′] **34** 1

curve [kürv] **79** 3

cushion [koosh′ ən] **28** 24

customer [kŭs′ tə mər] **15** 17

cut (v) [kŭt] **31** 9

cut (n) [kŭt] **40** 16

cutting board [kŭt′ ĭng börd′] **30** 26

cylinder [sĭl′ ĭn dər] **79** 26

cymbals [sĭm′ bəlz] **98** 18

daffodil [dăf′ ə dĭl] **60** 8

dairy cow [dër′ ē kow′] **81** 11

dairy farm [dër′ ē färm′] **81**

dairy products [dër′ ē prŏd′ ŭkts] **14** 4

daisy [dā′ zē] **60** 5

dam [dăm] **80** 18

dance [dăns] **99**

dancer [dăn′ sər] **99** 3

dark [därk] **24** 10

dashboard [dăsh′ börd′] **50** 19

date [dāt] **9** 23

daughter [dö′ tər] **3** 15

deck [dĕk] **27** 5, **58** 22

deer [dïr] **67** 26

defendant [də fĕn′ dənt] **43** 23

defense attorney [də fĕns′ ə tür′ nē]
43 22

Delaware [dĕl′ ə wär′] **72** 8

deli counter [dĕl′ ē kown′ tər] **14** 1

delivery boy [də lĭv′ ə rē boy′] **85** 10

delivery person [də lĭv′ ə rē pür′ sən]
49 10

dental care [dĕn′ təl kër′] **39**

dentist [dĕn′ tĭst] **39** 17

department store [də pärt′ mənt stör′]
44 5

depth [dĕpth] **79** 33

derrick [dĕr′ ĭk] **80** 2

deserts [dĕz′ ərts] **71**

desk [dĕsk] **28** 14, **76** 16, **83** 13

detective [də tĕk′ tĭv] **43** 2

diagonal [dī ăg′ ə nəl] **79** 20

diameter [dī ăm′ ə tər] **79** 12

dictionary [dĭk′ shə nër′ ē] **47** 24

diesel fuel [dē′ zəl fyoo′ əl] **80** 34

dig [dĭg] **26** 3

dime [dīm] **13** 29

dinghy [dĭng′ ē] **59** 18

dining room [dī′ nĭng room′] **29**

dipstick [dĭp′ stĭk′] **51** 58

dirt bike [dürt′ bīk′] **52** 8

disc jockey (DJ) [dĭsk′ jŏk′ ē]/[dē′ jā]
86 9

dirty [dür′ tē] **24** 5

dish drainer [dĭsh′ drā′ nər] **30** 2

dish towel [dĭsh′ tow′ əl] **30** 18

dishwasher [dĭsh′ wŏsh′ ər] **30** 1

dishwashing liquid
[dĭsh′ wŏsh ĭng lĭ′ kwĭd] **30** 10

disposable diaper
[dīs pō′ zə bəl dī′ pər] **33** 12

dissection kit [dĭ sĕk′ shən kĭt′] **78** 33

dive [dīv] **97** 14

dock [dŏk] **58** 28

doctor [dŏk′ tər] **39** 11

dogs [dögz] **69**

dogwood [dög′ wood′] **61** 28

doll [dŏl] **33** 28

doll house [dŏl′ hows′] **33** 25

dollar bills [dŏl′ər bĭlz′] **13** 25

dolly [dŏl′ ē] **56** 6

dolphin [dŏl′ fĭn] **68** 13

donkey [dŏng′ kē] **67** 23

door handle [dör′ hăn′ dəl] **50** 4

door lock [dör′ lŏk′] **50** 1

doorman [dör′ mən] **85** 11

down [down] **103** 3

down vest [down′ vĕst′] **19** 12

dragonfly [drăg′ ən flī′] **63** 4

drain [drān] **34** 9

drainpipe [drān′ pīp′] **27** 18

drapes [drāps] **28** 23

draw [drö] **77** 11

drawer [drör] **47** 5

dress [drĕs] **20** 22

dried fruits [drīd′ frōōts′] **9**

drill [drĭl] **39** 15

drink [drĭngk] **17** 2

drive [drīv] **97** 15

driveway [drīv′ wā′] **27** 1

drugstore [drŭg′ stör′] **45** 22

drum [drŭm] **98** 19

drummer [drŭm′ər] **99** 27

drumsticks [drŭm′ stĭks′] **98** 19a

dry [drī] **25** 14, **38** 9

dryer [drī′ər] **35** 24

duck [dŭk] **11** 25, **64** 25

(duck) pond [dŭk′ pŏnd′] **87** 8

dugout [dŭg′ owt′] **93** 13

dump truck [dŭmp′ trŭk′] **49** 14

dust [dŭst] **38** 15

dustpan [dŭst′ păn′] **35** 8

eagle [ē′ gəl] **64** 5

ear [ïr] **4** 34

(ear of) corn [ïr′ əv körn′] **6** 12

earmuffs [ïr′ mŭfs′] **19** 10

earrings [ïr′ ĭngz] **23** 1

Earth [ürth] **74** 8, **13**

east [ēst] **71** 73

East China Sea [ēst′ chī′ nə sē′] **70** 38

eat [ēt] **17** 1

eel [ēl] **65** 4

egg [ĕg] **18** 32, **64** 13

egg roll [ĕg′ rōl′] **18** 25

eggplant [ĕg′ plănt′] **7** 21

elbow [ĕl′ bō] **4** 8

electric drill [ĭ lĕk′ trĭk drĭl′] **37** 43

electric guitar [ĭ lĕk′ trĭk gĭ tär′] **99** 26

electric generator [ĭ lĕk′ trĭk gĕn′ ə rā tər] **80** 21

electrical tape [ĭ lĕk′ trĭ kəl tāp′] **37** 34

electrician [ĭ lĕk trĭ′ shən] **85** 6

electricity [ĭ lĕk trĭs′ ĭ tē] **80** 32

electronics [ĭ lĕk trŏn′ ĭks] **100**

elephant [ĕl′ ə fənt] **66** 17

elevator [ĕl′ ə vā′ tər] **45** 17, **80** 9

elm [ĕlm] **61** 36

embroidery [ĕm broi′ də rē] **101** 27

emergency brake [ĭ mür′ jən sē brāk′] **50** 15

emery board [ĕm′ ə rē börd′] **23** 24

encyclopedia [ĕn sī′ klə pē′ dē ə] **47** 25

end table [ĕnd′ tā′ bəl] **28** 29

end zone [ĕnd′ zōn′] **93** 23

energy [ĕn′ər jē] **80**

engagement ring [ĕn gāj′ mənt rĭng′] **23** 3

engine [ĕn′ jən] **51, 52** 32

engineer [ĕn′ jə nïr′] **55** 15

enter [ĕn′ tər] **77** 14

entrance ramp [ĕn′ trəns rămp′] **53** 21

envelope [ĕn′ və lōp′] **46** 16, **83** 31

equator [ĭ kwā′ tər] **71** 70

erase [ĭ rās′] **77** 3

eraser [ĭ rā′ sər] **76** 11

escarole [ĕs′ kə rōl′] **6** 7

esophagus [ĭ sŏf′ ə gəs] **5** 61

eucalyptus [yōō′ kə lĭp′ təs] **61** 27

Europe [yōōr′ əp] **70** 3

examining table [ĭg zăm′ ə nĭng tā′ bəl] **39** 6

exhaust pipe [ĭg zöst′ pīp′] **52** 33

exit ramp [ĕg′ zĭt rămp′] **53** 2

exit sign [ĕg′ zĭt sīn′] **53** 24

Express Mail (package) [ĭk sprĕs′ māl păk′ ĭj] **46** 23

extension cord [ĭk stĕn′ shən körd′] **36** 5

eye [ī] **5**

eye drops [ī′ drŏps′] **41** 10

eye shadow [ī′ shă′ dō] **23** 30

eyebrow [ī′ brow′] **5** 44

eyebrow pencil [ī′ brow pĕn′ səl] **23** 26

eyelashes [ī′ lăsh′ əz] **5** 46

eyelid [ī′ lĭd′] **5** 45

eyeliner [ī′ lī′ nər] **23** 33

fabric softener [făb′ rĭk sö′ fə nər] **35** 27

face [fās] **4** 1

face guard [fās′ gärd′] **92** 15

factory work [făk′ tə rē würk′] **85**

fairway [fĕr′ wā′] **95** 12

fall [föl] **96** 7

Fall [föl] **26**

family [făm′ ə lē] **3**

family restaurant [făm′ ə lē rĕs′ tər ənt] **16**

fan belt [făn′ bĕlt′] **51** 53

fare [fĕr] **55** 21

fare box [fĕr′ bŏks′] **54** 5

farmhouse [färm′ hows′] **81** 3

farmer [fär′ mər] **81** 7

farming [fär′ mĭng] **81**

fashion designer [făsh′ ən də zī′ nər] **86** 6

father [fŏdh′ ər] **3** 5

faucet [fö′ sĭt] **34** 17, 18

fawn [fön] **67** 27

feather [fĕdh′ər] **64** 7a

feather duster [fĕdh′ ər dŭs′ tər] **35** 2

fence [fĕns] **81** 9

fender [fĕn′ dər] **52** 10

ferry [fĕr′ ē] **58** 17

fever [fē′ vər] **40** 2

field [fēld] **81** 16

fields and courses [fēldz′ ənd kör′ səz] **95**

fig [fĭg] **9** 21

fighter plane [fī′ tər plān′] **48** 1

file cabinet [fīl′ kăb′ ə nət] **83** 21

file clerk [fīl′ klürk′] **83** 23

file folder [fīl′ fōl′ dər] **83** 22

filet [fĭ lā′] **11** 28

fill [fĭl] **26** 9

film [fĭlm] **100** 10, **100** 17

filter paper [fĭl′ tər pā′ pər] **78** 16

fin [fĭn] **65** 3b

finger [fĭng′ gər] **4** 25

fingernail [fĭng′ gər nāl′] **4** 23

fingerprints [fĭng′ gər prĭnts′] **43** 24

finish line [fĭn′ ĭsh līn′] **95** 21

fire [fīr] **28** 9, **42** 5

fire engine [fīr′ ĕn′ jən] **42** 2

fire escape [fīr′ ə skāp′] **42** 4

fire extinguisher [fīr′ ĭk stĭng′ gwĭ shər] **42** 11

fire fighter [fīr′ fī′ tər] **42** 10

fire hydrant [fīr′ hī′ drənt] **42** 9

fire truck [fīr′ trŭk′] **42** 3

firefighting [fīr′ fī′ tĭng] **42**

firefly [fīr′ flī′] **63** 17

fireplace [fīr′ plās′] **28** 8

first baseman [fürst′ bās′ mən] **93** 8

first quarter [fürst′ kwör′ tər] **74** 23

fish [fĭsh] **11** 26, **65**

fisherman [fĭsh′ ər mən] **58** 2

fishing [fĭsh′ ĭng] **88**

fishing boat [fĭsh′ ĭng bōt′] **58** 1

fishing line [fĭsh′ ĭng līn′] **88** 8

fishing net [fĭsh′ ĭng nĕt′] **88** 9

fishing rod [fĭsh′ ĭng rŏd′] **88** 7

flag [flăg] **76** 1, **82** 20, **95** 9

flame [flām] **29** 26, **78** 21

flamingo [flə mĭng′ gō] **64** 29

flanker [flăng′ kər] **93** 31

flannel shirt [flăn′ əl shürt′] **19** 3

flare [flër] **51** 41

flash [flăsh] **100** 7

flashlight [flăsh′ līt′] **35** 3

flask [flăsk] **78** 2

(flat) sheet [flăt′ shēt′] **32** 19

flatbed [flăt′ bĕd′] **49** 18

flight attendant [flīt′ ə tĕn′ dənt] **56** 20

flight deck [flīt′ dĕk′] **75** 10

flight engineer [flīt′ ĕn jə nïr′] **56** 17

flipper [flĭp′ ər] **68** 12a

flippers [flĭp′ ərz] **91** 36

floor [flör] **32** 29

Florida [flör′ ə də] **72** 9

florist [flör′ ĭst] **84** 11

flounder [flown′ dər] **65** 7

flowers [flow′ ərz] **60**

flute [flōōt] **99** 13

fly [flī] **63** 18

flying mammal [flī′ ĭng mă′ məlz] **66**

foal [fōl] **67** 22

foggy [fög′ ē] **25** 12

fold [fōld] **38** 1

food [fōōd] **6-18**

foot [fŏŏt] **5**

football [fŏŏt′ böl′] **92, 92** 13

football field [fŏŏt′ böl fēld′] **93**

forceps [för′ səps] **78** 28

forearm [för′ ärm′] **4** 9

forehead [för′ hĕd′] **4** 32

forelegs [för′ lĕgz′] **66** 3d

foreman [för′ mən] **85** 13

fork [förk] **29** 12

forklift [förk′ lĭft′] **58** 4

foul line [fowl′ līn′] **93** 9

foundation [fown dā′ shən] **82** 11

four-door hatchback [för′ dör hăch′ băk] **51**

fox [fŏks] **68** 6

fractions [frăk′ shənz] **79**

frame [frām] **28** 4

frame backpack [frām′ băk′ păk] **89** 28

freezer [frē′ zər] **14** 3, **30** 20

freezing [frē′ zĭng] **25** 11

french fries [frĕnch′ frīz′] **18** 28

French horn [frĕnch′ hörn′] **98** 26

fried chicken [frīd′ chĭk′ ən] **18** 29

Frisbee™ [frĭz′ bē] **90** 13

frog [frŏg] **65** 17

from [frŭm] **103** 10

front bumper [frŭnt′ bŭm′ pər] **51** 51

frozen foods [frō′ zən fōōdz′] **14** 2

fruit and vegetable market [frōōt′ ənd vĕj′ tə bəl mär′ kət] **44** 28

fruit tree [frōōt′ trē′] **81** 2

fruits [frōōts] **8**

fry [frī] **31** 15

frying pan [frī′ ĭng păn′] **30** 5

fuel truck [fyōō′ əl trŭk′] **49** 3

full moon [fŏŏl′ mōōn′] **74** 24

full slip [fŏŏl′ slĭp′] **22** 10

fullback [fŏŏl′ băk′] **93** 34

funnel [fŭn′ əl] **78** 17

fuselage [fyōō′ sə lŏj′] **57** 14

galaxy [găl′ ək sē] **74** 1

Ganges River [găn′ jēz rĭv′ ər] **71** 67

gangway [găng′ wā′] **58** 20

garage [gə rŏj′] **27** 2

garbage can [gär′ bĭj kăn′] **35** 31

garbage truck [gär′ bĭj trŭk′] **49** 6

garden hose [gär′ dən hōs′] **27** 14

gardenia [gär dēn′ yə] **60** 14

gardener [gärd′ nər] **85** 3

garlic [gär′ lĭk] **7** 25

garment bag [gär′ mənt băg′] **56** 1

garter belt [gär′ tər bĕlt′] **22** 14

(garter) snake [gär′ tər snāk′] **65** 9

gas gauge [găs′ gāj′] **50** 9

gas pump [găs′ pŭmp′] **53** 14

gas tank [găs′ tănk′] **50** 34

gas(oline) [găs′ ə lēn′] **80** 28

(gauze) bandage [göz′ băn′ dĭj] **39** 24

gauze pads [göz′ pădz′] **39** 25

gavel [găv′ əl] **43** 12

gear [gïr] **89** 27

gear changer [gïr′ chān′ jər] **52** 22

gearshift [gïr′ shĭft′] **50** 17

geometrical figures [jē′ ə mĕ′ trĭ kəl fĭg′ yərz] **79**

Georgia [jör′ jə] **72** 10

geyser [gī′ zər] **80** 5

gibbon [gĭb′ ən] **69** 15

gill [gĭl] **65** 3c

giraffe [jə răf′] **67** 29

girdle [gür′ dəl] **22** 15

girl [gürl] **2** 9

girl's frame [gürlz′ frām′] **52** 3

give [gĭv] **17** 9

glass [glăs] **12** 20

glasses [glăs′ əz] **21** 44

glider [glī′ dər] **57** 4

globe [glōb] **47** 19

glove [glŭv] **92** 12, **94** 11, **94** 15

glove compartment [glŭv′ kəm pärt′ mənt] **50** 20

gloves [glŭvz] **19** 1

glue [glōō] **36** 33, **76** 17

goal [gōl] **92** 25

goalie [gōl′ ē] **92** 24

goalpost [gōl′ pōst′] **93** 35

goat [gōt] **67** 28

Gobi Desert [gō′ bē dĕz′ ərt] **71** 54

golf [gŏlf] **94**

golf bag [gŏlf′ băg′] **95** 7

golf ball [gŏlf′ böl′] **94** 7

golf cart [gŏlf′ kärt′] **95** 8

golf course [gŏlf′ körs′] **95**

golfer [gŏl′ fər] **94** 10

goose [gōōs] **64** 26

gooseberries [gōōs′ bër′ ēz] **8** 11

gopher [gō′ fər] **66** 8

gorilla [gə rĭl′ ə] **69** 17

graduated cylinder [grăj′ ōō ā tĭd sĭl′ ən dər] **78** 25

grains [grānz] **60**

granddaughter [grănd′ dö′ tər] **2** 11

grandfather [grănd′ fö′ dhər] **3** 2

grandmother [grănd′ mŭ′ dhər] **3** 1

grandparents [grănd păr′ ənts] **2** 10

grandson [grănd′ sŭn′] **2** 12

grapefruit [grăp′ fr⊙ot′] **8** 7

grapes [grāps] **8** 1

graph paper [grăf′ pā′ pər] **78** 11

grass [grăs] **27** 15

grasses [grăs′ əz] **60**

grasshopper [grăs′ hŏp′ ər] **63** 6

grate [grāt] **31** 2

Great Sandy Desert
   [grāt′ săn′ dē dĕz′ ərt] **71** 55

green [grēn] **95** 10

greengrocer [grēn′ grō′ sər] **84** 7

grill [grĭl] **27** 22, **88** 12

grizzly bear [grĭz′ lē bër′] **69** 23

groceries [grō′ sə rēz] **15** 24

ground beef [grownd′ bēf′] **10** 2

grounding plug [grown′ dĭng plŭg′]
   36 7

guitar [gĭ tär′] **98** 11

Gulf of Alaska [gŭlf′ əv ə lăs′kə]
   70 17

Gulf of Guinea [gŭlf′ əv gĭn′ ē] **70** 25

Gulf of Mexico [gŭlf′ əv mĕk sə kō]
   70 19

gulfs [gŭlfs] **70**

gun [gŭn] **43** 7

gun turret [gŭn′ tür′ ət] **48** 12

gutter [gŭt′ ər] **27** 10, **94** 3

gymnast [jĭm′ nəst] **94** 23

gymnastics [jĭm năs′ tĭks] **94**

hacksaw [hăk′ sö′] **36** 18

hair [hër] **4** 30

hair dryer [hër′ drī′ ər] **34** 26

hairbrush [hër′ brŭsh′] **32** 7

hairdresser [hër′ drĕs′ ər] **84** 10

half (1/2) [hăf] **79** 30

half slip [hăf′ slĭp′] **22** 8

halfback [hăf′ băk′] **93** 33

hall [höl] **76** 12

ham [hăm] **10** 12

hamburger [hăm′bür′ gər] **18** 9

hammer [hăm′ ər] **36** 13

hammock [hăm′ ək] **27** 11

hamper [hăm′ pər] **34** 28

hand [hănd] **4**

hand brake [hănd′ brāk′] **52** 24

hand grenade [hănd′ grə nād′] **48** 29

hand towel [hănd′ tow′ əl] **34** 23

hand truck [hănd′ trŭk′] **87** 4

handball [hănd′ böl′] **94**, **94** 12

handcuffs [hănd′ kŭfs′] **43** 4

handicrafts [hăn′ dē krăfts′] **101**

handlebars [hăn′ dəl bärz′] **52** 2

hang [hăng] **38** 6

hang glider [hăng′ glī′ dər] **57** 6

hangar [hăng′ ər] **57** 17

hanger [hăng′ ər] **32** 2

hard hat [härd′ hăt′] **21** 28, **82** 4

harmonica [här mŏn′ ə kə] **98** 30

harness [här′ nəs] **89** 22

harp [härp] **98** 6

hat [hăt] **19** 18

hatchback [hăch′ băk′] **51** 43

hatchet [hăch′ ət] **36** 17

Hawaii [hə wŏ′ ē] **72** 11

hawk [hök] **64** 7

hay [hā] **81** 13

hazelnut(s) [hā′ zəl nŭt(s)′] **9** 30

head [hĕd] **4**, **36** 42a

(head of) cauliflower
   [hĕd′ əv köl ə flow′ ər] **6** 1

head protector [hĕd prə tĕk′ tər] **94** 14

headache [hĕd′ āk′] **40** 6

headboard [hĕd′ börd′] **32** 14

headlights [hĕd′ līts′] **51** 48

headphones [hĕd′ fōnz′] **100** 29

headrest [hĕd′ rĕst′] **50** 35

headset [hĕd′ sĕt′] **83** 2

heart [härt] **5** 64

heat [hēt] **80** 27

heating pad [hē′ tĭng păd′] **41** 3

hedge clippers [hĕj′ klĭp′ ərz] **27** 29

heel [hēl] **5** 50, **20** 5

heels [hēlz] **20** 25

height [hīt] **79** 34

helicopter [hĕl′ ə kŏp′ tər] **57** 2

helmet [hĕl′ mət] **42** 12, **52** 7, **92** 14

hem [hĕm] **101** 11

hem binding [hĕm′ bīn′ dĭng] **101** 12

herb(s) [ürb(z)] **6** 9

(herd of) cattle [hürd′ əv kăt′ əl] **81** 20

high [hī] **24** 11

high blood pressure [hī′ blŭd prĕsh′ ər]
   40 10

high chair [hī′ chër′] **16** 8

high heels [hī′ hēlz′] **20** 25

highway travel [hī′ wā trăv′ əl] **53**

hikers [hī′ kərz] **88** 2

hiking boots [hī′ kĭng b⊙ots′] **19** 9

hill [hĭl] **88** 4

Himalayas [hĭm′ ə lā′ əz] **70** 47

hind legs [hīnd′ lĕgz′] **66** 3b

hip [hĭp] **4** 16

hippopotamus [hĭp′ ə pŏt′ ə məs]
   66 14

hit [hĭt] **96** 1

hitchhiker [hĭch′ hī′ kər] **53** 9

hockey stick [hŏk′ ē stĭk′] **92** 18

hog [hög] **66** 30

hold [hōld] **17** 12, **58** 8

hole [hōl] **94** 8

holly [hŏl′ ē] **61** 37

holster [hōl′ stər] **43** 8

home plate [hōm′ plāt′] **93** 15

honeydew melon
   [hŭn′ ē d⊙o mĕl′ ən] **9** 35

hood [h⊙od] **51** 47

hoof [h⊙of] **66** 35b

hoofed mammals [h⊙oft′ măm′ əlz] **66**

hook [h⊙ok] **32** 1, **36** 16

hook and eye [h⊙ok′ ənd ī′] **101** 14

horn [hörn] **50** 12, **52** 5, **66** 16a

horse [hörs] **66** 21

horse racing [hörs′ rā′ sĭng] **94**

horse-drawn carriage
   [hörs′ drön kăr′ ĭj] **54** 33

horseback rider [hörs′ băk rī′ dər]
   87 6

horses [hörs′ əz] **81** 23

hose [hōz] **42** 8, **50** 57

hot [hŏt] **25** 7

hot air balloon [hŏt′ ër bə l⊙on′] **57** 1

hot dog [hŏt′ dög′] **18** 2

hot water faucet [hŏt′ wŏt ər fö′ sət]
   34 17

house plants [hows′ plănts′] **60** 39

household items [hows′ hōld ī′ təmz]
   15 15

household services
   [hows′ hōld sür′ və səz] **85**

housekeeper [hows′ kē′ pər] **85** 8

houses [how′ zəz] **27**

housework [hows′ würk′] **38**

Huang River [hwöng′ rĭv′ ər] **71** 68

hubcap [hŭb′ kăp′] **50** 36

Hudson Bay [hŭd′ sən bā′] **70** 18

human body [hyōō′ mən bŏd′ ē] **4**

hummingbird [hŭm′ ĭng bürd′] **64** 2

hump [hŭmp] **67** 33a

husband [hŭz′ bənd] **2** 3, **3** 12

hyacinth [hī′ ə sĭnth] **60** 10

hyena [hī ē′ nə] **68** 30

hypotenuse [hī pŏt′ə nōōs′] **79** 24

ice cream cone [īs′ krēm cōn′] **18** 36

ice hockey [īs′ hŏk′ ē] **92**

ice pack [īs′ păk′] **41** 4

ice skates [īs′ skāts′] **19** 15

ice skating [īs′ skā′ tĭng] 94

ice tray [īs′ trā′] **30** 21

icy [ī′ sē] **25** 16

Idaho [ī′ də hō′] **72** 12

ignition [ĭg nĭsh′ ən] **50** 14

iguana [ĭ gwŏ′ nə] **65** 13

Illinois [ĭl′ ə noy′] **72** 13

in [ĭn] **102** 7

in front of [ĭn frŭnt′ əv] **102** 6

in-box [ĭn′ bŏks] **83** 12

(index) finger [ĭn′ dĕks fĭng′ gər] **4** 25

Indian Ocean [ĭn′ dē ən ō′ shən′] **70** 13

Indiana [ĭn′ dē ăn′ ə] **72** 14

individual sports
     [ĭn′ də vĭj′ ōō əl spörts′] **94**

infection [ĭn fĕk′ shən] **40** 14

inflatable raft [ĭn flā′ tə bəl răft′] **59** 20

information desk
     [ĭn′ fər mā′ shən dĕsk′] **47** 22

injection [ĭn jĕk′ shən] **41** 8

injuries [ĭn′ jə rēz] **40**

insect bite [ĭn′ sĕkt bīt′] **40** 3

insects [ĭn′ sĕkts] **63**

instep [ĭn′ stĕp′] **5** 51

instruments [ĭn′ strə mənts]
     39 13, **56** 14, **98**

internal organs [ĭn tür′ nəl ör′ gənz] **5**

intersection [ĭn′ tər sĕk′ shən] **44** 11

interstate highway
     [ĭn′ tər stāt hī′ wā] **53** 1

intestines [ĭn tĕs′ tənz] **5** 67

into [ĭn′ tōō] **103** 12

Iowa [ī′ ə wə] **72** 15

iris [ī′ rəs] **5** 47, **60** 11

iron (n) [ī′ ərn] **35** 12

iron (v) [ī′ ərn] **38** 11

ironing board [ī′ ər nĭng börd′] **35** 13

jack [jăk] **32** 26b, **50** 38

jacket [jăk′ ət] **19** 17, **21** 33

jackhammer [jăk′ hăm′ər] **82** 22

jail [jāl] **43** 1

janitor [jăn′ ə tər] **85** 9

jar [jär] **12** 9

jaw [jö] **4** 38

jeans [jēnz] **19** 6

jeep [jēp] **48** 9

jelly [jĕl′ ē] **18** 31

jellyfish [jĕl′ ē fĭsh′] **62** 12

jet engine [jĕt′ ĕn′ jən] **57** 11

jet fuel [jĕt′ fyōō′ əl] **80** 31

(jet) plane [jĕt′ plān′] **57** 18

jeweller [jōō′ ə lər] **84** 12

jewelry [jōō′ əl rē] **23**

jewelry box [jōō′ əl rē bŏks′] **32** 4

jigsaw [jĭg′ sö] **36** 3

jockey [jŏk′ ē] **94** 21

jogging path [jŏg′ ĭng păth′] **87** 9

judge [jŭj] **43** 10

jukebox [jōōk′ bŏks′] **16** 12

jump [jŭmp] **96** 8

jungle gym [jŭng′ əl jĭm′] **87** 17

Jupiter [jōō′ pə tər] **74** 15

jury [jōōr′ ē] **43** 21

jury box [joor′ ē bŏks′] **43** 20

kangaroo [kăng′ gə rōō′] **66** 3

Kansas [kăn′ zəs] **72** 16

Kara Sea [kär′ ə sē′] **70** 31

kayak [kī′ ăk] **59** 17

Kentucky [kĕn tŭk′ ē] **72** 17

ketchup [kĕch′ əp] **16** 4

kettledrum [kĕt′ əl drŭm′] **98** 21

keyboard [kē′ börd′] **98** 1a, **100** 33

keyboard player [kē′ börd plā′ ər] **99** 22

kickstand [kĭk′ stănd′] **52** 9

kidney [kĭd′ nē] **5** 70

kidney bean(s) [kĭd′ nē bēn(z)′] **6** 13

kitchen [kĭch′ ən] **30**

kite [kīt] **91** 22

kitten [kĭt′ ən] **68** 5

knee [nē] **4** 19

knee socks [nē′ sŏks′] **22** 16

knife [nīf] **29** 15

knitting [nĭt′ ĭng] **101** 22

knitting needle [nĭt′ ĭng nē′ dəl] **101** 25

knuckle [nŭk′ əl] **4** 22

koala [kō ŏl′ ə] **66** 1

label [lā′ bəl] **46** 21

lacrosse [lə krös′] **92**

lacrosse stick [lə krös′ stĭk′] **92** 16

ladder [lăd′ ər] **42** 1, **82** 8

ladybug [lā′ dē bŭg′] **63** 14

lamb [lăm] **10** 13, **67** 24

lamp [lămp] **28** 28

lampshade [lămp′ shād′] **28** 27

landing gear [lăn′ dĭng gĭr′] **57** 15

lane [lān] **94** 4

lantern [lăn′ tərn] **88** 29

lapel [lə pĕl′] **20** 1

Laptev Sea [lăp′ tĕv sē′] **70** 33

last quarter [lăst′ kwör′ tər] **74** 25

launchpad [lönch′ păd′] **75** 15

laundry [lön′ drē] **35** 28

laundry basket [lön′ drē băs′ kət] **35** 29

laundry detergent [lön′ drē də tür′ jənt]
     35 25

lawn mower [lön′ mō′ ər] **27** 12

lead guitarist [lēd′ gĭ tär′ ĭst] **99** 25

leaf [lēf] **60** 36a

leave [lēv] **77** 13

left fielder [lĕft′ fēl′ dər] **93** 1

left guard [lĕft′ gärd′] **93** 26

left lane [lĕft′ lān′] **53** 5

left tackle [lĕft′ tăk′ əl] **93** 25

leg [lĕg] **4** 17, **10** 14, **11** 20

(legal) pad [lē′ gəl păd′] **83** 26

lemon [lĕm′ ən] **8** 9

Lena River [lē′ nə rĭv′ ər] **71** 66

length [lĕngth] **79** 36

lens [lĕnz] **100** 6

leopard [lĕp′ ərd] **68** 1

letter [lĕt′ ər] **46** 7

letter carrier [lĕt′ər kăr′ yər] **46** 3

lettuce [lĕt′əs] **6** 6

level [lĕv′əl] **82** 3

librarian [lī brër′ ē ən] **47** 23

library card [lī′ brër ē kärd′] **47** 3

library clerk [lī′ brër ē klürk′] **47** 1

license plate [lī′ səns plāt′] **50** 28

lid [lĭd] **30** 9

life jacket [līf′ jăk′ ət] **59** 1

life preserver [līf′ prə zür′ vər] **90** 9

lifeboat [līf′ bōt′] **58** 19, **90** 10

lifeguard [līf′ gärd′] **90** 6

lifeguard chair [līf′ gärd chër′] **90** 8

light (v) [līt] **17** 13

light (adj) [līt] **24** 9

light switch [līt′ swĭch′] **32** 25

lightbulb [līt′ bŭlb′] **35** 22

lighter [lī′ tər] **16** 30

lighthouse [līt′ hows′] **58** 14

lily [lĭl′ ē] **60** 3

lima bean(s) [lī′ mə bēn(z)′] **6** 16

lime [līm] **8** 10

line [līn] **58** 25

lines [līnz] **79**

linesman [līnz′ mən] **82** 17

lion [lī′ ən] **68** 3

lip [lĭp] **4** 43

lipstick [lĭp′ stĭk′] **23** 29

liquor (bottle) [lĭk′ər bŏt′ əl] **16** 22

listen [lĭs′ ən] **77** 6

little finger [lĭt′ əl fĭng′ gər] **4** 28

little league baseball [lĭt′ əl lēg bās′ böl] **92**

Little Leaguer [lĭt′ əl lēg′ ər] **92** 8

little toe [lĭt′ əl tō′] **5** 55

liver [lĭv′ ər] **5** 65

livestock [līv′ stŏk′] **81** 12

living quarters [lĭv′ ĭng kwör′ tərz] **75** 11

living room [lĭv′ ĭng rōōm′] **28**

lizard [lĭz′ ərd] **65** 15

llama [lŏm′ ə] **66** 15

loaf [lōf] **12** 7

loafer [lō′ fər] **21** 42

lobby [lŏb′ ē] **44** 2

lobster [lŏb′ stər] **10** 30, **62** 13

lock [lŏk] **52** 13

locker [lŏk′ ər] **76** 6

locksmith [lŏk′ smĭth′] **85** 4

log [lög] **28** 10

long [löng] **24** 2

long johns [löng′ jŏnz′] **22** 7

long sleeve [löng′ slēv′] **20** 15

loose [lōōs] **24** 4

(loose-leaf) paper [lōōs′ lēf pā′ pər] **76** 13

loudspeaker [lowd′ spē′ kər] **76** 3

Louisiana [lōō ē′ zē ăn′ ə] **72** 18

lounge chair [lownj′ chër′] **27** 24

low [lō] **24** 12

lunar eclipse [lōō′ nər ĭ klĭps′] **74** 6

lunar module [lōō′ nər mŏj′ ōōl] **75** 7

lunch box [lŭnch′ bŏks′] **20** 31

lunch truck [lŭnch′ trŭk′] **49** 8

lung [lŭng] **5** 63

machine gun [mə shēn′ gŭn′] **48** 25

magazine [măg′ ə zēn′] **47** 16

magnet [măg′ nət] **78** 27

magnifying glass [măg′ nə fī ĭng glăs′] **78** 15

magnolia [măg nōl′ yə] **61** 29

mail [māl] **46** 2

mail slot [māl′ slŏt′] **46** 13

mail truck [māl′ trŭk′] **46** 5

mailbag [māl′ băg′] **46** 4

mailbox [māl′ bŏks′] **46** 1

Maine [mān] **72** 19

maintenance [mān′ tə nəns] **95**

make (the bed) [māk′ dhə bĕd′] **38** 8

makeup [māk′ ŭp′] **23**

mallet [măl′ ĭt] **36** 11

mammals [măm′ əlz] **66-69**

man [măn] **2** 2

manager [măn′ ĭ jər] **83** 18

mandolin [măn′ də lĭn′] **98** 4

mane [mān] **66** 21a

mango [măng′ gō] **8** 5

manhole [măn′ hōl′] **45** 32

mantel [măn′ təl] **28** 7

mantis [măn′ tĭs] **63** 7

manual transmission [măn′ yōō əl trănz mĭsh′ ən] **50**

map [măp] **70**

maple [mā′ pəl] **61** 38

marigold [măr′ ə gōld′] **60** 6

marine [mə rēn′] **48** 18

Marines [mə rēnz′] **48** 17

Mars [märz] **74** 14

Maryland [mër′ ə lənd] **72** 20

mascara [mă skăr′ ə] **23** 28

mashed potatoes [măsht′ pə tā tōz] **18** 17

mask [măsk] **91** 35

Massachusetts [măs′ ə chōō′ sĭts] **72** 21

mast [măst] **59** 8

mat [măt] **50** 22

matches [măch′ əz] **16** 28

material [mə tür′ ē əl] **101** 4

math [măth] **79**

mattress [mă′ trəs] **32** 17

measurement [mĕzh′ ər mənt] **79**

meat [mēt] **10**

meatballs [mēt′ bölz′] **18** 11

mechanic [mə kăn′ ĭk] **84** 2

media [mē′ dē ə] **86**

medical care [mĕd′ ə kəl kër′] **39**

medicine [mĕd′ ə sən] **41**

medicine chest [mĕd′ ə sən chĕst′] **34** 14

medicine dropper [mĕd′ ə sən drŏp′ ər] **78** 26

Mediterranean Sea [mĕd′ ĭ tə rā′ nē ən sē′] **70** 24

melon [mĕl′ ən] **9** 35

menu [mĕn′ yōō] **16** 7

Mercury [mür′ kyə rē] **74** 11

merry-go-round [mër′ ē gō rownd′] **87** 5

message pad [mĕs′ ĭj păd′] **83** 25

messenger [mĕs′ən jər] **86** 19

metal detector [mĕt′ əl də tĕk′ tər] **56** 10

meteor [mē′ tē ər] **74** 5

meter [mē′ tər] **55** 23

mezzanine [mĕz′ ə nēn′] **99** 13

Michigan [mĭsh′ ə gən] **72** 22

microfilm [mī′ krə fĭlm′] **47** 13

microfilm reader [mī′ krə fĭlm rē′ dər] **47** 14

microscope [mī′ krə skōp′] **78** 30

microwave oven [mī′ krə wāv ŭv′ ən] **30** 23

middle finger [mĭd′ əl fĭng′ gər] **4** 26

milk [mĭlk] **14** 5

Minicam™ [mĭn′ ē kăm′] **100** 2

Minnesota [mĭn′ ə sō′ tə] **72** 23

mirror [mĭr′ ər] **32** 5

Mississippi [mĭs′ ə sĭp′ ē] **72** 24

Mississippi River [mĭs′ ə sĭp′ ē rĭv′ ər] **71** 58

Missouri [mĭ zŏŏr′ ē] **73** 25

mitt [mĭt] **27** 20

mittens [mĭt′ ənz] **19** 11

mixed vegetables [mĭkst′ vĕj′ tə bəlz]
  18 16

mixing bowl [mĭk′ sĭng bōl′] **30** 24

mobile [mō′ bēl] **33** 2

model [mŏd′ əl] **86** 5

Mojave Desert [mō hŏv′ ē dĕz′ ərt]
  71 48

money [mŭn′ ē] **12**

money order [mŭn′ ē ör′ dər] **46** 18

monitor [mŏn′ ə tər] **100** 32

monkey [mŭng′ ke] **69** 14

monkey wrench [mŭng′ kē rĕnch′]
  36 12

monorail [mŏn′ ə rāl′] **55** 29

Montana [mŏn tăn′ ə] **73** 26

Moon [mo͞on] **74** 9

mooring [mo͝or′ ĭng] **59** 19

moose [mo͞os] **67** 35

mop [mŏp] **35** 6

(mop) refill [mŏp′ rē′ fĭl] **35** 11

mortar [mör′ tər] **48** 28

mosquito [mə skē′ tō] **63** 13

motel [mō tĕl′] **90** 3

moth [mŏth] **63** 21

mother [mŭdh′ ər] **3** 4

motor oil [mōt′ ər oyl′] **80** 33

motor scooter [mōt′ ər sko͞o′ tər] **52** 29

motorboat [mōt′ ər bōt′] **59** 13

motorcycle [mōt′ ər sī′ kəl] **52** 30,
  53 19

mountain [mown′ tən] **89** 19

mountain climbing [mown′ tən klīm′ ĭng]
  89

mountain ranges [mown′ tən rān′ jəz] **71**

mouse [mows] **66** 9

mousetrap [mows′ trăp′] **35** 32

mouth [mowth] **4** 2

mover [mo͞o′ vər] **49** 12

movie camera [mo͞o′ vē kăm′ ə rə]
  100 15

moving van [mo͞o′ vĭng văn′] **49** 11

mow [mō] **26** 6

mum [mŭm] **60** 4

muscle [mŭs′ əl] **5** 62

mushroom(s) [mŭsh′ ro͞om(z)] **7** 30

music [myo͞o′ zĭk] **99**

musical comedy
  [myo͞o′ zə kəl kŏm′ ə dē] **99**

musical instruments
  [myo͞o′ zə kəl ĭn′ strə mənts] **98**

musician [myo͞o zĭsh′ ən] **99** 10

mussel(s) [mŭs′ əl(z)] **11** 34, **62** 3

mustache [mŭs′ tăsh] **4** 40

mustard [mŭs′ tərd] **18** 1

nail [nāl] **37** 41

nail clippers [nāl′ klĭp′ ərz] **23** 31

nail polish [nāl′ pŏl′ ĭsh] **23** 25

nailbrush [nāl′ brŭsh′] **34** 20

napkin [năp′ kĭn] **29** 14

natural gas [năch′ ər əl găs′] **80** 29

Navy [nā′ vē] **48** 13

Nebraska [nə brăs′ kə] **73** 27

neck [nĕk] **4** 4

necklace [nĕk′ lĭs] **23** 6

nectarine [nĕk′ tə rēn′] **8** 17

needle [nē′ dəl] **39** 26, **60** 34a, **101** 18

needlecrafts [nē′ dəl krăfts′] **101**

needlepoint [nē′ dəl poynt′] **101** 26

neighborhood parks
  [nā′ bər ho͝od pärks′] **87**

nephew [nĕf′ yo͞o] **3** 13

Neptune [nĕp′ to͞on] **74** 18

nest [nĕst] **64** 31

net [nĕt] **92** 23

Nevada [nə văd′ ə] **73** 28

new [no͞o] **24** 13

New Hampshire [no͞o′ hămp′ shər]
  72 29

New Jersey [no͞o′ jür′ ze] **73** 30

New Mexico [no͞o′ mĕk′ sə kō] **73** 31

new moon [no͞o′ mo͞on′] **74** 26

New York [no͞o′ yörk′] **73** 32

newscaster [no͞oz′ kăs′ tər] **86** 2

newspaper [no͞oz′ pā′ pər] **21** 48

newsstand [no͞oz′ stănd′] **45** 30

next to [nĕkst′ to͞o] **102** 11

nickel [nĭk′ əl] **13** 28

niece [nēs] **3** 14

Niger River [nī′ jər rĭv′ ər] **71** 61

night table [nīt′ tā′ bəl] **32** 27

nightgown [nīt′ gown′] **22** 21

nightstick [nīt′ stĭk′] **43** 9

Nile River [nīl′ rĭv′ ər] **71** 63

nipple [nĭp′ əl] **33** 18

north [nörth] **71** 71

North America [nörth′ ə mĕr′ ə kə]
  70 1

North Atlantic [nörth′ ăt lăn′ tĭk] **70** 11

North Carolina [nörth′ kăr ə lī′ nə]
  73 33

North Dakota [nörth′ də kō′ tə] **73** 34

North Pacific [nörth′ pə sĭf′ ĭk] **70** 9

North Sea [nörth′ sē′] **70** 21

nose [nōz] **4** 36, **57** 8

nostril [nŏs′ trĭl] **4** 37

nozzle [nŏz′ əl] **42** 17

nuclear reactor [no͞o′ klē ər rē ăk′ tər]
  80 13

nurse [nürs] **39** 19

nut [nŭt] **37** 39

nuts [nŭts] **9**

oak [ōk] **61** 33

oar [ör] **59** 22

oarlock [ör′ lŏk′] **59** 21

oats [ōts] **60** 23

Ob River [ŏb′ rĭv′ ər] **71** 64

oboe [ō′bō] **98** 15

obtuse angle [ŏb to͞os′ ăng′ gəl] **79** 5

occupations [ŏk′ yə pā′ shənz] **84-86**

ocean liner [ō′ shən lī′ nər] **58** 27

oceans [ō′ shənz] **70**

octopus [ŏk′ tə pəs] **62** 6

office [ö′ fĭs] **83**

office building [ö′ fĭs bĭl′ dĭng] **44** 1

officer [ö′ fĭ sər] **86** 13

Ohio [ō hī′ ō] **73** 35

oil [oyl] **38** 12

oil well [oyl′ wĕl′] **80** 1

ointment [oynt′ mənt] **41** 9

Oklahoma [ō′ klə hō′ mə] **73** 36

old [ōld] **24** 14

on [ŏn] **102** 5

on top of [ŏn tŏp′ əv] **102** 10

onion(s) [ŭn′ yən(z)] **7** 31

open [ō′ pən] **24** 15, **31** 3

optician [ŏp tĭsh′ ən] **84** 9

oral hygienist [ör′ əl hī jē′ nĭst] **39** 14

orange [ör′ ĭnj] **8** 8

orangutan [ə răng′ ə tăn′] **69** 18

orbit [ör′ bĭt] **74** 21

orchard [ör′ chərd] **81** 1

orchestra [ör′ kə strə] **99** 6

orchestra seating [ör/ kə strə sēt/ ĭng] **99** 12

orchid [ör/ kĭd] **60** 12

order [ör/ dər] **17** 5

Oregon [ör/ ə gən] **73** 37

organ [ör/ gən] **98** 29

ostrich [ŏs/ trĭch] **64** 12

otter [ŏt/ ər] **68** 10

out of [owt/ əv] **103** 7

outboard motor [owt/ börd mō/ tər] **59** 12

outer space [owt/ ər spās/] **74**

outlet [owt/ lət] **36** 6

oval [ō/ vəl] **79** 18

oven [ŭv/ ən] **30** 32

over [ō/ vər] **103** 8

overalls [ō/ vər ölz/] **21** 30

overcoat [ō/ vər kōt/] **19** 20

overhead projector
[ō/ vər hĕd prə jĕk/ tər] **76** 27

overpass [ō/ vər păs/] **53** 3

owl [owl] **64** 6

oyster(s) [oy/ stər(z)] **11** 33, **62** 2

pacifier [păs/ ə fī/ ər] **33** 22

pack [păk] **13** 16

package [păk/ ĭj] **12** 4, **46** 19

pad [păd] **83** 26

paddle [păd/ əl] **59** 3, **94** 18

pail [pāl] **90** 16

paint (v) [pānt] **26** 1

paint (n) [pānt] **37** 31

paintbrush [pānt/ brŭsh/] **37** 30

Painted Desert [pān/ təd dez/ ərt] **71** 49

painter [pān/ tər] **85** 7

painting [pān/ tĭng] **28** 5

(pair of) scissors [për/ əv sĭz/ ərz]
101 17

pajamas [pə jŏm/ əz] **22** 19

palm [pŏm] **4** 29, **61** 26

pan [păn] **37** 28

pancakes [păn/ kāks/] **18** 5

pancreas [pang/ krē əs] **5** 71

panda [păn də] **69** 20

panel truck [păn/ əl trŭk/] **49** 9

pansy [păn/ zē] **60** 2

panties [păn/ tēz] **22** 11

pants [pănts] **21** 27

pantyhose [păn/ tē hōz/] **22** 5

papaya [pə pī/ yə] **8** 6

paper [pā/ pər] **76** 13

paper clips [pā/ pər klĭps/] **83** 28

paper towels [pā/ pər tow/əlz] **35** 23

parachute [păr/ ə shoot/] **48** 6

parakeet [păr/ ə kēt] **64** 15

parallel lines [păr/ ə lĕl līnz/] **79** 4

paramedic [păr/ ə mĕd/ ĭk] **42** 7

Parana River [păr/ ə nŏ/ rĭv/ ər] **71** 60

parents [păr/ ənts] **2** 6

park [pärk] **87**

park ranger [pärk/ rān/ jər] **88** 5

parka [pär/ kə] **19** 8

parking lights [pär/ kĭng līts/] **51** 49

parking garage [pär/ kĭng gə rŏj/]
45 19

parking meter [pär/ kĭng mē/ tər]
45 20

parrot [păr/ ət] **64** 16

part [pärt] **4** 31

pass [păs] **96** 5

passenger [păs/ ĭn jər] **55** 25

passenger car [păs/ ĭn jər kär/] **53** 15

pasture [păs/ chər] **81** 6

patient [pā /shənt] **39** 20

patio [păt/ ē ō/] **27** 17

pattern [păt/ ərn] **101** 7

pattern piece [păt/ ərn pēs/] **101** 6

paw [pö] **69** 29a

pay [pā] **17** 7

pea(s) [pē(z)] **6** 17

peach [pēch] **9** 37

peacock [pē/ kŏk/] **64** 18

peak [pēk] **89** 20

peanut(s) [pē/ nŭt(s)/] **9** 28

pear [për] **8** 18

pedal [pĕd/ əl] **39** 18, **52** 19

pedestrian [pə dĕs/ trē ən] **44** 12

peel (n) [pēl] **9** 20a

peel (v) [pēl] **31** 5

pegboard [pĕg/ börd/] **36** 15

pelican [pĕl/ ə kən] **64** 24

pencil [pĕn/ səl] **76** 24

pencil eraser [pĕn/ səl ə rā/ sər] **76** 21

pencil sharpener
[pĕn/ səl shär/ pə nər] **76** 20, **83** 30

Pennsylvania [pĕn səl vān/ yə] **73** 38

penny [pĕn/ ē] **13** 27

penguin [pĕn/ gwĭn] **64** 27

people [pē/ pəl] **2**

pepper shaker [pĕp/ ər shā/ kər] **29** 9

pepper(s) [pĕp/ ər(z)] **7** 22

percussion [pər kŭsh/ ən] **98**

perfume [pür/ fyoom] **23** 27

periodicals section
[pïr/ ē ŏd/ ə kəlz sĕk/ shən] **47** 15

periscope [për/ə skōp/] **48** 8

perpendicular lines
[pür/ pən dĭk/ yə lər līnz/] **79** 2

Persian Gulf [pür/ zhən gŭlf /] **70** 28

personal computer (PC)
[pür/ sə nəl kŭm pyoo/ tər]/
[pē/ sē/] **100** 31

personnel [pür/ sə nĕl/] **48**

petal [pĕt/ əl] **60** 18b

petri dish [pĕt/ rē dĭsh/] **78** 3

petunia [pə toon/ yə] **60** 7

pharmacist [fär/ mə sĭst] **84** 1

phases of the moon
[fā/ zəz əv dhə moon/] **74**

pheasant [fĕz/ ənt] **64** 19

Phillips screwdriver
[fĭl/ ĭps skroo/ drī vər] **37** 25

phone [fōn] **32** 26

photocopier [fō/ tə kŏp/ ē ər] **83** 24

photocopy machine
[fō tə kŏp ē mə shēn/] **47** 18

photographer [fə tŏg/ rə fər] **86** 4

photography [fə tŏg/ rə fē] **100**

piano [pē ăn/ ō] **98** 1

piccolo [pĭk/ ə lō/] **98** 12

pick (v) [pĭk] **26** 7

pick (n) [pĭk] **98** 11a

pickup truck [pĭk/ ŭp trŭk/] **49** 4

pickax [pĭk/ ăks/] **82** 13

pickle [pĭk/ əl] **18** 8

picnic area [pĭk/nĭk ër/ ē ə] **88**

picnic basket [pĭk/ nĭk băs/ kət] **88** 13

picnic table [pĭk/ nĭk tā/ bəl] **88** 15

piece [pēs] **12** 22

pier [pïr] **58** 3

pierced earring [pïrst/ ïr/ ĭng] **23** 16

pigeon [pĭj/ ən] **64** 1

pill [pĭl] **41** 7

pillow [pĭl/ ō] **32** 16

pillowcase [pĭl/ ō kās/] **32** 15

pilot [pī′ lət] **56** 15

pin [pĭn] **23** 8, **94** 5, **101** 20

pincushion [pĭn′ koōsh′ ən] **101** 3

pine [pīn] **60** 34

pineapple [pīn′ ăp′ əl] **8** 4

ping-pong [pĭng′ pŏng′] **94**

ping-pong ball [pĭng′ pŏng böl′] **94** 19

pinking shears [pĭng′ kĭng shïrz′]
101 5

pipe [pīp] **16** 26, **35** 18

pipette [pī pĕt′] **78** 14

pit [pĭt] **8** 37a

pitcher [pĭch′ ər] **29** 4, **93** 12

pitcher's mound [pĭch′ ərz mownd′]
93 11

pitchfork [pĭch′ förk′] **81** 14

pizza [pēt′ sə] **18** 30

plaid [plăd] **24** 22

plane [plān] **57** 18

planets [plăn′ əts] **74**

plant (v) [plănt] **26** 4

plants (n) [plănts] **60**

plate [plāt] **29** 13

plateau [plă tō′] **88** 1

platform [plăt′ förm′] **54** 11

playground [plā′ grownd′] **87** 15

playpen [plā′ pĕn′] **33** 30

pleasure boating [plĕzh′ ər bō′ tĭng] **59**

pliers [plī′ ərz] **36** 19

plug [plŭg] **37** 43d

plum [plŭm] **9** 34

plumber [plŭm′ ər] **85** 1

plunger [plŭn′ jər] **35** 14

Pluto [ploo′ tō] **74** 19

pocket [pŏk′ ət] **21** 41

pod [pŏd] **6** 17a

podium [pō′ dē əm] **99** 7

poinsettia [poyn sĕt′ē ə] **60** 15

poison ivy [poy′ zən ī′ vē] **61** 45

poison oak [poy′ zən ōk′] **61** 43

poison sumac [poy′ zən soo′ măk]
61 44

poisonous plants [poy′ zə nəs plănts′]
61

polar bear [pōl′ ər bër′] **69** 22

pole [pōl] **94** 34, **95** 14

police officer [pə lēs′ öf′ ə sər] **43** 6

police station [pə lēs′ stā′ shən] **43**

polish [pŏl′ ĭsh] **38** 3

polka dot [pō′ kə dŏt′] **24** 19

pond [pŏnd] **87** 8

pony [pō′ nē] **67** 20

poplar [pŏp′ lər] **61** 30

porch [pörch] **27** 6

porcupine [pör′ kyə pīn′] **66** 11

pork [pörk] **10** 6

pork chops [pörk′ chŏps′] **18** 15

port [pört] **58**

porter [pör′ tər] **56** 5

porthole [pört′ hōl′] **58** 21

post [pōst] **23** 18

post office [pōst′ öf′ ĭs] **44** 9, **46**

postal worker [pōs′ təl wür′ kər] **46** 14

postcard [pōst′ kärd′] **46** 17

postmark [pōst′ märk′] **46** 9

pot [pŏt] **30** 13

pot holder [pŏt′ hōl′ dər] **30** 34

potato chips [pə tā′ tō chĭps′] **18** 4

potato(es) [pə tā′ tō(z)] **7** 23

potty [pŏt′ ē] **33** 33

pouch [powch] **66** 3c

pouched mammals [powcht′ măm′ əlz]
66

poultry [pōl′ trē] **10**

pour [pör] **31** 4

power lines [pow′ ər līnz′] **80** 24

power sander [pow′ ər săn′ dər] **37** 26

power saw [pow′ ər sö′] **27** 25

power station [pow′ ər stā′ shən] **80** 20

prepositions [prep′ ə zĭ′ shənz]
102, 103

primates [prī′ māts] **69**

print [prĭnt] **24** 21

printer [prĭn′ tər] **83** 4

printout [prĭnt′ owt′] **83** 8

prints [prĭnts] **100** 11

prism [prĭz′ əm] **78** 1

private jet [prī′ vət jĕt′] **57** 3

produce [prŏd′ oōs] **14** 9

programs [prō′ grămz] **99** 17

projector [prə jĕk′ tər] **100** 16

propane gas [prō′ pān găs′] **80** 30

propeller plane [prə pĕl′ ər plān′] **57** 7

prosecuting attorney
[prŏ′ sə kyoō tĭng ə tür′ nē] **43** 17

prune [proōn] **9** 22

public library [pŭb′ lĭk lī′ brër ē] **47**

public transportation
[pŭb′ lĭk trăns pər tā′ shən] **54**

public telephone [pŭb′ lĭk tĕl′ ə fōn]
44 7

puck [pŭk] **92** 17

pump [pŭmp] **13** 14, **52** 21

pumpkin [pŭmp′ kĭn] **7** 26

punishment [pŭn′ ĭsh mənt] **43**

pupil [pyoō′ pəl] **5** 48

puppy [pŭp′ ē] **69** 27

purse [pürs] **20** 23

push [poōsh] **26** 12

putter [pŭt′ ər] **94** 9

puzzle [pŭz′ əl] **33** 31

pyramid [pïr′ ə mĭd′] **79** 25

quantities [kwŏn′ tə tēz] **12**

quarter [kwör′ tər] **11** 18, **13** 30,
79 31

quarterback [kwör′ tər băk′] **93** 32

quill [kwĭl] **66** 11a

quilting [kwĭl′ tĭng] **101** 32

rabbit [răb′ ĭt] **66** 13

raccoon [ră koōn′] **68** 7

race track [rās′ trăk′] **95**

(racing) handlebars
[rā′ sĭng hăn′ dəl bärz] **52** 2

rack [răk] **47** 17, **78** 8

racket [răk′ ĭt] **94** 2

racquet [răk′ ĭt] **94** 29

racquetball [răk′ ĭt böl′] **94** 30

radiator [rā′ dē āt′ ər] **51** 56

radio [rā′ dē ō′] **50** 18

radish(es) [răd′ ĭsh (əz)] **7** 29

radius [rā′ dē əs] **79** 14

raft [răft] **89** 16

rafters [răf′ tərz] **82** 1

rafting [răf′ tĭng] **89**

rags [răgz] **35** 4

rain boots [rān′ boōts′] **19** 25

raincoat [rān′ kōt′] **21** 38

rainy [rān′ ē] **25** 1

raise (one's hand) [rāz′ wŭnz hănd′]
77 1

raisin(s) [rā′ zən(z)] **9** 24

rake (v) [răk] **26** 10

rake (n) [răk] **27** 30

ranch [rănch] **81**

ranch house [rănch/ hows/] **27**

ranching [rănch/ ĭng] **81**

rapids [răp/ ĭdz] **89** 17

rash [răsh] **40** 1

raspberries [răz/ běr/ ēz] **8** 16

rat [răt] **66** 7

rattle [răt/ əl] **33** 21

rattlesnake [răt/ əl snāk/] **65** 10

razor [rā/ zər] **23** 20

razor blades [rā/ zər blādz/] **23** 23

read [rēd] **77** 4

real estate agent [rēl/ ə stāt ā/ jənt]
    85 5

rear bumper [rĭr/ bŭm/ pər] **50** 42

rearview mirror [rĭr/ vyoō mĭr/ ər]
    50 7

receipt [rə sēt/] **15** 20, **55** 24

receiver [rə sē/ vər] **100** 21

receptionist [rə sĕp/ shə nəst] **86** 17

recliner [rə klī/ nər] **28** 16

records [rĕk/ ərdz] **100** 23

rectangle [rĕk/ tăng/ gəl] **79** 19

Red Sea [rĕd/ sē/] **70** 29

redwood [rĕd/ wŏŏd/] **61** 25

(reel of) film [rēl/ əv fĭlm/] **100** 17

referee [rĕf/ ə rē/] **93** 22, **94** 16

reference section
    [rĕf/ ə rəns sĕk/ shən] **47** 21

(reference) librarian
    [rĕf/ ə rəns lī brēr/ e ən] **47** 23

refill [rē/ fĭl/] **35** 11

refinery [rə fī/ nə rē] **80** 12

reflector [rə flĕk/ tər] **52** 25

refreshment stand
    [rə frĕsh/ mənt stănd/] **90** 2

refrigerator [rə frĭj/ ə rā/ tər] **30** 19

reins [rānz] **94** 22

relationshops [rə lā/ shən shĭps/] **2**

remedies [rĕm/ ə dēz] **41**

remote control [rə mōt/ kən trōl/]
    28 17

repair [rə për/] **38** 10

repairperson [rə për/ pür/ sən] **84** 5

reporter [rə pör/ tər] **86** 11

reptiles [rĕp/ tĭlz] **65**

rescue [rĕs/ kyoō] **42**

restaurant [rĕs/ tə rənt] **16**

retriever [rə trē/ vər] **69** 26

return address [rə türn/ ă drĕs/] **46** 8

rhinoceros [rī nŏs/ ə rəs] **66** 16

Rhode Island [rōd/ ī/ lənd] **73** 39

rice [rīs] **60** 21

ride [rīd] **97** 13

rider [rī/ dər] **54** 6

rifle [rī/ fəl] **48** 21

right angle [rīt/ ăng/ gəl] **79** 23

right fielder [rīt/ fēl/ dər] **93** 3

right guard [rīt/ gärd/] **93** 28

right lane [rīt/ lān/] **53** 7

right tackle [rīt/ tăk/ əl] **93** 29

right triangle [rīt/ trī/ ăng gəl] **79** 22

rind [rīnd] **8** 8b

ring(s) [rĭng(z)] **23** 2, **74** 16a, **94** 17

ring binder [rĭng/ bīn/ dər] **76** 14

ring finger [rĭng/ fĭng/ gər] **4** 27

ring stand [rĭng/ stănd/] **78** 19

rink [rĭngk] **94** 25

Rio Grande River [rē/ ō grănd/ rĭv/ ər]
    71 57

rivers [rĭv/ ərz] **71**

road sign [rōd/ sīn/] **53** 23

road work [rōd/ würk/] **82**

roadrunner [rōd/ rŭn/ ər] **64** 32

roast [rōst] **10** 3, **10** 8

roasting pan [rōs/ tĭng păn/] **30** 17

robes [rōbz] **43** 11

robin [rŏb/ in] **64** 9

rock group [rŏk/ groōp/] **99**

rocket [rŏk/ ət] **75** 13

rocks [rŏks] **88** 11

rocking chair [rŏk/ ĭng chër/] **33** 16

Rocky Mountains [rŏk/ ē mown/ tənz]
    71 40

rodents [rō/ dənts] **66**

roll [rōl] **12** 11, **18** 19

(roll of) film [rōl/ əv fĭlm/] **100** 10

roller [rōl/ ər] **37** 29

rolling pin [rōl/ ĭng pĭn/] **30** 25

rolodex [rōl/ ə dĕks/] **83** 14

rooster [roō/ stər] **64** 21

roof [roōf] **27** 4

root [roōt] **60** 35d

rope [rōp] **89** 23

rose [rōz] **60** 18

rotor [rō/ tər] **57** 2a

rough [rŭf] **95** 6

router [row/ tər] **37** 37

row [rō] **47** 11, **81** 18

rowboat [rō/ bōt/] **59** 23

Rub/ al Khali Desert
    [roōb/ ăl kŏl/ ē dĕz/ ərt] **71** 52

rubber tubing [rŭb/ ər toōb/ ĭng] **78** 18

rudder [rŭd/ ər] **59** 5

rug [rŭg] **32** 28

ruler [roō/ lər] **76** 23

run [rŭn] **96** 6

rung [rŭng] **82** 9

runner [rŭn/ ər] **91** 23, **94** 31

runway [rŭn/ wā/] **57** 19

saddle [săd/ əl] **94** 20

safety glasses [săf/ tē glăs/ əz] **78** 12

safety goggles [săf/ tē gŏg/ əlz] **94** 28

safety pin [săf/ tē pĭn/] **33** 11

Sahara Desert [sə hër/ ə dĕz/ ərt]
    71 51

sail [sāl] **59** 9

sailboard [sāl/ börd/] **59** 15

sailboat [sāl/ bōt/] **59** 4

sailor [sāl/ ər] **48** 14

salad bowl [săl/ əd bōl/] **29** 25

salad dressing [săl/ əd drĕs/ ĭng] **18** 12

salamander [săl/ ə măn/ dər] **65** 14

salesperson [sālz/ pür/ sən] **86** 12

salt shaker [sŏlt/ shā/ kər] **29** 10

sand (v) [sănd] **26** 14

sand (n) [sănd] **90** 31

sand dunes [sănd/ doōnz/] **90** 12

sand trap [sănd/ trăp/] **95** 11

sandal [săn/ dəl] **20** 19

sandbox [sănd/ bŏks/] **87** 13

sandcastle [sănd/ kăs/ əl] **91** 32

sandpaper [sănd/ pā/ pər] **37** 27

sandwich [sănd/ wĭch] **16** 16

sanitation worker
    [săn ə tā/ shən wür/ kər] **49** 7

Saturn [săt/ ərn] **74** 16

saucepan [sŏs/ păn/] **30** 8

saucer [sŏ/ sər] **29** 21

sausage [sŏ/ sĭj] **10** 7

saw [sŏ] **36** 8

saxophone [săk/ sə fōn/] **98** 24

scaffolding [skăf/ əl dĭng] **82** 7

scale [skāl] **14** 7, **34** 32, **78** 4

scallop(s) [skăl/ əp(s)] **11** 35, **62** 10

scarecrow [skër′ krō′] **81** 19

scarf [skärf] **19** 19

scenery [sē′ nə rē] **99** 2

school [skōol] **76, 77**

science lab [sī′ əns lăb′] **78**

scissors [sĭz′ ərz] **101** 17

scoreboard [skör′ börd] **93** 19

scorpion [skör′ pē ən] **63** 8

scouring pad [skowr′ ĭng păd′] **30** 11

scrape [skrāp] **26** 15

scraper [skrāp′ ər] **36** 14

screen [skrēn] **27** 19, **100** 14

screw [skrōō] **37** 42

screwdriver [skrōō′ drī′ vər] **37** 24

scrub [skrŭb] **38** 2

scuba tank [skōō′ bə tăngk′] **91** 37

sea gull [sē′ gŭl′] **64** 4

sea horse [sē′ hörs′] **65** 1

Sea of Japan [sē′ əv jə păn′] **70** 36

Sea of Okhotsk [sē′ əv ō kŏtsk′]
   70 35

seafood [sē′ fōōd′] **10**

seal [sēl] **68** 12

seam [sēm] **101** 10

seas [sēz] **70**

seat [sēt] **52** 16, **54** 2

seat belt [sēt′ bĕlt] **50** 23

second baseman [sĕk′ ənd bās′ mən]
   93 7

secretary [sĕk′ rə tĕr′ ē] **83** 11

section [sĕk′ shən] **8** 8a, **79** 15

security [sə kyŏor′ ə tē] **56**

security guard [sə kyŏor′ ə tē gärd′]
   56 9, **86** 14

sedan [sə dăn′] **51**

seed [sēd] **8** 8c

seesaw [sē′ sö′] **87** 18

serve [sürv] **17** 3, **96** 2

service area [sür′ vəs ër′ ē ə] **53** 11

sevice court [sür′ vəs kört′] **95** 1

service line [sür′ vəs līn′] **95** 3

set (the table) [sĕt′ dhə tā′ bəl] **17** 8

sewing [sō′ ĭng] **101**

sewing machine [sō′ ĭng mə shēn′]
   101 1

shade [shād] **33** 1

shaft [shăft] **80** 10

shampoo [shăm pōō′] **34** 8

shank [shăngk] **36** 43b

shark [shärk] **65** 5

shaving cream [shā′ vĭng krēm′] **23** 22

sheep [shēp] **67** 25, **81** 10

sheet [shēt] **32** 19

sheet music [shēt′ myōō′ zĭk] **98** 2

shelf [shĕlf] **14** 6, **47** 26

shell [shĕl] **48** 27, **62** 1a, **65** 18a,
   90 40

shellfish [shĕl′ fĭsh′] **11**

shepherd [shĕp′ ərd] **69** 28

shingle [shĭng′ gəl] **82** 2

ship [shĭp] **58** 9

shirt [shürt] **21** 46

shock absorbers [shŏk′ əb zör′ bərz]
   52 31

shoe [shōō] **21** 49

shoelace [shōō′ lās′] **20** 7

shoot [shōōt] **97** 16

shop worker [shŏp′ wür′ kər] **85** 12

shopping bag [shŏp′ ĭng băg′] **20** 18

shopping basket [shŏp′ ĭng băs′ kət]
   14 8

shopping cart [shŏp′ ĭng kärt′] **15** 19

short [shört] **24** 1

short sleeve [shört′ slēv′] **20** 21

shorts [shörts] **20** 14

shortstop [shört′ stŏp′] **93** 5

shoulder [shōl′ dər] **4** 5, **53** 22

(shoulder) bag [shōl′ dər băg′] **21** 35

shovel (n) [shŭv′ əl] **27** 31, **82** 15,
   90 17

shovel (v) [shŭv′ əl] **26** 13

shower cap [show′ ər kăp′] **34** 3

shower curtain [show′ ər kür′ tən] **34** 5

shower head [show′ ər hĕd′] **34** 4

shrimp [shrĭmp] **11** 31, **62** 8

shutter [shŭt′ ər] **27** 8

shuttle car [shŭt′ əl kär′] **80** 8

side [sīd] **79** 10

side mirror [sīd′ mïr′ ər] **50** 2

sideburn [sīd′ bürn′] **4** 33

sidewalk [sīd′ wök′] **45** 25

Sierra Madre [sē ër′ ə mŏ′ drē] **71** 42

silo [sī′ lō] **81** 4

silverware [sĭl′ vər wër′] **29** 22

simple animals [sĭm′ pəl ăn′ ə məlz] **62**

singer [sĭng′ ər] **99** 24

sink [sĭngk] **34** 19

sister [sĭs′ tər] **3** 10

sister-in-law [sĭs′ tər ən lö′] **3** 8

six-pack [sĭks′ păk′] **13** 13

skate (n) [skāt] **94** 26

skate (v) [skāt] **97** 9

skein [skān] **101** 24

ski [skē] **95** 17

ski boot [skē′ bōōt′] **95** 15

ski cap [skē′ kăp′] **19** 16

ski lift [skē′ lĭft′] **95** 18

ski slope [skē′ slōp′] **95**

skier [skē′ ər] **94** 35

skis [skēz] **94** 33

skin [skĭn] **9** 37b

skirt [skürt] **21** 36

skunk [skŭngk] **68** 8

slacks [slăks] **20** 4

sleeping bag [slē′ pĭng băg′] **89** 26

sleepwear [slēp′ wër′] **22**

slice (n) [slīs] **13** 21

slice (v) [slīs] **31** 10

slide [slīd] **78** 31, **87** 12

slide projector [slīd′ prə jĕk′ tər]
   100 13

slides [slīdz] **100** 12

sling [slĭng] **39** 3

splippers [slĭp′ ərz] **22** 18

slug [slŭg] **62** 4

small [smöl] **24** 7

smoke [smōk] **42** 15

smoke detector [smōk′ də tĕk′ tər]
   33 15

smokestack [smök′ stăk′] **58** 18,
   80 22

snacks [snăks] **14** 18

snail [snāl] **62** 1

snake [snāk] **65** 9

snap [snăp] **101** 13

sneakers [snē′ kərz] **20** 11

snorkel [snör′ kəl] **91** 34

snow plow [snō′ plow′] **49** 5

snowy [snō′ e] **25** 3

soap [sōp] **34** 15

soap dish [sōp′ dĭsh′] **34** 6

soccer [sŏk′ ər] **92**

soccer ball [sŏk′ ər böl′] **92** 26

socks [sŏks] **22** 17

sofa [sō′ fə] **28** 25

soft drink [söft′ drĭngk′] **16** 11

softball [söft′ böl′] **92, 92** 10

solar collector [sō′ lər kə lĕk′ tər] **80** 17

solar eclipse [sō′ lər ĭ klĭps′] **74** 10

solar system [sō′ lər sĭs′ təm] **74**

soldier [sōl′ jər] **48** 16

sole [sōl] **20** 6

solid [sŏl′ əd] **24** 20

solid figures [sŏl′ əd fĭg′ yərz] **79**

son [sŭn] **3** 16

Sony Walkman [sō′ nē wök′ mən] **100** 30

sore throat [sör′ thrōt′] **40** 12

south [sowth] **71** 72

South America [sowth′ ə mër′ ə kə] **70** 2

South Atlantic [sowth′ ăt lăn′ tək] **70** 12

South Carolina [sowth′ kăr ə lī′ nə] **73** 40

South China Sea [sowth′ chi′ nə sē′] **70** 39

South Dakota [sowth′ də kō′ tə] **73** 41

South Pacific [sowth pə sĭf′ ək] **70** 10

space probe [spās′ prōb] **75** 4

space program [spās′ prō′ grăm] **75**

space shuttle [spās′ shŭt′ əl] **75** 14

space station [spās′ stā′ shən] **75** 1

space suit [spās′ so͞ot′] **75** 6

spacecraft [spās′ krăft′] **75**

spaghetti [spə gĕt′ ē] **18** 10

spaniel [spăn′ yəl] **69** 24

spare ribs [spër′ rĭbz′] **10** 10

spare tire [spër′ tīr′] **51** 39

sparrow [spăr′ ō] **64** 10

spatula [spăch′ə lə] **27** 21

speaker [spē′ kər] **28** 21, **100** 24

speed limit sign [spēd′ lĭm ət sīn′] **53** 8

speedometer [spə dŏm′ə tər] **50** 10

spider [spī′ dər] **63** 16

spinach [spĭn′ əch] **6** 8

spinal cord [spī′ nəl körd′] **5** 58

spiral notebook [spī′ rəl nōt′ bo͝ok] **76** 15

split [splĭt] **11** 17

split end [splĭt′ ĕnd′] **93** 24

spoke [spōk] **52** 26

sponge [spŭnj] **34** 7

(sponge) mop [spŭnj′ mŏp′] **35** 6

(spool of) thread [spo͞ol′ əv thrĕd′] **101** 2

spoon [spo͞on] **29** 8

sports car [spörts′ kär′] **53** 17

sports [spörts] **92-97**

spotlight [spöt′ līt′] **99** 4

sprain [sprān] **40** 13

spray can [sprā′ kăn′] **13** 24

spray starch [sprā′ stärch′] **35** 21

spread [sprĕd] **17** 11

Spring [sprĭng] **26**

sprinkler [sprĭng′ klər] **27** 13, **87** 14

sprocket [sprŏk′ ət] **52** 20

square [skwër] **79** 9

squid [skwĭd] **62** 5

squirrel [skwür′ əl] **66** 10

stage [stāj] **99** 5

staircase [stër′ kās] **28** 12

stake [stāk] **89** 30

stamp [stămp] **46** 10

stands [stăndz] **93** 10

staple remover [stāp′ əl rə moo′ vər] **83** 29

stapler [stāp′ lər] **83** 27

star [stär] **74** 4

starfish [stär′ fĭsh′] **62** 7

starting gate [stär′ tĭng gāt′] **95** 20

station [stā′ shən] **55** 18

station wagon [stā′ shən wăg′ ən] **50**

steak [stāk] **10** 5, **11** 29, **18** 21

steam [stēm] **31** 12

steamer [stēm′ ər] **30** 3

steering wheel [stür′ ĭng wēl′] **50** 8

stem [stĕm] **8** 2a, **60** 1a

step [stĕp] **28** 13

stepladder [stĕp′ lăd′ ər] **35** 1

stereo cassette player [stĕr′ ē ō kə sĕt plā′ ər] **100** 25

stereo system [stĕr′ ē ō sĭs′ təm] **28** 20

stern [stürn] **58** 11

stethoscope [stĕth′ ə skōp′] **39** 9

stewing meat [stoo′ ĭng mēt] **10** 4

stick [stĭk] **12** 5

stick shift [stĭk′ shĭft′] **50** 24

sting [stĭng] **63** 8a

stingray [stĭng′ rā′] **65** 6

stir [stür] **31** 1

stitch [stĭch] **101** 19

stitches [stĭch′ əz] **39** 21

stockings [stŏk′ ĭngz] **22** 6

stomach [stŭm′ ək] **5** 66

stomachache [stŭm′ ək āk′] **40** 7

stool [stool] **78** 34

stopper [stŏp′ ər] **34** 10, **78** 10

stork [störk] **64** 30

stove [stōv] **30** 30

straight line [strāt′ līn′] **79** 1

(strand of) beads [strănd′ əv bēdz′] **23** 7

strap [străp] **54** 8

straw [strö] **16** 10

strawberry [strö′ bër′ ē] **8** 15

strawberry shortcake [strö′ bër ē shört′ kāk] **18** 26

stream [strēm] **88** 6

street [strēt] **45** 31

street cleaner [strēt′ klē′ nər] **49** 1

street sign [strēt′ sīn′] **44** 8

streetcar [strēt′ kär′] **55** 30

streetlight [strēt′ līt′] **45** 29

stretch [strĕch] **95** 19

stretch bandage [strĕch′ băn′ dĭj] **40** 13a

stretcher [strĕch′ ər] **39** 12

stretchie [strĕch′ ē] **33** 19

string [strĭng] **46** 20, **98** 10a

string bean(s) [strĭng′ bēn(z)′] **6** 15

strings [strĭngz] **98**

striped [strīpt] **24** 17

stroller [strō′ lər] **33** 14

student [stoo′ dənt] **76** 19

stuffed animal [stŭft′ ăn ə məl] **33** 27

subject [sŭb′ jəkt] **47** 10

submarine [sŭb′ mə rēn′] **48** 7

subway [sŭb′ wā′] **54**

subway station [sŭb′ wā stā′ shən] **44** 16

sugar (packet) [shoog′ ər păk′ ət] **16** 13

sugar bowl [shoog′ ər bōl′] **29** 23

sugarcane [shoog′ ər kān′] **60** 20

suitcase [soot′ kās′] **56** 7

Summer [sŭm′ ər] **26**

sun [sŭn] **74** 7, **80** 3

sunbather [sŭn′ bā′ dhər] **90** 19

sundae [sŭn′ dē] **18** 23

sunflower [sŭn′ flŏw′ ər] **60** 19

sunglasses [sŭn′ glăs′ əz] **90** 14

sunny [sŭn′ ē] **25** 4

(sunnyside-up) egg
  [sŭn′ ē sīd ŭp′ ĕg′] **18** 32

sunroof [sŭn′ rŏof′] **51** 44

suntan lotion [sŭn′ tăn lō′ shən] **91** 39

supermarket [sōo′ pər mär′ kət] **14**

surf [sürf] **97** 12

surfboard [sürf′ bȯrd′] **91** 25

surgery [sŭr′ jə rē] **41** 2

suspect [sŭs′ pĕkt] **43** 3

swan [swŏn] **64** 28

sweatband [swĕt′ bănd′] **20** 12

sweater [swĕt′ ər] **19** 7, **19** 13, **19** 23

sweatpants [swĕt′ pănts′] **20** 10

sweatshirt [swĕt′ shürt′] **20** 8

sweep [swēp] **38** 7

swimmer [swĭm′ ər] **91** 28

swing [swĭng] **33** 24

swings [swĭngz] **87** 16

switch [swĭch] **37** 43c

switchboard [swĭch′ bȯrd′] **83** 3

switchboard operator
  [swĭch′ bȯrd ŏp′ ə rā tər] **83** 1

swordfish [sȯrd′ fĭsh′] **65** 3

synthesizer [sĭn′ thə sī′ zər] **99** 21

syringe [sə rĭnj′] **39** 27

syrup [sĭr′ əp] **18** 6

T-shirt [tē′ shürt′] **21** 29

table [tā′ bəl] **29** 7

tablecloth [tā′ bəl klȯth′] **29** 16

tablet [tăb′ lət] **41** 6

taco [tŏ′ kō] **18** 24

tadpole [tăd′ pōl′] **65** 16

tail [tāl] **57** 10, **65** 3a, **66** 3a

taillight [tāl′ līt′] **50** 31

tailor [tā′ lər] **84** 6

take [tāk] **17** 10

takeoff [tāk′ ŏf′] **57**

Takla Makan Desert
  [tŏk′ lə mə kŏn′ dĕz′ ərt] **71** 53

tambourine [tăm′ bə rēn′] **98** 17

tank [tăngk] **48** 10

tank top [tăngk′ tŏp′] **20** 13

tanker [tăngk′ ər] **58** 15

tap [tăp] **16** 20

tape [tāp] **46** 22

tape measure [tāp′ mĕzh′ ər] **36** 21,
  101 15

taxi [tăk′ sē] **55**

taxi stand [tăk′ sē stănd′] **55** 28

taxicab [tăk′ sē kăb′] **55** 27

tea [tē] **16** 15

teacher [tē′ chər] **76** 4

teakettle [tē′ kĕt′ əl] **30** 28

team sports [tēm′ spȯrts′] **92**

teapot [tē′ pŏt′] **29** 19

tear [tër] **77** 9

teddy bear [tĕd′ ē bër′] **33** 3

tee [tē] **95** 13

telephone [tĕl′ ə fōn′] **83** 15

telescope [tĕl′ ə skōp′] **74** 22

television [tĕl′ ə vĭzh′ ən] **28** 18, **100** 5

teller [tĕl′ ər] **86** 15

temperature [tĕm′ pər ə chər] **25** 6

Tennessee [tĕn′ ə sē′] **73** 42

tennis [tĕn′ əs] **94**

tennis ball [tĕn′ əs bȯl′] **94** 1

tennis court [tĕn′ əs kȯrt′] **95**

tent [tĕnt] **89** 24

tentacle [tĕn′ tə kəl] **62** 12a

terminal [türm′ ə nəl] **51** 55, **58** 29

terminal building [türm′ ə nəl bĭl′ dĭng]
  57 16

termite [tür′ mīt] **63** 11

terrier [tĕr′ ē ər] **69** 25

test tube [tĕst′ tōob′] **78** 9

Texas [tĕk′ səs] **73** 43

textbook [tĕkst′ bŏok′] **76** 26

theater [thē′ ə tər] **99**

thermometer
  [thər mŏm′ ə tər] **25** 5, **78** 22

thermos [thür′ məs] **88** 14

thigh [thī] **4** 18, **11** 19

thimble [thĭm′ bəl] **101** 21

third (1/3) [thürd] **79** 32

third baseman [thürd′ bās′ mən] **93** 4

thorn [thȯrn] **60** 18c

thread [thrĕd] **37** 42b, **101** 2

three-piece suit [thrē′ pēs sōot′] **21** 40

throat [thrōt] **5** 59

through [thrōo] **103** 1

throw [thrō] **97** 10

thumb [thŭm] **4** 24

thumbtack [thŭm′ tăk′] **76** 25

ticket [tĭk′ ət] **55** 16, **56** 4

ticket window [tĭk′ ət wĭn′ dō] **55** 19

tie (n) [tī] **21** 47

tie (v) [tī] **77** 12

tie clip [tī′ klĭp′] **23** 14

tie pin [tī′ pĭn′] **23** 13

tiger [tī′ gər] **68** 2

tight [tīt] **24** 3

tighten [tī′ tən] **38** 4

tight end [tīt′ ĕnd′] **93** 30

tights [tīts] **19** 14

tile [tīl] **34** 27

timer [tī′ mər] **78** 13

timetable [tīm′ tă′ bəl] **55** 20

tip [tĭp] **55** 22

tire [tīr] **50** 37, **52** 28

tissues [tĭsh′ ōoz] **32** 13

title [tī′ təl] **47** 9

to [tōo] **103** 9

toast [tōst] **18** 34

toaster [tōs′ tər] **30** 16

toe [tō] **5** 54

toenail [tō′ nāl′] **5** 56

toilet [toy′ lət] **34** 29

toilet brush [toy′ lət brŭsh′] **34** 31

toilet paper [toy′ lət pā′ pər] **34** 30

toiletries [toy′ lə trēz] **23**

token booth [tō′ kən bōoth′] **54** 13

tollbooth [tōl′ bōoth′] **53** 27

tomato(es) [tə mā′ tō(z)] **6** 19

tongs [tŏngz] **78** 29

tongue [tŭng] **4** 41

tongue depressor [tŭng′ də prĕs′ ər]
  40 12a

toolbox [tōol′ bŏks′] **36** 23

toolshed [tōol′ shĕd′] **27** 28

tooth [tōoth] **4** 42

toothache [tōoth′ āk′] **40** 9

toothbrush [tōoth′ brŭsh′] **34** 21

toothless mammals [tōoth′ ləs măm′ əlz]
  66

toothpaste [tōoth′ pāst′] **34** 16

tortoise [tȯr′ təs] **65** 18

tossed salad [tȯst′ săl′ əd] **18** 13

touch [tŭch] **77** 2

touring handlebars
[tŏŏr′ ĭng hăn′ dəl bärz] **52** 12

tow truck [tō′ trŭk] **49** 2

toward [törd] **103** 4

towel rack [tow′ əl răk′] **34** 25

towrope [tō′ rōp′] **59** 11

toy chest [toy′ chĕst′] **33** 29

track [trăk] **54** 10, **94** 32

track and field [trăk′ ənd fēld′] **94**

tractor [trăk′ tər] **81** 15

tractor trailer [trăk′ tər trā′ lər] **49** 15

traffic cop [trăf′ ək kŏp′] **44** 10

traffic light [trăf′ ək līt′] **45** 21

trailer [trā′ lər] **53** 10

train [trān] **55**

training wheels [trān′ ĭng wēlz′] **52** 1

transcript [trăn′ skrĭpt] **43** 15

transfer [trăns′ fər] **54** 4

transformer [trăns för′ mər] **80** 25

transmission towers
[trănz mĭsh′ ən tow′ ərz] **80** 23

transportation [trăns′ pər tā′ shən] **54**

transporter [trăns′ pör tər] **49** 17

trash basket [trăsh′ băs′ kət] **44** 15

trash can [trăsh′ kăn′] **87** 11

travel agent [trăv′ əl ā′ jənt] **84** 4

traveler [trăv′ ə lər] **56** 3

tray [trā] **16** 33

tray table [trā′ tā′ bəl] **56** 22

treatments [trēt′ mənts] **41**

tree [trē] **61** 35

trees [trēz] **60**

triangle [trī′ ăng′ gəl] **79** 6

tricycle [trī′ sĭ kəl] **52** 6

trigger [trĭg′ ər] **48** 22

tripod [trī′ pod] **100** 9

trim [trĭm] **26** 8

trombone [trŏm bōn′] **98** 23

trough [tröf] **81** 25

trout [trowt] **65** 2

trowel [trow′ əl] **27** 27

truck [trŭk] **49**, **53** 25

truck driver [trŭk′ drī′ vər] **49** 16

trumpet [trŭm′ pət] **98** 25

trunk [trŭngk] **51** 40, **61** 35b, **66** 17a

tub [tŭb] **12** 6

tuba [tōō′ bə] **98** 27

tube [tōōb] **13** 15, **91** 29

tugboat [tŭg′ bōt′] **58** 13

tulip [tōō′ ləp] **60** 1

turkey [tür′ kē] **10** 23, **64** 20

turnip [tür′ nəp] **6** 34

turn signal lever [türn′ sĭg nəl lĕ′ vər]
50 11

turn signal lights [türn′ sĭg nəl līts′]
51 50

turnstile [türn′ stīl′] **54** 12

turntable [türn′ tā′ bəl] **100** 18

turtle [tür′ təl] **65** 12

(turtleneck) sweater
[tür′ təl nĕk swĕ′ tər] **19** 13

tusk [tŭsk] **66** 17b

TV antenna [tē′ vē ăn tĕn′ ə] **27** 3

tweezers [twē′ zərz] **78** 32

twig [twĭg] **61** 33a

(two-door) sedan [tōō′ dör sə dăn′] **51**

type [tīp] **77** 10

typewriter [tīp′ rī′ tər] **83** 10

typing chair [tī′ pĭng chër′] **83** 17

typist [tī′ pəst] **83** 6

U.S. mailbox [yōō′ ĕs māl′ bŏks] **46** 6

U.S. Postal System
[yōō′ ĕs pōs′ təl sĭs təm] **46**

ukulele [yōō′ kə lā′ lē] **98** 3

umbrella [ŭm brĕl′ ə] **20** 24

umpire [ŭm′ pīr] **92** 1, **93** 17

uncle [ŭng′ kəl] **3** 3

under [ŭn′ dər] **102** 8

underpants [ŭn′ dər pănts′] **22** 3

undershirt [ŭn′ dər shürt′] **22** 1

underwear [ŭn′ dər wër′] **22**

uniform [yōō′ nə förm′] **21** 45, **92** 9

United States of America
[yōō nī′ təd stāts′ əv əmër′ ə kə] **72**

universe [yōō′ nə vürs′] **74**

up [ŭp] **103** 11

upper arm [ŭp′ ər ärm′] **4** 7

Urals [yŏŏr′ əlz] **71** 46

uranium rods [yōō rā′ nē əm rŏdz′]
80 15

Uranus [yŏŏr′ ə nəs] **74** 17

usher [ŭsh′ ər] **99** 16

Utah [yōō′ tö] **73** 44

utility pole [yōō tĭl′ ə tē pōl′] **80** 26

utility room [yōō tĭl′ ə tē rōōm] **35**

(V-neck) sweater [vē′ nĕk swĕt′ ər]
19 23

vacuum [văk′ yōōm] **38** 14

vacuum cleaner [văk′ yōōm klē′ nər]
35 16

valve [vălv] **52** 27

van [văn] **53** 26

vase [vās] **28** 6

VCR (videocassette recorder)
[vē′ sē är′]/
[vĭd′ ē ō kə sĕt′ rə kör′ dər] **100** 4

vegetables [vĕj′ tə bəlz] **6**

vehicles and equipment
[vē′ ə kəlz ənd ə kwĭp′ mənt] **48**

vein [vān] **5** 68

vendor [vĕn′ dər] **87** 3

vent [vĕnt] **50** 21

Venus [vē′ nəs] **74** 12

verbs [vürbz] **17**, **26**, **31**, **38**, **77**, **96**

Vermont [vür mŏnt′] **73** 45

vest [vĕst] **21** 39

video [vĭd′ē ō] **100**

video camera [vīd′ ē ō kăm′ ə rə]
100 1

videocassette (tape)
[vĭd′ ē ō kə sĕt′ tāp′] **100** 3

vine [vīn] **61** 42

viola [vē ōl′ ə] **98** 8

violet [vī′ ə lət] **60** 16

violin [vī ə lĭn′] **98** 7

Virginia [vər jĭn′ yə] **73** 46

vise [vīs] **37** 36

visor [vĭz′ ər] **50** 5

volleyball [vŏl′ ē böl′] **92**, **92** 22

waders [wā′ dərz] **88** 10

waist [wāst] **4** 13

waiter [wā tər] **16** 5

waitress [wā′ trəs] **16** 2

walk [wök] **77** 8

walker [wök′ ər] **33** 23

wall [wöl] **28** 3

wall unit [wöl′ yōō′ nət] **28** 19

wall-to-wall carpeting
[wöl′ tə wöl kär′ pə tĭng] **28** 15

wallet [wöl′ ət] **20** 9

walnut(s) [wöl′ nət(s)] **8** 29

walrus [wöl′ rŭs] **68** 11

warm [wörm] **25** 8

wash [wŏsh] **38** 16

washcloth [wŏsh′klöth′] **34** 22

washer [wŏsh′ər] **37** 40

washing machine
[wŏsh′ĭng mə shēn′] **35** 30

Washington [wŏsh′ĭng tən] **73** 47

wasp [wŏsp] **63** 20

wastepaper basket
[wāst′ pā pər băs′ kət] **34** 13

watch [wŏch] **23** 10

watchband [wŏch′ bănd′] **23** 11

water (n) [wŏt′ ər] **42** 16, **91** 30

water (v) [wŏt′ ər] **26** 5

water fountain [wŏt′ ər fown′ tən]
87 19

water glass [wŏt′ ər glăs′] **29** 6

waterfall [wŏt′ər föl] **80** 11, **89** 18

water-skier [wŏt′ər skē′ ər] **59** 10

watercress [wŏt′ər krĕs′] **6** 5

watering can [wŏt′ər ĭng kăn′] **27** 16

watermelon [wŏt′ər mĕl′ ən] **9** 26

wave [wāv] **91** 24

weapon [wĕp′ənz] **48**

weather [wĕdh′ər] **25**

weather forecaster
[wĕdh′ər för′ kăst ər] **86** 1

weather satellite [wĕdh′ər săt′ ə līt]
75 3

weaving [wē′ vĭng] **101** 30

web [wĕb] **63** 15

wedding ring [wĕd′ĭng rĭng′] **23** 4

weights [wāts] **78** 5

west [wĕst] **71** 74

West Virginia [wĕst′ vər jĭn′ yə] **73** 48

wet [wĕt] **25** 15

wet suit [wĕt′ sōot′] **91** 38

whale [wāl] **68** 9

wheat [wēt] **60** 22

wheat farm [wēt′ färm′] **81**

(wheat) field [wēt′ fēld′] **81** 16

wheel [wēl] **52** 4

wheelbarrow [wēl′ băr′ ō] **27** 32,
82 23

wheelchair [wēl′ chër′] **39** 2

whistle [wĭs′ əl] **90** 5

whole [hōl] **11** 27, **79** 29

whole (chicken) [hōl′ chĭk′ ən] **11** 16

width [wĭdth] **79** 35

wife [wīf] **2** 4

willow [wĭl′ ō] **61** 31

wind [wĭnd] **80** 4

windbreaker [wĭnd′ brā′ kər] **19** 5

windlass [wĭnd′ ləs] **58** 23

windmill [wĭnd′ mĭl′] **80** 19

window [wĭn′ dō] **27** 7, **46** 15

window cleaner [wĭn′ dō klē′ nər]
35 10

windpipe [wĭnd′ pīp′] **5** 60

windshield [wĭnd′ shēld′] **51** 45

windshield wiper [wĭnd′ shēld wī′ pər]
50 6

windsurfer [wĭnd′ sür′ fər] **59** 14

windy [wĭn′ dē] **25** 13

wine [wīn] **16** 19

wine glass [wīn′ glăs′] **29** 5

wing [wĭng] **11** 22, **57** 9, **63** 4a,
64 1a

Winter [wĭn′ tər] **26**

wipe [wīp] **38** 5

wire [wīr] **37** 35

wire mesh screen [wīr′ mĕsh skrēn′]
78 6

Wisconsin [wĭs kŏn′ sən] **73** 49

witness [wĭt′ nəs] **43** 13

witness stand [wĭt′ nəs stănd′] **43** 18

wolf [wŏolf] **69** 29

woman [wŏom′ən] **2** 1

wood [wŏod] **36** 4

wood plane [wŏod′ plān′] **37** 32

woodpecker [wŏod′ pĕk′ ər] **64** 17

woods [wŏodz] **89** 32

woodwinds [wŏod′ wĭndz′] **98**

wool [wŏol] **101** 23

word processor [würd′ prŏ′ sĕs ər]
83 7

work gloves [würk′ glŭvz′] **27** 26

workbench [würk′ bĕnch′] **36** 22

workshop [würk′ shŏp′] **36**

world [würld] **70**

worm [würm] **62** 11

wrench [rĕnch] **36** 10

wrist [rĭst] **4** 21

write [rīt] **77** 7

writer [rī′ tər] **86** 7

Wyoming [wī ō′ mĭng] **73** 50

X ray [ĕks′ rā′] **39** 1

X ray screener [ĕks′ rā skrē′ nər] **56** 11

xylophone [zī′ lə fōn′] **98** 31

yam [yăm] **7** 24

Yangtze River [yăng′ sē rĭv′ ər] **71** 69

yarn [yärn] **101** 31

Yellow Sea [yĕl′ ō sē′] **70** 37

Yenisey River [yĕn′ ə sā′ rĭv′ ər]
71 65

Yukon River [yōo′ kŏn rĭv′ ər] **71** 56

zebra [zē′ brə] **66** 18

zinnia [zĭn′ ē ə] **60** 13

zip code [zĭp′ kōd′] **46** 12

zipper [zĭp′ ər] **101** 16

zoo [zōo] **87** 1

zucchini [zōo kē′ nē] **7** 27

ក 4 4

កងថ្មើរជើង 48 15

កងនាវាចរ 48 13

កងម៉ារីន 48 17

កងអាកាស 48 19

កង់ 50 37, 52 4, 52 15

កង់ៗបី 52 6

កង់សាស់ 72 16

កង់សីគ្ករ 51 39

កង់សំរាប់ជិះលេងនៅកន្លែង
-ដែលគ្មានផ្លូវស្រួលបួល 52 8

កង់សំរាប់ដាក់ឲ្យក្មេងរៀនជិះកង់ 52 1

កង់ហ្គរ 66 3

កង្កែប 65 17

កជើង 5 49

កញ្ចក់ 32 5

កញ្ចក់ខាងមុខ 51 45

កញ្ចក់នៅចំហៀង 50 2

កញ្ចក់មើលទៅខាងក្រោយ 50 7

កញ្ចប់ 12 8, 13 16, 13 17

កញ្ចប់ដាក់ឥវ៉ាន់ 15 25

កញ្ចប់ធ្វើតាមប៉ុស្ត៍ 46 19

(កញ្ចប់) ធ្វើឆ្នាក់លៀនបំផុត 46 23

កញ្ច្រែង 92 20

កញ្ជើដាក់ខោអាវប្រឡាក់ 34 28

កញ្ជើដាក់ខោអាវយកទៅបោក 35 29

កញ្ជើសំរាប់ដាក់គ្រឿងពិចនិច 88 13

កញ្ជើ 90 5

កញ្ជ្រោង 68 6

កដៃ 4 21

កណ្ដុរប្រម៉េះ 66 9

កណ្ដុរប្រែង 66 7

កណ្ដូប 63 6

កណ្ដូបសេះ 63 7

កណ្ដៀរ 63 11

កន្ទក 14 8

កន្ទ្រលឲ្យាក្រុស 92 16

កន្ទ្រៃ 101 17

កន្ទ្រៃកាត់កុំឲ្យរសាត់ 101 5

កន្ទុបប្រើហើយបោះចោល 33 12

កន្ទុបសំពត់ 33 13

កន្ទុយ 57 10, 65 3a, 66 3a

កន្ទុលវាល 40 1

កន្ទុំរុយ 63 4

កន្ទ្លាត 63 9

កន្លែងកប៉ាល់ហោះចូល
-ចត ឬ ចូលផ្លូវសដុល 57 17

កន្លែងក្មេងលេង 87 15

កន្លែងខ្ញីសៀវភៅ 47 2

កន្លែងគណៈវិនិច្ឆ័យអង្គុយ 43 20

កន្លែងគិតលុយ 15 26

កន្លែងចតឡ្យាន 45 19

កន្លែងចិញ្ចឹមគោយកទឹកដោះ 81 A

កន្លែងចិញ្ចឹមសត្វ 81 C

កន្លែងចូលចាក់សាំង 53 11

កន្លែងចំហាយទឹកបាញ់ចេញពីក្នុងដី 80 5

កន្លែងញាត់ខ្សែភ្លើង 36 6

កន្លែងញាំុស្រាកំសាន្ត 16 B

កន្លែងដាក់កាតសៀវភៅ 47 4

កន្លែងដាក់ដីខ្សាច់ឲ្យក្មេងលេង 87 13

កន្លែងដាក់ដីស 76 9

កន្លែងដាក់ប្រដាប់ប្រដាផ្សេងៗ 27 28

កន្លែងដាក់ពិនុបង្ហាញ
-(នៅពេលកំពុងលេង) 93 19

កន្លែងដាក់សាច់កក 30 20

កន្លែងដាក់ស្រោមដៃ 50 20

កន្លែងដាក់ឥវ៉ាន់ 51 40, 56 21, 57 12, 76 6

កន្លែងដុតឧស្ម័នក្នុងផ្ទះ 28 8

កន្លែងដេរឆ្នួងថ្នល់ 44 4

កន្លែងដេកសម្រាក 75 11

កន្លែងដែលគេមិនថែទាំកាត់ស្មៅ 95 6

កន្លែងតាក់សីឈប់ 55 28

កន្លែងត្រង់ខ្នងជើងជាប់នឹងមេជើង 5 52

កន្លែងទិញញាក់ (សំរាប់ជិះម៉ែត្រ) 54 13

កន្លែងទឹកហូរក្រូចខ្លាំង 89 17

កន្លែងធ្វើពិនិច 88

កន្លែងបង្ករទឹក 34 9

កន្លែងបញ្ចេះម៉ាស៊ុន 50 14

កន្លែងបញ្ជូរកង់ចត 52 14

កន្លែងបន្ថខ្យល់ភ្លើងឆ្នាប់នឹងឆុងអាគុយ 51 55

កន្លែងបាញ់បង្គោះ 75 15

កន្លែងបោះបាល់ 94 4

កន្លែងផុកឥវ៉ាន់ 75 9

កន្លែងផុកឥវ៉ាន់ក្នុងនាវា 58 8

កន្លែងផ្លូវកាត់គ្នា 44 11

កន្លែងព្យូរក្សៀង 34 25

កន្លែងព្យូរខោអាវ 32 3

កន្លែងយកលុយថ្លៃផ្លូវឡៗ 53 27

កន្លែងយកសៀវភៅចេញ 47 2

កន្លែងយកឥវ៉ាន់ទៅប្រគល់
-ឲ្យគេដាក់ក្នុងយន្តហោះ 56 27

កន្លែងយន្តបថពីរកាត់ប្រទាក់គ្នា 53 4

កន្លែងរត់ចេញទៅក្រៅពេលភ្លើងឆេះផ្ទះ 42 4

កន្លែងរថយន្តឈ្មួល(បីស)ឈប់ 44 13

កន្លែងរទេះភ្លើងឈប់ 55 18

បិលីក្រម

កន្លែងរៀបចំមូបនៅចង្រ្កានបាយ
-(ដូចគុតែធ្វើជាប់នៅនឹងជញ្ជាំង) 30 27

កន្លែងលក់តែម 46 15

កន្លែងលក់មូបភ្លិនស្រេច 14 1

កន្លែងលក់នំ (ដុត) 44 6

កន្លែងលក់សំបុត្រ 55 19

កន្លែងលាងដៃ ចាន ។ល។ 34 19

កន្លែងលេងតេននីស 95 A

កន្លែងលេងប៉័តាំង 94 25

កន្លែងលេងហាន់បល ។ល។ 94 13

កន្លែងវាយ 98 1a

កន្លែងសង់សំណង់ 82 A

កន្លែងសិកខ្មែរ 32 26b

កន្លែងសិកសំបុត្រថ្មី 46 13

កន្លែងសាក្សីអង្គុយ 43 18

កន្លែងសំរាប់ខ្យល់ចូល 50 21

កន្លែងសំរាប់ស្តោះទឹកមាត់ 39 16

កន្លែងសំរាប់ស្រាវជ្រាវរក
-សៀវភៅនិងឯកសារផ្សេងៗ 47 21

កន្លែងសំរាប់អ្នកបើកបរ 75 10

កន្លែងសំរាប់អ្នកលេងអង្គុយ 93 13

កន្លែងសួប្រេងកាត 80 12

កន្លែងអង្គុយ 54 1

កន្លែងអង្គុយយ៉ាងដាច់គ្នា 16 9

កន្លែងអង្គុយញញាំស្រា 16 24

កន្លែងអាំងសាច់ 30 33

កន្លែងអ្នកចោលបាល់ 93 11

កន្លែងអ្នកជិះឈរចាំរថភ្លើង 54 11

កន្លែងអ្នកបើកបរ 56 13

កន្លែងអ្នកស្តាប់ ឬ មើលនៅមុខគេ 99 12

កន្លែងអ្នកអង្គុយមើល 89 10

កន្លះ 79 30

កន្សែងជូតខ្លួនតូច 34 23

កន្សែងជូតខ្លួន (ធំៗ) 34 24

កន្សែងជូតចាន 30 18

កន្សែងវុត 19 19

កន្សែងសំរាប់ក្រាលអុយមាត់សមុទ្រ 90 15

កន្សែ (នាវា) 58 11

កបាល់នេសាទត្រី 58 1

កបាល់ហោះរ៉េអាក់ស្យុង 57 18

កបាល់ហោះប៉ែរ្រតងកជន 57 3

កបាល់ហោះទ្បៀង 57 B

កបាល់ហោះតតម៉ាស៊ីន 57 4

កម្មករវាងចក្រ 85 12

កម្មករសង់ផ្ទះ 82 14

កម្មវិធី 99 17

កម្រាល 32 29, 50 22

កម្រាលគ្របគ្រែ 32 23

កម្រាលដើមទី 93 15

កម្រាលតុ 29 16

កម្រាលពូក (ធម្មតា) 32 19

កមារ 20 1, 20 20

កាក់ 13 26

កាឌីណាល់ 64 11

កាណារី 64 14

កាណុក 48 11

កាណុត 59 13

កាណ្ឌ (ទូកអុំម្យ៉ាងក្បាល
-និងកន្សៃសំបើត) 59 2

កាតបណ្ណាល័យ 47 3

កាតប៉ុស្ត័ស្តាល់ 46 17

កាតសៀវភៅ 47 6

កាត់ 31 9, 103 6

កាត់ជាប្ដ 11 18

កាត់ (តាមកួងសៀនបញ្ជាំង) 103 1

កាត់ ឬ ច្បៀរជាបន្ទះៗឬជុំៗ 31 6

កាត់ស្ទើ 26 6

កាតាប 21 37

កាតីប 19 2

កាតីបពាក់លេងស្អី 19 16

កាតុង 12 1

កាន់ 17 12

កាន់ហ្ស្រាល់ 72 16

កាប៊ុប 26 9

កាប៊ុបស្លាយ 21 35

កាម៉េវ៉ាចករីឌីអូ 100 1

កាយ៉ាក់ (ទូកអុំម្យ៉ាងតូចហើយ
-បិទជិតគ្រង់ចង្កេះអ្នកអុំ) 59 17

ការកាត់សំពត់ជាបន្ទះតូចៗ
-ឲ្យនជ្រុងហើយដេរភ្ជាប់គ្នា 101 32

ការចាក់ថ្នាំ 41 8

ការចែកសំបុត្រ 46 A

ការចុះលើលោកខែ 75 B

ការជូសជុលនិងការថែទាំ 85 A

ការដេកសំរាកពេលមានជម្ងឺ 41 1

ការថតរូប 100 8

ការនេសាទត្រី 88

ការបង្កើតធាមពល 80 B

ការប្រើប្រាស់ហើយនិង
-ផលិតផលផ្សេងៗ 80 C

ការរត់ប្រណាំង 94

ការវះកាត់ 41 2

ការទ្បើងជិះយន្តហោះ 56

ការ៉ុត 7 32

ការរំមដាក់ផ្ទែលើ 18 23

កាល់គុលទ្បេទ័រ 100 34

កាលីហ្ស៊ូរនី 72 5
កាលីហ្ស៊ូរនីញ៉ា 72 5
ការ៉ 37 33, 76 17
កាសទ្រនាប់ 37 40
កាសែត 21 48
កាស្សែត 100 26
ការហ្ស៊ូ 18 35
កិច្ចការក្នុងរោងចក្រ 85 C
កិច្ចការដេរប៉ាក់ផ្សេងៗទៀត 101 B
កិច្ចការតាមផ្លូវថ្នល់ 82 B
កិច្ចការធនាគារ 86 B
កិនទឹកតី 72 17
កីឡាកាយសម្ព័ន្ធ 94
កីឡាបាល់ទន់ 92
កីឡាបាល់ទាត់ 92
កីឡាបាល់វាយ 94
កីឡាបាស់ស្កេតបូល ឬ បាល់បោះ 92
កីឡាបូលលិញ 94
កីឡាប្រដាល់ 94
កីឡាប្រណាំងសេះ 94
កីឡារ៉ូលស្ខេបូល ឬ បាល់ទះ 92
កីឡាហាន់បូល 94
កីឡាហុកគី 92
កីឡាហុលហ្ស៍ 94
កីឡាហ្ស៊ីតបូល 92
កីឡាឡាក្រុស 92
កីឡាឡើងភ្នំ 89
កុងតាក់ 32 25, 37 43c
កុងតាក់សំរាប់ផ្ដុះទាំងមូល 35 5
កុងហ្សា 98 20
កុន 100 C
កុនណិចទឹកឺត 72 7

កុមារអ្នកលេងរបហ្ស៊ីបល 92 8
កុយរមាស 66 16a
កូន 2 7
កូនក្រមុំ 33 28
កូនកុក 65 16
កូនខ្លើយ 28 24
កូនខ្លើយដោតមួល 101 3
កូនខ្លាឃុំញ៉ាត់សំឡ្បី 33 3
កូនគោ 67 31
កូនគោល 92 17
កូនដៃត 2 5
កូនចៀម 67 24
កូនផ្ទេ 69 27
កូនឆ្នាំង 30 8
កូនឆ្មា 68 5
កូនជញ្ជីង 78 5
កូនជើង 5 55
កូនឈូស 67 27
កូនដៃ 4 28
កូនតុដាក់ជិតក្បាលគ្រែ 32 27
កូនតុ (ដាក់នៅចុងសូហ្វា) 28 29
កូនថ្មង 88 9
កូនប្រុស 3 16
កូនមាន់ 64 22
កូនសត្វញ៉ាត់សំឡ្បី 33 27
កូនសិស្ស 76 19
កូនសេះ 67 20
កូនសេះ ឬ លា (អាយុតិចជាងមួយឆ្នាំ) 67 22
កូនស្ពៃក្ដោប 6 4
កូនស្រី 3 15
កូនហ្ស៊ីតា 98 3
កូវ 31 1

កូឡ្យាប 60 18
កូឡ្យ៉ាដ្យ 72 6
ក្ញ 6 17a
កែងជើង 5 50
កែងដៃ 4 8
កែងស្បែកជើង 20 5
កែប 52 16, 94 20
កែវ 12 9, 13 20, 18 6, 100 6
កែវទឹក 29 6
កែវពិត្រ្កីក 78 15
កែវពិសោធន៍ 78 9
កែវពាក់មុជទឹក 91 35
កែវពិសោធន៍ 78 31
កែវមានកម្រិតចំណុះ 78 25
កែវមានមាត់ធំហើយមានចង្អូរចាក់ 78 23
កែវយ៉ិត 74 22, 90 7
កែវយ៉ិតនាវាមុជទឹកសំរាប់
  -មើលពីក្រោមទឹក 48 8
កែវស្រាទំពាំងបាយជូរ 29 5
កៃ 48 22
កោណ 59 28, 79 28
កោស 26 15, 31 2
កៅស៊ូ 52 28
កៅស៊ូពាក់ហែលទឹក
  -(ពាក់នៅចុងជើង) 91 36
កៅឡ្យា 66 1
កៅអី 29 17, 44 14
កៅអីកូនក្រុង 16 8
កៅអីកូនដៃត 50 33
កៅអីខាងក្រោយ 50 32
កៅអីខ្នស់ 16 25
កៅអី (គ្មានស្ព័ផ្អែក) 78 34

បិលិក្រម

កៅអីងីកងោក **33** 16

កៅអីដាច់ពីគ្នា **50** 16

កៅអីតម្រួតមើលមនុស្សហែលទឹក **90** 8

កៅអីទម្រេត **28** 16

កៅអីមានកង់សំរាប់

-មនុស្សពិការដើរមិនរួច **39** 2

កៅអីសំរាប់អង្គុយវាយដាក់ទីឡូ **83** 17

កៅអីអង្គុយទម្រេតលេង **90** 20

កៅអីអង្គុយលេង **87** 10

កៅអីអង្គុយសណ្ដូក **27** 24

កុំព្យូទ័រ **76** 8, **83** 16, **100** E

កុំព្យូទ័រធុនតូច (ពីស៊ី) **100** 31

កំភួនជើង **4** 20

កំភួនដៃ **4** 9

កំដៅ **25** 6, **80** 27

កំណត់ហេតុ **43** 15

កំប៉ុង **12** 10

កំប៉ុងបាញ់ **13** 24

កំប៉េ **89**

កំប្រុក **66** 10

កំពស់ **79** 34

កំពឹស **7** 25a

កំពូល **79** 21

កំពូលភ្នំ **89** 20

កំសៀវដាំទឹក **30** 28

កាំ **52** 26, **66** 11a, **79** 14

កាំជណ្ដើរ **28** 13, **82** 9

កាំជ្រួច **75** 13

កាំបិត **29** 15

កាំភ្លើង **43** 7

កាំភ្លើងត្បាល់ **48** 28

កាំភ្លើងយន្ត **48** 25

កាំភ្លើងវែង **48** 21

ក្ងាន **64** 26

ក្អែក **64** 18

ក្ដាន់ **67** 26

ក្ដាម **11** 36, **62** 9

ក្ដារក្បាលគ្រែ ឬ អ្វីដែលប្រើជំនួស **32** 14

ក្ដារក្រាល **32** 29

ក្ដារខៀន **76** 5

ក្ដារចុងជើងគ្រែ **32** 24

ក្ដារ(ជិះលេង)បះចុះបះឡើង **87** 18

ក្ដារជិះលេងលើរលក **91** 25

ក្ដារប៉ាណូ **92** 19

ក្ដារបិទប្រកាស **76** 7

ក្ដារព្យួរប្រដាប់ប្រដារជាង **36** 15

ក្ដារសំរាប់តោងហែល **91** 27

ក្ដារសំរាប់អ៊ុតខោអាវ **35** 13

ក្ដោង **59** 9

ក្ដៅ **25** 7

ក្ដៅបន្តិចៗ **25** 8

ក្ដៅឧណ្ហៗ **25** 8

ក្បាល **4** C

ក្បាល (កប៉ាល់) **58** 5

ក្បាលខ្សែក្រវ៉ាត់ **20** 17

ក្បាលជើងក្រានដុតឧស្ម័ន (ហ្គាស់)

-កំដៅធ្វើម្ហូបអាហារ **30** 29

ក្បាលដោះ **33** 18

ក្បាលដោះបៀមលេង **33** 22

ក្បាលបំពង់ទឹកលត់ភ្លើង **42** 17

ក្បាលផ្កាឈូក (ងូតទឹក) **34** 4

ក្បាលភ្ជាប់ខ្សែដី **36** 7

ក្បាលម៉ាស៊ីនទឹកក្ដៅ **34** 17

ក្បាលម៉ាស៊ីនទឹកត្រជាក់ **34** 18

ក្បាលម៉ាស៊ីនទឹកលត់ភ្លើង **40** 9

ក្បាលម៉ាស៊ីនទឹកសំរាប់ផឹក **87** 19

ក្បាលសំរាប់មួលភ្ជាប់ផ្លែ

-ដែកខួងទៅនឹងតួដែកខួង **37** 43 b

ក្បាលស្ពី **37** 42 a

ក្បាលឡោស៊ី **37** 39

ក្បូន **89** 16

ក្បូនកៅស៊ូ **59** 20

ក្មួយប្រុស **3** 13

ក្មួយស្រី **3** 14

ក្មេងប្រុស **2** 8

ក្មេងស្រី **2** 9

ក្រខ្វក់ **24** 5

ក្រចកជើង **5** 56

ក្រចកដៃ **4** 23

ក្រចក (សំរាប់ដេញហ្គីតា) **98** 11a

ក្រចក(សេះ, គោ។ល។) **67** 35 b

ក្រចាប់សមុទ្រ **62** 7

ក្រញាំជើង **68** 2a, **69** 29 a

ក្រដាស **76** 13

ក្រដាសកត់ពាក្យ

-បណ្ដាំ (ធម្មតាតាមតេឡេហ្វូន) **83** 25

ក្រដាសខាត់ **37** 27

ក្រដាសគិតលុយ **16** 14

ក្រដាសគូរហ្គ្រាហ្វិក **78** 11

ក្រដាសចេញពីម៉ាស៊ីនវាយអក្សរ **83** 8

ក្រដាសជិះបីសបន្ត **54** 4

ក្រដាសជូតដៃ **29** 14, **35** 23

ក្រដាសជូតមុខមាត់ **32** 13

ក្រដាសតម្រង **78** 16

ក្រដាសបង្គន់ **34** 30

ក្រដាសប្រាក់ដុល្លារ **13** 25

ក្រដាសភ្លេង 98 2

ក្រដាសរកសៀវភៅ 47 12

ក្រដាសសរសេរធុនធំ 83 26

ក្រដាសសើមៗសំរាប់សំអាតកូនង៉ាពេលដូរ

-កន្ទប 33 8

ក្រណាត់ 101 4

ក្រណាត់ចំដើង (ថ្មែរ) 101 12

ក្រណាត់ដូតដើង 34 12

ក្រណាត់លាងមុខមាត់ 34 22

ក្រណាត់សំរាប់ដូតធួលី 35 4

ក្រណាត់សំរាប់ដូត(ស្ដើងៗ) 39 25

ក្រប 28 4

ក្របសៀវភៅសរសេរមានកង 76 14

ក្របសំរាប់ដាក់សំណុំ

-រឿង, បញ្ជី ឬ ក្រដាសផ្សេងៗ 83 22

ក្រពា 65 8

ក្រពះ 5 66

ក្រពះនោម 5 72

ក្រវ៉ាត់ក 21 47

ក្រវិល 23 1

ក្រវិលកីប 23 5

ក្រវិលរាំងនន 34 2

ក្រវិលសំរាប់ត្រចៀកចោះ 23 16

ក្រឡ្យ 12 9

ក្រឡ្យាឈើត្រង់ 24 18

ក្រឡ្យាស់ខ្លាស់ 23 8

ក្រានបៃរិ 8 13

ក្រាស 32 6

ក្រុមបេហ្យ៉ូប៊ីលកុមារ 92

ក្រុមផ្លាយ   (ខ្លាឃ្មុំធំ) 74 3

ក្រុមភ្លេងរ៉ុកកាន់រ៉ូល 99 C

ក្រុមស្ត្រីអ្នកស្រែកលើកទិកចិត្ត 93 20

ក្រុមអ្នកចម្រៀង 99 18

ក្រកុស 60 9

ក្រច 8

ក្រួចឆ្នោរ 8 10

ក្រួចឆ្នោរលើៀង 8 9

ក្រួចថ្ងុងអាមេរិកាំង 8 7

ក្រួចពោធិសាត់ 8 8

ក្រែមលាបបបូរមាត់ 23 29

ក្រោម, នៅក្រោម (ធ្លាស) 102 3

ក្រោល 81 24

ក្រោលគោនិងកន្លែងដាក់ឥវ៉ាន់ 81 5

ក្រេះសុង 65

ក្លាយ 40 14

ក្លារីណេត 98 16

ក្លៀក 4 10

ក្លែ 36 10

ក្លែធំ(ម្យ៉ាង) 36 12

ក្លែក 64 3

ខាត់ 38 3

ខិតឌីប 16 4

ខូរក្បាល 5 57

ខែងឌឹតសួន្យ 74 26

ខែពេញវង់ 74 24

ខាកិឡ្យាដើងរវែង 20 10

ខាកូរបៀយ 19 6

ខាកោស្ៀពាក់លុយទិក 88 10

ខាខ្ញី 20 14

ខាគ័រដ័រវ៉ៃយ 21 27

ខាដើងរវែង 20 4

ខាបៀយ 81 21

ខាទ្រនាប់ 22 3

ខាទ្រនាប់ប៊ីគីនី 22 11

ខាទ្រនាប់រឹប 22 12

ខាទ្រនាប់អ្នកអត្តពលកម្ម 22 4

ខារឹប 19 14

ខាស្លាប់ភ្លៅ 22 2

ខាសៀ្យកបែហលទិក 91 33

ខាអារវកៅស្ៀពាក់ចុះទិក 91 38

ខាអារង្អតទិក 90 18

ខាអារវជាប់គ្នាឃ្ញុបដើងសំរាប់កូនង៉ា 33 19

ខាអារវប្រឡ្យាក់ត្រូវប៉ាក 35 28

ខាអារវសៀ្យកពាក់លេងទិក 90 18

ខាអារវសៀ្យកពិក្នុងកុំឲ្យរងា 22 7

ខាអារវអ្នកអារវកាស 75 6

ខារៀម (សំរាប់ពាក់ធ្វើការ) 21 30

ខ្លី 62 1

ខ្ងេសមុទ្រ 62 12

ខ្ញីបារាំង 7 31

ខ្ញីមស 7 25

ខុយ 63 8

ខុះ 30 5

ខ្លុង 4 11

ខ្លុងដើង 5 51

ខ្លើយ 32 16

ខ្លាះដៃ 43 4

ខុង់រាប 88 1

ខ្លស់ 24 11

ខ្លើដៃ 76 24

ខ្លើដៃគួសចិញ្ជើម 23 26

ខ្យង 62 1

ខ្យងស្ថិត 11 33, 62 2

ខ្យង (ពតស្លូក) 62 4

ខ្យល់ 80 4

ខ្យល់ខ្លាំង 25 13

បញ្ជីក្រម

ខ្លាឃ្មុំ 69

ខ្លាឃ្មុំខ្មៅ 69 21

ខ្លាឃ្មុំផ្កាត 69 23

ខ្លាឃ្មុំស 69 22

ខ្លាឃ្មុំស្រុកចិន 69 20

ខ្លាធំ 68 2

ខ្លារខិន 68 1

ខ្លី 24 1

ខ្លែង 91 22

ខ្លែងមានមនុស្សគោងជិះ 57 6

ខ្លែប 8 8a

ខ្លាច 17 14

ខ្សាចសំរាប់ធ្វើជាឧបសគ្គ 95 11

ខ្សៀ 16 26

ខ្សែ 32 26a, 46 20, 52 23, 89 23, 98 10a

ខ្សែក 23 6

ខ្សែក្រវ៉ាត់ 20 16, 50 23

ខ្សែក្រវ៉ាត់ពាក់ជាមួយ

-ស្រោមជើងនិទ្បូង 22 14

ខ្សែងដ្កាល 51 53

ខ្សែដៃ 23 9

ខ្សែទាញឱ្យឡានឈប់ 54 1

ខ្សែនាឡិកា 23 11

ខ្សែបញ្ចប់ការប្រណាំង 95 21

ខ្សែផ្តាច់ព្រាត់ 95 21

ខ្សែភ្លើង 37 35, 80 24

ខ្សែភ្លើងសំរាប់បន្ទប្យវៃង 36 5

ខ្សែមាស 23 5

ខ្សែរុត 101 16

ខ្សែសណ្ដោង 59 11

ខ្សែសន្ទូច 88 8

ខ្សែស្បែកជើង 20 7

ខ្សែហាលខោអាវ 35 19

(ខ្សែ)អង្កា 23 7

ខ្សែអាត់ថតវីឌីអូ 100 3

គន្ធាលគោប្រុស 81 21

គន្ធាលគោស្រី 81 22

គណនេយ្យករ 86 18

គណៈវិនិច្ឆ័យ 43 21

គន្ធងអង់វង់ 74 21

គន្លាក់ម្រាមដៃ 4 22

គន្លឹះទាញទ្វារបិទ 50 4

គម្របកង់ 50 36

គម្របចង្ក្រៀង 28 27

គម្របម៉ាស៊ីន 51 47

គិលានុបដ្ឋាយិកា 39 19

គីបិត 98 1a

គីបិត(កុំព្យូទ័រ) 100 33

គុក 43 1

គុកគី 18 22

គុម្ពោត 61 41

គូទ 4 15

គុប 79 27

គូប 79 27

គូរ 77 11

គោញ្ជី 67 32

គោឈ្មោល 67 34

គំនូរ 28 5

គំនូររេខាគណិត 79 B

គំនូររេខាគណិតចំណុះ 79 C

គំរូ (ទាំងមូល) 101 7

គ្រប 30 9

គ្របភាគ់ 52 10

គ្រាប់ 8 8c, 9 37a

គ្រាប់កាំភ្លើង 48 26

គ្រាបឋិសណ៉ិត 9 32

គ្រាប់ (ថ្នាំតូច) 41 7

គ្រាប់ (ថ្នាំមូលសំប៉ែត) 41 6

គ្រាប់ (ថ្នាំរាងមូលទ្រវែង) 41 5

គ្រាប់ប៉ែក 48 3

គ្រាប់ប៉ែកដៃ 48 29

គ្រាប់ (ផ្លែឈើដែលគេទទួលទាន) 9

គ្រាប់វិលណ៉ិត 9 29

គ្រាប់ហេហ្វ្រិសណ៉ិត 9 30

គ្រាប់ស្វាយចន្ទី 9 27

ត្រីស្បូ្យងតែម 60 4

ត្រី៖ 82 11

គ្រុន 40 2

គ្រូបង្រៀន 76 4

គ្រូពេទ្យ 39 11

គ្រូពេទ្យជំនួយ 42 7

គ្រូពេទ្យធ្មេញ 39 17

គ្រសារបស់លោកស្រីម៉ៃរ៉ីស្មិត 3

គ្រឿងចងប្រទាក់ប្រទិនសំរាប់

-យោងទាញ ឬភ្ជាប់នឹងអ្វីទៀត 89 22

គ្រឿងចងស្បែកជើងភ្ជាប់ទៅនឹងស្គី 95 16

គ្រឿងទុកប្ញល់ហោះចុ្យខ្លួសពីជើ 57 15

គ្រឿងបរិភោគកំសាន្ត 15 18

គ្រឿងប្រក់ 82 2

គ្រឿងប្រើប្រាស់ក្នុងផ្ទះ 15 15

គ្រឿងផ្សាយពត៌មាននិងសិល្បៈ 86 A

គ្រឿងព្យូរលើគ្រេឿ្យកូនដាំមើល 33 2

គ្រឿងភ្លេងដែលមានអណ្ណាត 98

គ្រឿងភ្លេងផ្លុំធ្វើពីស្ពាន់ 98

គ្រឿងភ្លេងផ្សេងៗទៀត 98

គ្រឿងភ្លេងមានខ្សែ 98

គ្រឿងភ្លេង វាយ ឬ គោះ 98
គ្រឿងភ្លេងអេឡិចត្រូនិច 99 21
គ្រឿងភ្លេងអេឡិចត្រូនិចរាប់ស្លាប់ 100 D
គ្រឿងសម្រាប់ជិះឆ្លើដំណើរផ្សេងៗទៀត 55 E
គ្រឿងសំអិតសំអាងខ្លួន 23 B
គ្រឿងស្ងេរ៉ែអូ 28 20
គ្រឿងស្រូបយកថាមពលព្រះអាទិត្យ 80 17
គ្រឿងអលង្ការ 23 A
គ្រេច 40 13
គ្រែ 32 21
គ្រែកូនង៉ែត 33 4
គ្រែសែងអ្នកជម្ងឺ 39 12
គ្រុំសមុទ្រ (ម្យ៉ាង) 11 35
ឃ្លុងដើងក្រានគ្រូ 28 7
ឃ្លុំ 63 19
ងាវ 11 33, 62 2
ចង 77 12
ចង្កា 4 3
ចង្កះ 99 9
ចង្កះរ៉ាយស្ងួរ 98 19a
ចង្កូត 59 5
ចង្កៀង 28 28, 89 29
ចង្កៀងមានអំពូលច្រើន 29 3
ចង្កេះ 4 13
ចង្ក្រាន 30 30, 89 25
ចជ្រឹត 63 5
ចង្កាយ 81 14
ចង្អុលដៃ 4 25
ចង្អុលដៃកណ្ដាល 4 26
ចង្អូរ 94 3
ចង្ឆើរអាំងសាច់ 27 22
ចង្ឆៀត 24 3

ចតុរ័ង្ស 79 19
ចតុរ័ង្សកែងស្មើ 79 9
ចន្ទគ្រាស 74 6
ចន្ទល់ 52 9
ចន្លាស 78 32
ចន្លោះ 81 19
ចបត្រសេះ 82 13
ចាក់ 31 4
ចាក់ទ្រីក្ស 101 22
ចាន 13 23, 29 1
ចានគោះបារី 16 29
ចានចិញ្ចើមមេរោគ 78 3
ចានដាក់ថ្នាំលាប 37 28
ចានដាក់នំប៉័ងនិងប៊ីរ 29 11
ចានដាក់សាឡាត់ 29 25
ចានទាប 29 13
ចានលាយគ្រឿង 30 24
ចានសាប៊ី 34 6
ចានសំប៉ែត 29 13
ចាបស្រក 64 10
ចាប់ 96 4
ចាល់ 24 14
ចិញ្ចើម 5 44
ចិញ្ចើមថ្នល់ 45 26
ចិញ្ចៀន 23 2
ចិញ្ចៀនភ្ជាប់ពាក្យ 23 3
ចិញ្ចៀនអាពាហ៍ពិពាហ៍ 23 4
ចិញ្ញាំ 31 11
ចិតសំបក 31 5
ចុងខាងមុខ (កប៉ាល់ហោះ) 57 8
ចុងចោទ 43 23
ចុងទី 93 23

ចូក 26 13
ចូល 77 14
ច្បៀន 31 15
ច្បៀម 67 25, 81 10
ចេក (មួយស៊ីត) 8 20
ចេញ 77 13
ចេញលុយ 17 7
ចៃឈ្លើ 18 31
ចៃរ 59 22
ចោល 97 10
ចៅក្រម 43 10
ចៅប្រុស 2 12
ចៅស្រី 2 11
ចំការ 81 16
ចំការឈើផ្លែ 81 1
ចំការដាំស្រូវសាលី 81 B
ចំណិត 13 21
ចំណុចកណ្ដាល 79 13
ចំនួនគត់ 79 29
ចំពុះ 64 3a, 64 24a
ចំពុះទា 11 34, 62 3
ចំពុះទុង 48 24
ចំហ 24 15
ចំហុយ 31 12
ចំអិន 17 4
ចុះ, ចុះពី (ជើងល) 103 3
ចុះអំ្រ 25 12
ច្រកដើរ 14 10
ច្រកដើរទៅមក 56 23
ច្រកតាមនៅរៀននាវា 58 20
ច្រកនៅចន្លោះបន្ទប់រៀនសំរាប់ទៅមក 76 12
ច្រមុះ 4 36

ចំណិក្រម

ច្រវា 59 3, 59 22

ច្រវាក់ 52 18

ច្រាសសិតសក់ 32 7

ច្រាស 37 30

ច្រាសដុសក្រចក 34 20

ច្រាសដុសធ្មេញ 34 21

ច្រាសដុសលាងបង្គន់ 34 31

ច្រិប 26 8

ច្រាំងចោត 89 21

ឆកសមុទ្របាហ្រិន 70 16

ឆកសមុទ្របិនហ្គាល 70 32

ឆកសមុទ្រហុតសុន 70 18

ឆត្រ 20 24

ឆត្រ (ធំៗសំរាប់ប្រើនៅពេល
-ទៅលេងមាត់សមុទ្រ ។ល។) 90 21

ឆត្រយោង 48 6

ឆឡៀង្ស 79 27

ឆា 31 15

ឆាក 99 5, 98 7a

ឆាកកំប្លែងមានតន្ត្រី 99 ৮

ឆាប (គ្រឿងភ្លេង) 98 18

ឆែក 15 27

ឆែទ្យ (គ្រឿងតន្ត្រីម្យ៉ាង
-ដូចវីយ៉ូឡុងតែធំជាង) 98 9

ឆៃថាវបាវាង 7 34

ឆៃយ៉ចិន 18 25

ឆ្កែ 69

ឆ្កែចចក 69 29

ឆ្កែបៃហៃ្យ 69 28

ឆ្កេម្យ៉ាងគេចិញ្ចឹមសំរាប់ឲ្យពាំ
-សត្វដែលគេបាញ់ធ្លាក់យកមកឲ្យ 69 26

ឆ្នេម្យ៉ាងតូចល្បមស្លឹកត្រចៀកឆ្លាក់
-ទាបមានរោមទន់ហើយវញ 69 24

ឆ្នេម្យ៉ាងតូចហើយរហ័សរហួន 69 25

ឆ្នុក 34 10, 78 10

ឆ្នុកដប 16 18

ឆ្នុត 24 17

ឆ្នុតខ្វេងគ្នា 24 22

ឆ្នុតញ្ជើស 20 12

ឆ្នាំង 30 13

ឆ្នាំងកាសឡើរ៉ូល 30 14

ឆ្នាំងអ៊ុត 35 12

ឆ្នា 68 4

ឆ្នាំទី 92 24

ឆ្លងកាត់ (ទឹក) 103 6

ឆ្លាម 65 5

ឆ្មឹងជំនីរ 10 10

ឆ្មឹងបាក់ 40 15

ជក់ 76 18, 37 30

ជង្គង់ 4 19

ជម្រុក 81 4

ជញ្ជីង 14 7, 34 32, 78 4

ជញ្ជាំង 28 3

ជណ្ដើរ 28 12, 35 1, 42 1

ជណ្ដើរយោង 45 17

ជន្លែន 62 11

ជម្រៅ 79 33

ជំរលុប 76 21

ជាងកាត់ខោអាវ 84 6

ជាងកាត់សក់ 84 3

ជាងជួសជុល 84 5

ជាងជួសជុលឡ្យាន 84 2

ជាងឈើ 85 2

ជាងតខ្សែភ្លើង 85 6

ជាងតបំពង់ទឹក 85 1

ជាងធ្វើសក់ 84 10

ជាងធ្វើសៅ 85 4

ជាងបន្តខ្សែភ្លើង 82 17

ជាងសង់ផ្ទះ 82 5

ជាន់ខាងលើ (ចាប់ពីជាន់ទីៗឡើង) 99 14

ជាន់ទី២ នៅក្នុងរោងមហោស្រព 99 13

ជាយ (សំពត់, អាវ ។ល។) 101 11

ជាយថ្ល 53 22

ជិះ 97 13

ជិះក្បូនលេង 89

ជិះបន្ទះក្ដារលើរលក 97 12

ជីក 26 3, 26 13

ជីដូន 3 1

ជីដូនជីតា 2 10

ជីតា 3 2

ជីវឡ្យារ 78 17

ជួត 38 5 , 38 9

ជួត ឬ បោសធូលី 38 15

ជួរ 47 11, 81 18

ជួរភ្នំកូកាស៊្យ 71 45

ជួរភ្នំរ៉កគី 71 40

ជួរភ្នំស្យេរ៉ាម៉ាទ្រេ 71 42

ជួរភ្នំហេមពាន្ត 71 47

ជួរភ្នំអង់ឌីហ្ស្ 71 43

ជួរភ្នំអាប៉ាឡ្យាស៊្យាន 71 41

ជួរភ្នំអាលព៍ 71 44

ជួរភ្នំអ៊ូរ៉ាល់ 71 46

ជួរភ្នំស្យេរ៉ាម៉ាទ្រេ 71 42

ជួរ ឬ ឌងភ្នំ 71

ជួសជុល 38 10

ជើង 4 17, 11 20

ជើង (ការម៉ៅវ៉ា) 100 9

ជើងក្រាន 30 30

ជើងក្រានគ្រួ 28 8

ជើងក្រោយ 66 3b

ជើង(ចាប់ពីកជើងទៅក្រោម) 5 E

ជើងទ្រទ្យេន 29 28

ជើងមុខ 66 3d

ជើងសក់ (ត្រង់ផ្ដាល់) 4 33

ជុវិញ (សៀនបញ្ញាងភ្លើង) 103 2

ជំនួយពេទ្យ 39 8

ជំនួយពេទ្យធ្មេញ 39 14

ជំនួយអ្នកបំរើ 16 3

ជំពួលទិក 62 12

ជំពូក 47 10

ជាំ 40 17

ជាំ(ប្រទ្យេង) ភ្នែក 40 5

ជ្រេង 13 22, 44 3, 79 10

ជ្រេង (នៃរង្ខង់មូល) 79 15

ជ្រេងសំរាប់ចូលសែរវិសផ្ដាក់ 95 1

ជ្រេញ 30 26

ជ្រោះជ្រៅ 88 3

ឈិបម៉ង់ (សត្តម៉៉ាង
-ដូចកំប្រុកតែតូចជាង) 66 6

ឈឹក 40 12

ឈឹក្បាល 40 6

ឈឹចង្កេះ 40 8

ឈឹធ្មេញ 40 9

ឈឹពោះ 40 7

ឈូងសមុទ្របៃស៊ីក 70 28

ឈូងសមុទ្រមិចហ្ស៊ីកកូ 70 19

ឈូងសមុទ្រហ្ក្ដិណេ 70 25

ឈូងសមុទ្រអាឡ្បាស្ដា 70 17

ឈូ ស 26 13, 26 15, 31 2

ឈេ្លី 36 4

ឈេី្រក្រហម 61 25

ឈេី្ក្ធ្ឆាប 39 7

ឈេី្ក្ដំកល់បាល 95 13

ឈេី្រ្ផ្ដេ 81 2

ឈេី្រ្វ្ញ 94 34

ឈេី្រ្សំរាប់ធ្ឆឹងដើរ ឬ លោត 94 24

ឈេី្រ្សំរាប់វុញ 95 14

ឈ្នាន 39 18, 52 19

ឈ្នាន់ដាក់លេខ 50 25

ឈ្ល្ញាះស្យើរិភៅ 47 9

ឈ្ល្ស 67 26

ញ៉ញ៉រ 36 13

ញ៉ីរិយ៉ឺក 73 32

ញ៉ូវិយ៉ឺក 73 32

ញ៉ុំ 17 1, 17 2

ដកវុត 61 28

ដងក្ដោង 59 8

ដងខ្ទួ 4 A

ដងចង្កូត 50 13

ដងសន្ថច 88 7

ដង្ឃាប 36 19, 78 28

ដង្ឃុវមេអំប៉ៅ 63 1

ដង្ខ្យើប 62 13a, 78 7, 78 28, 78 29

ដង្ខ្យើបខ្ចាស់ក្រវ៉ាត់ 23 14

ដង្ខ្យើបហាលខោអាវ 35 20

ដផ្ឆំ 37 36

ដផ្ឆាល់ 80 19

ដផ្ឆាល់ពិជាន 28 1

ដប 78 2, 33 17, 12 3

ដបដាក់ខ្យល់ 91 37

ដបឧស្ស៊ុនសំរាប់លត់ភ្លើង 42 11

ដប ឬ កំប៉ុងប្រាំមួយស្រាក់ជាប់គ្នា 13 13

ដាហុ្ធិល 60 8

ដាក់ប្រេង 38 12

ដ៏ខ្យាច់ 91 31

ដ៏ស 76 10

ដុតក្នុងឪ្យ 31 14

ដុស 38 2

ដួង 8 3

ដួរ (កម្រាល) 38 13

ដួហ្ក្ាំង 68 13

ដួល 96 7

ដើម 60 1a, 61 35 b

ដើមឈេី្ 61, 61 35

ដើមដេ 4 7

ដើរ 77 8

ដេរប៉ាក់ 101 A

ដេហ្ក្រិ 60 5

ដែកកេះ 16 30

ដែកខ្ជង 36 9

ដែកខ្ជងខ្យេភ្លើង 37 43

ដែកខ្ចាស់ 83 28

ដែកគាប 36 2

ដែកគោល 37 41

ដែកគោលចុច 76 25

ដែកគ្រឹប 51 38

ដែកឆាយ 81 14

ដែកឈ្ល្ស 37 32

ដែកព្ជូរវ៉ាងនន 34 1

ដែកសំរាប់សិកច្រវ៉ាំ 59 21

ដែលកក 25 11

មិលិក្រម

ដែលមានទឹកកកកកក **25** 16

ដែឡាវែរ **72** 8

ដៃ **4** 6, **4** B, **62** 12a

ដៃកង់ប្រណាំង **52** 2

ដៃចង្កូត **50** 8

ដៃធម្មតា **52** 12

ដៃ (ម៉ាស៊ីនច្រៀង) **100** 20

ដុំ **12** 7, **12** 11, **12** 5, **13** 18 , **13** 22

(ដុំ) ចំបើង **81** 13

ដុំបួនជ្រុងសំរាប់ឲ្យក្មេង

-ដាក់បន្តុបគ្នាលេង **33** 32

ដុំហ្វិល **100** 17

ដុំ (ហ្វីល) **100** 10

ដុំឡែន ឬ អម្បោះ **101** 24

ដំណើរប្រែប្រួលទៅវិញ

-ទៅមកនៃព្រះចន្ទ **74** C

ដំបង **43** 9

ដំបងយក្ស **61** 40

ដំបងលេងហុលហ្វ៍ (ម្យ៉ាង) **94** 9

ដំបងវាយ **95** 5

ដំបង (វាយកូនគោល) **92** 18

ដំបងវាយបាល់ **92** 5

ដំបូល **27** 4

ដំរី **66** 17

ដំរីទឹក **66** 14

ដំឡូងចៀន **18** 28

ដំឡូងជ្វា **7** 24

ដំឡូងដុតក្នុងឡ **18** 20

ដំឡូងបារាំង **7** 23

ដំឡូងស្ងោរកិន **18** 17

ដាំ **26** 4

ឌិស្ត្រិច(អូហ្វ)កូឡុមប៊ីយ៉ា **73** 51

ណិចតារីន **8** 17

ណិបទូន **74** 18

ណេប្រាស្កា **73** 27

ណេវ៉ាដា **73** 28

តង់ **89** 24

តម្រងខ្យល់ **51** 52

តម្រងមូត្រ **5** 70

តម្រឹម **26** 8

តម្រួតចរាចរ **44** 10

តម្រួតផ្លូវថ្នល់ **44** 10

តម្រួតមើលមនុស្សហែលទឹក **90** 6

តម្រួតសន្តិសុខ **56** 9

តម្រួតសាលាកាត់ក្តី **43** 19

តម្រួតឧទ្យាន **88** 5

តាក់ស៊ី **55** D

តាកូ **18** 24

តាប្លូ **99** 2

តារា **74** 4

តារ៉ាងកត់ពត៌មានអ្នកជម្ងឺ **39** 10

តារ៉ាងប្រាប់ម៉ោងរទេះ

-ភ្លើងចេញ ឬ មកដល់ **55** 20

តិចសាស់ **73** 43

តិចហ្សាស់ **73** 43

តិណទេសប្រើជាគ្រឿងសម្ល ឬ ថ្នាំ **6** 9

តិណ្ណឹស្ស៊ី **73** 42

តឹង **24** 3

តុ **28** 14, **29** 7, **32** 9, **76** 16, **83** 13

តុកាហ្វេ **28** 26

តុក្កតា **33** 28

តុចៅក្រម **43** 16

តុជាង **36** 22

តុដាក់ថាសបរិភោគបាយ **56** 22

តុដាក់ម្ហូប **29** 29

តុដូរកន្ទប **33** 9

តុពត៌មាន **47** 22

តុពិចនិច **88** 15

តុពិនិត្យអ្នកជម្ងឺ **39** 6

តុ (សំរាប់ធ្វើការពិសោធន៍) **78** 24

តូច **24** 7

តូបលក់សារពត៌មាន **45** 30

តូបលក់ភេសជ្ជៈ **90** 2

តួកង់ប្រុស **52** 11

តួកង់ស្រី **52** 3

តួប្រុស **99** 19

តួស្រី **99** 20

តួយន្តហោះ **57** 14

តេវេ **28** 18, **100** 5

តេឡេហ្វូន **32** 26, **83** 15

តេឡេហ្វូនសាធារណៈ **44** 7

តែ **16** 15

តែននីស **94**

តែម **46** 10

តែរម៉ុស **88** 14

តោ **68** 3

តំប៊ួរិន **98** 17

ត្បាញ **101** 30

ត្រគាក **4** 16

ត្រង់ (បង្ហួច) **102** 1

ត្រង់ស្វ័មម៉ាទ័រ **80** 25

ត្រចៀក **4** 34

ត្រជាក់ **25** 10

ត្រជាក់ខ្លាំង **25** 11

ត្រជាក់បន្តិច **25** 9

ត្រប់ **7** 21

ត្របក 60 18b
ត្របកភ្នែក 5 45
ត្រសក់ 7 20
ត្រសក់ជ្រក់ 18 8
ត្រសក់ស្រូវកងគឺទ្បុ៩ 9 36
ត្រសក់ស្រូវហុនណេង 9 35
ត្រសេះ 64 17
ត្រាបុ័ស្ដ៍ 46 9
ត្រាក់ទ័រ 81 15
ត្រាក់ទ័រឈ្លូសដី 82 27
ត្រាក់ទ័រមានប្រដាប់
-កាយដីនៅពីក្រោយ 82 26
ត្រី 11 26, 65 A
ត្រីកាត់ជាកង់ៗ 11 29
ត្រីកោណ 79 6
ត្រីកោណមានមុម៩០ដីក្រមួយ 79,22
ត្រីខ្លីង 65 4
ត្រីបាខ្សែន 68 9
ត្រីសមុទ្រម្យ៉ាងមានមាត់ស្រួចវលែម 65 3
ត្រីយ័ហ៊ុ 62 5
ត្រីអណ្ដាតផ្ដែ 65 7
ត្រេលិវ 53 10
ត្រែ 98 25
ត្រែបារាំង 98 26
ត្រែសម្លេងធំ 98 27
ត្រៅ (ត្រីម្យ៉ាង) 65 2
ត្រុំបូន 98 23
ត្រុំប៉េ័ត 98 25
ថង់ 20 18, 66 3c
ថង់សំបុត្រ 46 4
ថជលិក និង ឧរង្គសត្វ 65 B
ថត 47 5

ថនិកសត្វមានថង់,
-គ្មានផ្ទៃ ឬចេះហើរ 66
ថនិកសត្តួរស់នៅក្នុងទឹក 68
ប្រភពថាមពល 80 A
ថាស 16 33
ថាសដាក់សាច់អាំង 30 17
ថាសទឹកកក 30 21
ថាស (មានផ្ទៃ) 52 20
ថាសម៉ាស៊ីន 100 23
ថ្ម 28 6
ថ្មដាក់ស្ករ 29 23
ថ្មដាក់ក្រេម 29 24
ថ្មទឹក 29 4
ថេប 46 22
ថាំង 12 6
ថេបរុំខ្សែរភ្លើង 37 34
ថ្គាម 4 38
ថ្គាស 4 32
ថ្ងៃ 25 4, 80 3, 74 7
ថ្ងងនេសាទរ្ត្រី 88 9
ថ្ងល់ 45 31
ថ្នាក់ដាក់សៀវរភៅ 47 26
ថ្ងេរ 101 10, 101 19
ថ្នាំកក់សក់ 34 8
ថ្នាំក្រហម (សំរាប់ផាត់ថ្ងាល់) 23 32
ថ្នាំគូររភ្នែក 23 33
ថ្នាំជាប្រេង ឬ ក្រមួន 41 9
ថ្នាំដាក់ភ្នែក 41 10
ថ្នាំដាក់ឡ្យខោអារវទន់ 35 27
ថ្នាំដុសធ្មេញ 34 16
ថ្នាំញ្យាបាលរោគ 41
ថ្នាំលាងអង្គុច 35 10

ថ្នាំលាប 37 31
ថ្នាំលាបក្រចក 23 25
ថ្នាំលាបត្របកភ្នែក 23 30
ថ្នាំលាបរោមភ្នែក 23 28
ថ្នាំលាបស្បែកកូនង៉ែត 33 6
ថ្នាំលាបស្បែកហាលថ្ងៃ 91 39
ថ្នាំសំរាប់បោកខោអារវប្រឡាក់ខ្លាំង 35 26
ថ្ងាល់ 4 35
ធុ 88 11
ធ្មិ 24 13
ធ្មើម 5 65
ធ្មែញ្មល 55 21
ធ្មៅះ 40 13
ទ 27 10
ទង 8 2a
ទង់ 82 20, 95 9
ទង់ជ័យ 76 1
ទទិង 79 35
ទទួលទាន 17 1
ទន្លេកុងហ្គោ 71 62
ទន្លេនីល 71 63
ទន្លេនីហ្គេ 71 61
ទន្លេប៉ៅរ៉ាំណា 71 60
ទន្លេមីស្ស៊ីពី 71 58
ទន្លេយ៉ង់សេ 71 69
ទន្លេយុកន 71 56
ទន្លេយៃនីសេ 71 65
ទន្លេវិយោក្រន់ដេ 71 57
ទន្លេហ្វង ឬ ហ្វាង 71 68
ទន្លេហ្គៃ 71 67
ទន្លេឡ្យណា 71 66
ទន្លេអាម៉ាហ្សូន 71 59

 មិនិទ្បក្រម

ទន្លេអុប្ប 71 64

ទន្លេ ឬ ស្ទឹង 71

ទន្រ្យាយ 66 13

ទម្លក់ 23 17

ទស្សនារវដ្ដី 47 16

ទស្សនិយភាព 99 2

ទា 11 25, 64 25

ទាត់ 96 3

ទាប 24 12

ទារក 2 5

ទាហានកងអាកាស 48 20

ទាហានជើងគោក 48 16

ទាហានជើងទឹក 48 14

ទាហានម៉ារីន 48 18

ទិច 63 8a

ទិប 55 22

ទិសខាងកើត 71 73

ទិសខាងជើង 71 71

ទិសខាងត្បូង 71 72

ទិសខាងលិច 71 74

ទី 92 25

ទិងមោងបន្លាចសត្វ 81 19

ទីជម្រាលសំរាប់លេងស្គី 95 C

ទីទុយ 64 6

ទីធ្លា (នៅមែបក្រោលគោ) 81 8

ទីវាល (សំរាប់លេងហ្គុលហ្វ៍) 95 12

ទីរី 28 18, 100 5

ទិសម្រាប់មនុស្សដើរនៅវែងខាងផ្លូវ 45 25

ទឹក 91 30, 42 16

ទឹកដោះគោ 14 5

ទឹកធ្លាក់ 89 18, 80 11

ទឹកប៉េងប៉ោះ 11 4

ទឹកសាឡ្បាត់ 18 12

ទឹកអប់ 23 27

ទឹកអប់សំរាប់លាប
-ក្រោយពេលកោរពុកមាត់ 23 21

ទុង 64 24

ទុយ្យោ 78 18

ទូកក្តោង 59 4

ទូកតូចៗសំរាប់ប្រើពេលកប៉ាល់លិច 58 19

ទូកផ្សករបស់ផេ្លរៗ 58 12

ទូកយ៉ាងតូចត្បានម៉ាស៊ីន 59 18

ទូកសម្រាប់ប្រើនៅពេលមានអាសន្ន 90 10

ទូកអុំ 59 23

ទូដាក់ចាន 29 2

ទូដាក់តាំងក្នុងបន្ទប់ទទួលភ្ញៀវ 28 19

ទូដាក់ថ្នាំពេទ្យ 34 14

ទូដាក់បញ្ញី 83 21

ទូដាក់មួបកក 30 20

ទូដាក់សៀវរភៅ 83 20, 28 22

ទូដាក់ឥវ៉ាន់ (នៅចង្រ្កានបាយ) 30 22

ទូទឹកកក 30 19

ទូប 13 15

ទូមានថត 32 30

ទូរទស្សន៍ 28 18 100 5

ទូរទេះភ្លើង 54 9

ទូរស័ព្ទ 32 26, 83 15

ទូរស័ព្ទសាធារណៈ 44 7

ទូលាយ 24 4

ទូលិប 60 1

ទូរណរីវិស 37 24

ទូណរីវិសក្បាលជ្រុង 37 25

ទ្យៀន 29 27

ទេរម្ម៉ែមែត្រ 25 5, 78 22

ទោង 33 24, 87 16

ទោច 69 15

ទោចក្រយាន 52 15

ទោចក្រយានយន្ត 53 19, 52 30

ទៅក្នុង (វន្ល) 103 12

ទៅ, ឆ្ពោះ (កន្លែងលេខ) 103 9

ទៅ, ឆ្ពោះ (វន្ល) 103 4

ទិនប់ទឹក 80 18

ទំពក់ 36 16

ទំពក់និងដែកសំរាប់ផ្គុក 101 14

ទំពក់សំរាប់ព្យួរ 32 1

ទំពាំងបាយជូរ (មួយចង្កោម) 81 1

ទំពាំងបាយជូរក្រៀម 9 24

ទំពាំងបារាំង 6 18

ទំហ្បី 23 1

ទាំងមូល 11 27

ទ្រនាប់ 50 22

ទ្រនាប់កែវ 16 27

ទ្រនាប់ពែង 29 21

ទ្រនិចនិងគ្រឿងស្តួងផេ្លរៗ 56 14

ទ្រងដាក់ឲ្យកូនង៉ាអង្គុយលេង 33 30

ទ្រងដឹកកម្មករចុះឡើង 80 9

ទ្រង 4 12, 11 21

ទ្វារខាងក្រោយបើកឡើងលើ 51 43

ទ្វារចាប់ផ្ដើមការប្រណាំងសេះ 95 20

ទ្វារចូលទៅកន្លែងដាក់ឥវ៉ាន់ 57 13

ទ្វីប 70

ទ្វីបអង់តាកទិច 70 7

ទ្វីបអាមេរិកខាងជើង 70 1

ទ្វីបអាមេរិកខាងត្បូង 70 2

ទ្វីបអាស៊ី 70 5

ទ្វីបអាប្រ្ហិក 70 4

ទ្រូបអ័រ័ុប 70 3
ទ្រូបអូស្ត្រាលី 70 6
ផុង 12 6, 15 16, 90 16
ផុងដាក់គ្រឿងក្តេងលេង 33 29
ផុងដាក់ចំណីឱ្យសត្វ 81 25
ផុងដាក់សំរាប 35 31, 44 15
ផុងដីកជញ្ជូនធ្យូងថ្ម 80 8
ផុងទឹក 35 15
ផុងទឹកកក 91 41
ផុងសំរាម 34 13, 87 11
ផុងសាំង 50 34
ផុងស្រោចផ្កា 27 16
ផុងអាកុយ 51 54
ផំ 3 3, 24 8
ផ្ទូ (នៃរង្គង់មូល) 79 16
ផ្ទើរ 14 6, 47 17
ផ្ទេញ 4 42
ធ្យូងថ្ម 80 7
ផ្ទាក់ 96 7
ផ្ទាក់ទឹកកក 25 3
ផ្ទាក់ទ្យាហ្កឹតបិល 93 B
ផ្ទាក្រោយផ្ទះ 27 C
ផ្ទាលេងបេបៀបិល 93 A
ផ្ទើម្ភប 17 4
ផ្ទើឱ្យខ្លាច 17 14
ធ្យូងសំរាប់អាំងសាច់ 27 23
នបសំពត់ 89 26
នីរការ៉ាំវ៉្បែណា 73 33
នីរដាកូតា 73 34
នាងដៃ 4 27
នាវាចម្លង 58 17
នាវាចំបាំង 48 5

នាវាជិះលេងមានកន្លែង
-រស់នៅដួចក្នុងផ្ទះ 59 16
នាវាដឹកនាំទ្យ៉ាំងផ្លុកគរវ៉ាន់ធំៗ 58 9
នាវាដឹកយន្តហោះចំបាំង 48 4
នាវាផ្លុកវត្ថុវារ 58 15
នាវាមុជទឹក 48 7
នាវាសណ្ដោង 58 13
នាវាសមុទ្រដឹកអ្នកដំណើរ 58 27
នាទ្យ៉ិកា 23 10, 76 2
នាទ្យ៉ិកាវេទ៍ 32 8
និម្ភាបនិក 86 8
និស្ស្រិត 76 19
នូម៉ែចហ្ស៊ីក្ 73 31
នូយ៉័ក 73 32
នូហាស៊ីរ 73 29
នូហ្ស៊ីហេ្សរ 73 30
នូនស្រី 60 14
នៅក្នុង (ថត) 102 7
នៅក្រោម (ត្) 102 8
នៅក្រោយ (កៅអី) 102 9
នៅខាងក្រោយ (កៅអី) 102 9
នៅចន្លោះ (ខ្លើយ) 102 4
នៅជិត (ទ័រ) 102 11
នៅ (បង្គច) 102 1
នៅមុខ (ក្រានគ្រូ) 102 6
នៅលើ (ផ្ការខៅ) 102 2
នៅលើ (ត្) 102 10
នំចំណីដុតក្នុងទ្យ 14 11
នំបីស្ត្ងី 18 27
នំប៉័ង 14 12, 18 7
នំប៉័ងមួលៗត្ូចៗ 18 19
នំប៉័ងអាំង 18 34

នំសំរាប់ញ៉ាត់ពែស្ត្រឹម 18 36
នំស្ត្រ្បែរិសតខេក 18 26
បងថ្លៃប្រស 3 11
បងថ្លៃស្ត្រី 3 8
បងប្រស 3 9
បងប្អូនជីដួនមួយ 3 7
បងស្រី 3 10
បង់ 17 7
បង់សំរាប់បង់សីម័ង 39 24
បង់ស្ត្ិត 46 22
បង់ហ្ស្ 98 5
បង់ប្អូបន្ទុះសំពត់បង់សីម័ងយឺត 40 13a
ប័ង់សេ 60 2
បង្កសមុទ្រ 62 13
បង្កង (សមុទ្រ) 11 30
បង្កង់ ឬ ផ្នាង 82 1
បង្ការនៃដៃ 15 20, 28 11, 55 24
បង្កន់ 34 29
បង្គោល (កីឡ្យាប្ូលលិញ្ញ) 94 5
បង្គោលខ្សែភ្លើងត្ូច (ធម្មតាយក
-ដើមឈើទាំងមូលមួយដើមមកធ្វើ) 80 26
បង្គោលខ្សែភ្លើងធំ 80 23
បង្គោលចននាវា 58 26
បង្គោលទី 93 35
បង្គា (បង្គច) 27 8
បង្គេ្បៀរ 94 22
បង្គច 27 7
បង្គចដំបូល 51 44
បង្គចនាវា 58 21
បង្ងែកក្បាល 50 35
បញ្ញីឈ្យោះមួប 16 7
បណ្ឌិះដែកល្បួស 78 6

ចំណិត្តក្រម

បណ្ដូល **6** 12a

បណ្ដោយ **79** 36

បណ្ណាគារ **45** 18

បំណ្ណបណ្ណាល័យ (សំរាប់ខ្ចីសៀវភៅ) **47** 3

បត់ **38** 1

បន្ទប់ប្ងនជ្រុងតូចៗ **83** 5

បន្ទប់សំរាប់ចូល ឬ ចេញពីអាគារ **44** 2

បន្ទប់អ្នកជិះ **56** 19

បន្ទប់អ្នកមើល **99** 11

បន្ទាត់ **76** 23, **79** A

បន្ទាត់កាត់គ្នា ៩០ ដឺក្រេ **79** 2

បន្ទាត់កោង **79** 3

បន្ទាត់ក្រោយបំផុត **95** 4

បន្ទាត់ត្រង់ **79** 1

បន្ទាត់បាល់ចេញក្រៅ **93** 9

បន្ទាត់វាយសេរវិស **95** 3

បន្ទាត់ស្រប **79** 4

បនុក **58** 10

បន្ទះកែវ **78** 31

បន្ទះក្ដារមានក្ដោង **59** 15

បន្ទះក្ដារសិកទៅក្រោមចំកណ្ដាល
-ទូកដើម្បីកុំឲ្យឃ្លោង ឬ រសាត់ **59** 6

បន្ទះឈើ **82** 16

·បន្ទះឈើសង្កត់មើលបំពង់ក **40** 12a

បន្ទះដែកស្បែកជើងលេងប៉ាតាំង **94** 27

បន្ទា **60** 18c

បន្លែច្រើនមុខលាយគ្នា **18** 16

បន្លែផ្លែឈើ **14** 9

បប្ធរមាត់ **4** 43

បម្រើ **17** 3

បរិចារកិច្ចតាមផ្ទះ **85** B

បរិភោគ **17** 1

បសុសត្ត **81** 12

បា **22** 16

បាចដំខ្យាច់ **26** 14

បាញ់ **97** 16

បាត **79** 7

បាតដៃ **4** 29

បាត្ស្បែកជើង **20** 6

បាន់ដេត **39** 4

បារី **16** 31

បាល់តែននីស **94** 1

បាល់ទន់ **92** 10

បាល់ (រាងមូលទ្រវែង) **92** 13

បាល់(សំរាប់លេង)កីឡ្យាបាល់វាយ **94** 30

បាល់សំរាប់លេងតែននីស **94** 1

បាល់សំរាប់លេងនៅមាត់សមុទ្រ **90** 11

បាល់ (សំរាប់លេងបាល់ទាត់) **92** 26

បាល់ (សំរាប់លេងបាល់ទះ) **92** 22

បាល់ (សំរាប់លេងបាស់ស្កេតបិល) **92** 21

បាល់(សំរាប់លេង)ប៊ូលលិញ **94** 6

បាល់សំរាប់លេងហាន់បិល **94** 12

បាល់(សំរាប់លេង)ហ្គូលហ្វ **94** 7

បាល់ **98** 10

បាស់ស្ទីន **98** 14

បាល់រ៉ាំង **39** 16

បាទ្បូ **99** A

បាឡូងហោះដោយសារកំដៅក្ដៅ **57** 1

បាឡូងហោះមានម៉ាស៊ីន **57** 5

បិតទឹកខ្មិប **60** 17

បិទ **24** 16, **77** 5

បីស **53** 20, **54** A

បុគ្គលិក **48** B

បុគ្គលិកថ្នាក់ខ្ពស់ **86** 13

បុងហ្ស៉ោ **98** 22

បុប្ផ **60**

ប៊ូក **67** 33a

ប៊ូមនិងម៉ាស៊ីនបោសសំអាតផ្ទះ **38** 14

ប៊ូនជ្រុងស្មើ **79** 9

ប៊ូនជ្រុងទ្រវែង **79** 19

បើក **24** 15, **31** 3

បើក (ឡានឯលៗ) **97** 15

បេកុន **10** 11, **18** 33

បេរ៉េ **19** 22

បេហ្សរ៍ **93** 6

បេហ្សរ៍បិល **92**

បៃតគីវ៉ាវ **7** 33

បោស **38** 7

ប៉ោម **8** 2

បំបែក **31** 7

បំពង់ **48** 23

បំពង់ក **5** 59

បំពង់កែវសំរាប់ប៊ូមវត្ថុវរ **78** 14

បំពង់កៅស៊ូ **78** 18

បំពង់ខ្យល់ **5** 60

បំពង់ដកដផ្ញើមក្នុងទឹក **89** 34

បំពង់ទឹក **27** 14, **35** 18, **51** 57

បំពង់ទឹក (ធ្វើអំពីសំពត់ ឬ កៅស៊ូ) **42** 8

បំពង់បង្ហូរទឹក **27** 18

បំពង់បីត **16** 10

បំពង់ផ្សែង **27** 9, **52** 33, **58** 18, **80** 22

បំពង់អាហារ **5** 61

បំពង់ដកដផ្ញើមក្នុងទឹក **91** 34

បំពង់អ៊ុយវ៉ានិញ៉ម **80** 15

បំពេញ **26** 9

បេះ **26** 7

បេះដូង 5 64

ប្ចោះ 97 10

ប្ចោះទៅឲ្យ 96 5

ប្ផី 2 3, 3 12

ប្រក្រតីទិន 83 9

ប្រជៀវ 66 4

ប្រដាប់កាត់ក្រចក 23 31

ប្រដាប់កិប 83 27

ប្រដាប់កំដៅខ្លួន 41 3

ប្រដាប់កោរពុកមាត់ 23 20

ប្រដាប់កោស 36 14

ប្រដាប់ក្មេងដុះនោម 33 33

ប្រដាប់ក្មេងលេងមានកាំឡេីងចុះ
-ឆ្មើអំពីលេីសំរាប់ឲ្យក្មេងឡេីងលេង 87 17

ប្រដាប់ខាត់ក្រចក 23 24

ប្រដាប់ខារ 58 23

ប្រដាប់ខ្ចង 39 15

ប្រដាប់គងដៃ 50 3

ប្រដាប់គិតលេខ 100 34

ប្រដាប់ចងទូកកុំឲ្យរសាត់ 59 19

ប្រដាប់ចងស្ពាយ ឬ ចងបន្ទោរ 39 3

ប្រដាប់ចាក់ភ្ឈេងដាក់លុយ 16 12

ប្រដាប់ចិតសម្រួចខ្មៅដៃ 76 20, 83 30

ប្រដាប់ចំហុយ 30 3

ប្រដាប់ចាំងភ្លេីង 52 25

ប្រដាប់ច្រក ឬដាក់ទុក 12 2

ប្រដាប់ឆែករកលោហធាតុ 56 10

ប្រដាប់ជូតទឹកភ្លៀង 50 6

ប្រដាប់ជូតផ្ទះ (ធ្វើពីអេប៉ុងមានដង) 35 6

ប្រដាប់ដាក់យ៉ាង 82 21

ប្រដាប់ដាក់ទឹកកកស្ពី 41 4

ប្រដាប់ដាក់ទំនិញឲ្យទៅខ្លួនឯង 15 23

ប្រដាប់ដាក់បាយទៅធ្វើការ 21 31

ប្រដាប់ដាក់ម្រេចរោយ 29 9

ប្រដាប់ដាក់លខ 50 17

ប្រដាប់ដាក់អំបិលរោយ 29 10

ប្រដាប់ដាក់ឪវ៉ាន់រ្វញ 56 6

ប្រដាប់ដុសឆ្នាំង 30 11

ប្រដាប់ដូរលេខ 50 24, 52 22

ប្រដាប់ដោះដែកកិប 83 29

ប្រដាប់ទាញឪវ៉ាន់មកខ្លួនឯង 56 12

ប្រដាប់ទ្រាប់ដែកុំឲ្យក្តៅ 30 34

ប្រដាប់ធ្វើការហេ 30 31

ប្រដាប់បញ្ចាំងរូបពីលើអ្នកមេីល 76 27

ប្រដាប់បញ្ចាំងស្លេ 100 13

ប្រដាប់បញ្ចាឯឲ្យចត្រនិច 28 17

ប្រដាប់បេីកកំប៉ុង 30 4

ប្រដាប់បេីកដប 30 6

ប្រដាប់ប្រដាផ្សេងៗ 89 27

ប្រដាប់បន្ថក់ផ្ទាំ 78 26

ប្រដាប់បាច ឬ បាញ់ទឹក 87 14

ប្រដាប់បាញ់ទឹកស្រោចស្មៅ 27 13

ប្រដាប់បិទរបួស 39 4

ប្រដាប់ប្អូមកង់ឡ្ងាន 53 13

ប្រដាប់ប្អូមបញ្ចេញ 13 14

ប្រដាប់ប្អូមភេសជ្ជៈ 16 20

ប្រដាប់បេីកន្ទកដប 16 17

ប្រដាប់បាំងកុំឲ្យថ្ងៃចាំង 50 5

ប្រដាប់ពាក់ការពារក្បាល 94 14

ប្រដាប់ពាក់ការពារខាអារ 16 6

ប្រដាប់ពាក់កុំឲ្យលង់ទឹក 59 1

ប្រដាប់ពាក់ស្តាប់ 83 2, 100 29

ប្រដាប់ព្យូរខាអារ 32 2

ប្រដាប់មូលភ្ជាប់ទំហ៊្បីទៅនឹងត្រចៀក 23 19

ប្រដាប់មើលម៉ែ្ក្រូហ៊ុល 47 14

ប្រដាប់រំអិលលេង 87 12

ប្រដាប់លាបថ្នាំ 37 29

ប្រដាប់លុញមេ្ហៅ 30 25

ប្រដាប់វាស់ប្រេងសាំង 50 9

ប្រដាប់វាស់ល្បឿន 50 10

ប្រដាប់សិក 37 43d

ប្រដាប់សៀតកាំភ្លេីង 43 8

ប្រដាប់សំរាប់កូត 98 7a

ប្រដាប់សំរាប់ចងពួរទៅផែ 58 26

ប្រដាប់សំរាប់ចុកសំរាម 35 8

ប្រដាប់សំរាប់ដាក់តម្រៀប 78 8

ប្រដាប់សំរាប់ដាក់ឲ្យស្រស់ទឹក 30 7

ប្រដាប់សំរាប់ដុតហ្គាសកំដៅ 78 20

ប្រដាប់សំរាប់ទ្វែរពីសោធន៍
-ពេលដុតភ្លេីងពីក្រោម 78 19

ប្រដាប់ (សំរាប់ធ្វើអ្វីមួយ) 39 13

ប្រដាប់សំរាប់បិទបេីកភ្លេីងបត់ 50 11

ប្រដាប់សំរាប់វៈកាត់ 78 33

ប្រដាប់សំរាប់លុប 76 11

ប្រដាប់សំរាប់សប់បន្ទូរស្អៈ 35 14

ប្រដាប់សំរាប់ស្ងួយទៅទីខ្ពស់ 82 18

ប្រដាប់សំរាប់អ្នកជិះយរគោង 54 8

ប្រដាប់សំរាប់ឲ្យដឹងថាមានភ្លេីងនេះផ្ទះ 33 15

ប្រដាប់ស្ងង់ស្តាប់ស្ងួតនិងបេះដូង 39 9

ប្រដាប់ស្ងង់ប្រេងម៉ាស៊ីន 51 58

ប្រដាប់ស្ងង់ឲ្យដឹងថាស្ងើឆ្មីឬមិនស្ងើ 82 3

ប្រដាប់ស្ងួច 58 6

ប្រដាប់ស្ងៀីករិបត្រកាក 22 15

ប្រដាប់អ្រ្ជន់ឲ្យកូនឡ្ងាស្តាប់ 33 21

ប្រដាប់អាំងនំប៉័ង 30 16

ប្រដាប់អាំងសាច់ 88 12

បិលិក្រម

ប្រធាន 47 10

ប្រចែល 65 6

ប្រពន្ធ 2 4

ប្រព័ន្ធព្រះអាទិត្យ 74 B

ប្រភាគ 79 D

ប្រមោយ 66 17 a

ប្រស្រីភ្នែក 5 47

ប្រហោងជណ្តើរយោងឡើងចុះ 80 10

ប្រហោងសំរាប់ចុះទៅធ្វើការក្រោមដី 45 32

ប្រអប់ 12 1, 12 4, 13 12, 13 17

ប្រអប់ច្របាច់ 13 15

(ប្រអប់)ឈើគុស 16 28

ប្រអប់ដាក់គ្រឿងអលង្ការ 32 4

ប្រអប់ដាក់លុយបង់ថ្លៃបឺស 54 5

ប្រអប់ដាក់សំបុត្រ ឬ

-ក្រដាសចូល ឬមកជល់ 83 12

ប្រអប់ផ្លូរលេខ 50 24

ប្រអប់លេខ 50 17

ប្រអប់លេខប្រើដៃ 50 B

ប្រអប់លេខស៊ីយប្រវត្តិ 50 A

ប្រអប់សំបុត្រ 46 1

ប្រអប់សំបុត្រ(តាមផ្ទាល់) 46 6

ប្រអប់សំរាប់ដាក់ប្រដាប់ប្រដាជាង 36 23

ប្រាក់កាស 13

ប្រាសាទធ្វើអំពីខ្សាច់ 91 32

ប្រប៉ែន 80 30

ប្រក្រាម 99 17

ប្រប៉ីស 67 26

ប្រេងកាតឧស្ម័ន 80 30

ប្រេងនីយេហ្បេល 80 34

ប្រេងម៉ាស៊ីន 80 33

ប្រេងសាំង 80 28

ប្រេងសាំងសំរាប់កប៉ាល់

-ហោះរ៉េអាក់ស្យុង 80 31

ប្រែសណីយ៍ស្ថាន 44 9, 46 B

ប្រ៉ាំង 52 17

ប្រ៉ាំសែន 13 28

ប្អូងផ្នុះ 82 6

ប្អូកឈ្ពោះផ្លូវ 44 8

ប្អូកប្រាប់ផ្លូវចេញ 53 24

ប្អូកប្រាប់ពតិមានអ្នកបើកបរ 53 23

ប្អូកប្រាប់ល្បៀនដែលអនុញ្ញាតឱ្យបើក 53 8

ប្អូកលេខឧទ្យាន 50 28

ប្អូកសរសេរអាស័យដ្ឋាន 46 21

ប្អូកសំគាល់ខ្លួន 43 5

ប្អិនដ៏វៀ 30 12

ប្អុក 33 32

ប្អូនថ្លៃប្រុស 3 11

ប្អូនថ្លៃស្រី 3 8

ប្អូនប្រុស 3 9

ប្អូនស្រី 3 10

ប៉ាំងដា 69 20

ប៉ាំតិញូមិទ័រ 45 20

ប៉ាំណូនៅមុខអ្នកបើក 50 19

ប៉ាំត 17 11

ប៉ាំតាំង 19 15, 94

ប៉ាំន់ការហ្ស 29 18

ប៉ាំន់ខេក 18 5

ប៉ាំន់តែ 29 19

ប៉ាំវ៉ាស៊កខាងក្រោយ 51 42

ប៉ាំវ៉ាស៊កខាងមុខ 51 51

ប្អិនឆ្ងិន 64 27

ប្អិនស៊ីវ៉ានី 73 38

ប៉ុ 98 13

ប៉ុស្ស៍ 44 9, 46 B

ប៉ុស្ស៍ប៉ូលីស 43 A

ប៉ុតេគ្គឈិប 18 4

ប៉េងប៉ោះ 7 19

ប៉េទូនិញ្ញា 60 7

ប៉ែល 27 31, 82 15, 90 17

ប៉ែស 9 37

ប៉្រាណូ 98 1

ប៉ីវច 61 32

ប៉ីវ៉ីវ 66 12

ប៉ិច 76 22

ប៉ីតិល 63 10

ប៉ីយ៉េវ 16 23

ប៉ីវ 18 18

ប៉ីហ្សុ្រង 67 19

ប៉ុត 19 21

ប៉ុឡ្ចង 37 38

ប៉្អូក់បឺវ 8 12

ប៉្អូបឺវ 8 14

ប៉្អូហ្ចេ 64 8

ផ្ទីក 17 2

ផ្ចបប៉្ចី 61 30

ផ្ទៃ 58 3, 58 28

ផ្ទៃនដី 47 19, 74 8, 74 13

ផ្ទា 60

ផ្ទា, ផ្ចោះពួម 24 21

ផ្ទាក្រពុំ 60 18a

ផ្ទាឈ្ចូករតន៍ 60 19

ផ្ទាយ 74 4

ផ្ទាយដុះកន្ទុយ 74 2

ផ្ទាយព្រះគ្រោះ 74

ផ្ទាសាយ 40 11

បញ្ជីក្រម

ផ្លាំងគំរូ 101 6

ផ្លះតៀម 27 A

ផ្លះបាយឡ្យកបាយឡ្យ 33 25

ផ្លះមានតែមួយជាន់ 27 A

ផ្លះពីរជាន់ (មានជណ្ដើរ) 27 B

ផ្លះរបស់អ្នកស្រែចំការ 81 3

ផ្លះល្យេង 45 23

ផ្លែកត្រង់នៃផ្ទះវប្រណាំងសេះ (ធម្មតានៅ
-ខាងមុខអាគារអ្នកអ្គុយមើល) 95 19

ផ្លែករាបស្ម៊ើនៅលើនាវា 58 22

ផ្លូវ 45 31

ផ្លូវកប៉ាល់ហោះឡ្យើងចុះ 57 19

ផ្លូវកាត់ពីលើ 53 3

ផ្លូវចូលទៅផ្លូវរឳំ 53 21

ផ្លូវចេញ 53 2

ផ្លូវជិះសេះ 87 7

ផ្លូវដែក 54 10

ផ្លូវទឹក 88 6

ផ្លូវរត់ 94 32

ផ្លូវសំរាប់រត់ហាត់ប្រាណ 87 9

ផ្លូវឡ្យានចូល 27 1

ផ្ទៃ 37 43a

ផ្ទែកាំបិតកោរពុកមាត់ 23 23

ផ្ទៃលើក្រៀម 9

ផ្ទៃលើតូចៗ 8

ផ្ទៃទំហ៊ឺ 23 18

ផ្ទៃផ្ទឹ 9 34

(ផ្ទៃ) ពោត 6 12

ផ្ទៃព្រានក្រៀម 9 22

ផ្ទៃឡ្វាបារាំងក្រៀម 9 21

ផ្ទៃសែន 61 33b

ផ្ទៃស្រល់ 61 34b

ផ្សារលក់បន្លែនិងផ្លែឈ៊ើ 45 28

ផ្ស៊ីត 7 30

ផ្ស្យុង 42 15

ពង 64 13

ពងមាន់ចៀនឥតប្រេ 18 32

ពពៃ 67 28

ព៍យសេតក្ប្រា 60 15

ព៍រ 8 18

ពស់កណ្ដឹង 65 10

ពស់វែក 65 11

ពស់(ឥតមានពិសម៉្យាងមាន
-នៅទ្ឹបអាមេរិកខាងជ្ឹង) 65 9

ពិជាន 28 2

ពិណ (ប្រទេសអឺរុប) 98 6

ពិតហ្ប្រា 18 30

ពិល 35 3

ពីងប៉ុង 94

ពីងប៉ុង 94 19

ពីងពាង 63 16

ពី, ចេញពី (ទឹក) 103 7

ពី, ចេញពី (កន្លែងលេខ) 103 10

ពី, ចេញពី (រង្វ) 103 5

ពីក្ខុឡ្យ 98 12

ពីលើ (ស្ថាន) 103 8

ពុកចង្កា 4 39

ពុកមាត់ 4 40, 62 1b

ពុះ 26 11

ពុះជាព៍រ 11 17

ពូ 3 3

ពូក 32 17

ពូកកៅស៊ូ (ផ្ទុំខ្យល់) 91 26

ពូកយ៉ាងកំ៉ឡ្យទ្ឆ្កិចនឹងក្រែ 33 5

ពូថៅ 36 17, 42 14

ពូរ (សំរាប់ចងនាវា) 58 25

ព៍ពង 29 20, 13 19

ពោង 90 9

ពោង (បង្គោញផ្លូវនាវា) 58 16

ពោត 60 24

ពោះ 4 14

ពោះរៀន 5 67

ពោះរៀនកង់ឡ្យាន 91 29

ព្រាប 64 1

ព្រិស៊្ម 78 1

ព្រុយ 65 3b

ព្រុយហុកខាងមុខ (ដូចដៃ) 68 12a

ព្រោន 11 31, 62 8

ព្រ៊ំ 32 28

ព្រ៊ំក្រាលពេញបន្ទប់ 28 15

ព្រះចន្ទ 74 9

ព្រះចន្ទខ្ខ្ខិត 74 23

ព្រះចន្ទពេញបូរមី 74 24

ព្រះចន្ទរនោច 74 25

ព្រះធរណី 74 8, 74 13

ព្រះអាទិត្យ 80 3, 74 7

ញ៉្ស្រ៊ីវ 62 6

ញ៉្សរ 38 6

ភីសាម៉ា 22 19

ភូមិឪ្សរខា 71 70

ភូយ 32 20

ភូយញ្ញាត់សំឡ៊ី 32 22

ភោ 68 10

ភេសជ្ជ: 14 14

ភេសជ្ជ:ឥតមានស្រា 16 11

ភោជនីយដ្ឋានគ្រួសារ 16 A

 បញ្ជីរក្រម

ភ្នាក់ភ្លើងកំបេ៉ 89 31

ភ្នាក់ងារខាងការធ្វើដំណើរ 84 4

ភ្នាក់ងារប៉ូលិស 43 6

ភ្នាក់ងារប្រៃសណីយ៍ 46 14

ភ្នកខ្យាច់ 90 12

ភ្នែក 5 D

ភ្នំ 89 19

ភ្នំទាបៗ 88 4

ភ្នក 66 17b

ភ្នូ 74 19

ភ្លើង 28 9

ភ្លើងខាងក្រោយ 50 31

ភ្លើងចរាចរ 45 21

ភ្លើងចត 51 49

ភ្លើងនេះ 42 5

ភ្លើងឆយក្រោយ 50 30

ភ្លើងបញ្ជាំង 99 4

ភ្លើងបត់ 51 50

ភ្លើងប៉ភ្លឺថ្មល់ 45 29

ភ្លើងមុខ 51 48

ភ្លើងសំរាប់ពេលអាសន្ន 51 41

ភ្លើងប្រ្បាំង 50 29

ភ្លៀង 25 1

ភ្លៅ 4 18, 10 14, 11 19

មនុស្សដែលគេសង្ស័យ 43 3

មនុស្សប្រុស 2 2

មនុស្សស្រី 2 1

ម៉រជេ 48 28

មហាសមុទ្រ 70

មហាសមុទ្រទឹកកខាងជើង 70 8

មហាសមុទ្រប៉ាស៊ីហ្វិកខាងជើង 70 9

មហាសមុទ្រប៉ាស៊ីហ្វិកខាងត្បូង 70 10

មហាសមុទ្រអង់តាកទិក 70 14

មហាសមុទ្រអាត្លង់ទិកខាងជើង 70 11

មហាសមុទ្រអាត្លង់ទិកខាងត្បូង 70 12

មហាសមុទ្រឥណ្ឌា 70 13

មា 3 3

មាត់ 4 2

មាត់ព្រៃ 48 23

មានថ្ងៃល្អ 25 4

មានផ្កាមូលៗ (ពាសពេញ) 24 19

មានពពកច្រើន 25 2

មានភ្លៀង 25 1

មាន់ 11 24, 64 23

មាន់ច្បៀន 18 29

មាន់ល្មោល 64 21

(មាន់) ទាំងមូល 11 16

មាន់បារាំង 11 23, 64 20

ប៉ុនកិន 30 12

ប៉ុនបៅសផ្ទះ 35 16

ប៉ុនភ្លើង 80 20

ប៉ុនអ៊ីវ៉ប៊រ 59 12

ប្ការ៉ូ 23 28

មិនសើម 25 14

មិនស្រអាប់ 24 9

មីណោស្តា 72 23

មីហ្សូរី 73 25

មីនិកាំ (ម៉ាស៊ីនថតវីឌីអូ) 100 2

មីស៊ីស្ស៊ីពី 72 24

មីស៊ីហ្ស៊ិន 72 22.

មុ 4 1

មុត 40 16

មុមតួចជាង ៩០ ដឺក្រេ 79 8

មុមធំជាង ៩០ ដឺក្រេ 79 5

មុមមានកម្រិត ៩០ ដឺក្រេ 79 23

ម្ពតាត 18 1

ម្ពហ្ម 67 35

ម្ពុក 19 18, 92 11, 92 14

ម្ពុកដេក 21 28, 42 12, 82 4

ម្ពុកមានរប៉ាំងមុខ 21 43

ម្ពុកពាក់ងួតទឹក 34 3

ម្ពុក (សំរាប់ពាក់ជិះកង់ ឬ ម៉ូតូ) 52 7

ម្ពុកអ្នករវាយបាល 92 6

មួយកាក់ 13 29

មួយភាគបី 79 32

មួយភាគបួន 79 31

មេម 60 8a

មេល 77 4

មេក្រុមកម្មករ 85 13

មេគោយកទឹកដោះ 81 11

មេជើង 5 53

មេដេក 78 27

មេដៃ 4 24

មេភ្លេង 99 8

មេអំបៅ 63 3

មេក 61 35a, 60 1a

មេក (ក្ដចៗ) 61 33a

មេវិឡ្យាន់ 72 20

ម្ពូល 39 26, 100 19, 101 18

ម្ពូលខ្លាស់ 33 11

ម្ពូលខ្លាស់ក្រវ៉ាត់ 23 13

ម្ពូលចាក់ទ្រីក្ស 101 25

ម្ពូលចាក់ផ្នក 101 29

ម្ពូលបារាំង 101 20

ម្ពាយ 3 4

ម្ពាយធំ 3 6

ម្ហាយមីង 3 6

ម្ហេស 7 22

ម្ហាល់ 8 4

ម្រាមជើង 5 54

ម្ហ្វេព្រាំសេន 13 30

ម្ហេរ្យបាញ់ខោអាវអ៊ុតដើម្បីច្បូវវ៉ារិង 35 21

ម្ហេរ្យបោកខោអាវ 35 25

ម្ហេរ្យលាបកូនង៉ែត 33 7

ម្ហេរ្យ ឬ ទឹកសំរាប់ដុសលាង 35 9

ម្ហបកក 14 2

ម្ហបកំប៉ុង 14 13

ម្ហបធ្វើអំពីទឹកដោះគោ 14 4

ម្ហបសមុទ្រ 11 C

ម្ហបអាហារ 15 24

ម៉ង់ដ្ហូលីន 98 4

ម៉ាក់ណូឡ្យ៉ា 61 29

ម៉ាល់ 74 14

ម៉ាស្ហាឈ្មសេត 72 21

ម៉ាស៊ីន 51 F, 52 32

ម៉ាស៊ីនកាត់របងកូនឈើ 27 29

ម៉ាស៊ីនកាត់ស្មៅ 27 12

ម៉ាស៊ីនកិន 30 12

ម៉ាស៊ីនខាត់ 37 26

ម៉ាស៊ីនខួងថ្ម (ប្រើម្ហៅំខ្យល់, ធម្មតាគេច្រើន
-ប្រើសំរាប់ជីកតាល់ថ្មក្រាលថ្នល់) 82 22

ម៉ាស៊ីនគិតលុយ 15 21

ម៉ាស៊ីនគិតលេខ 83 19

ម៉ាស៊ីនចាក់កាសែ្សត 100 22

ម៉ាស៊ីនចាក់កាសែ្សតស្ទេរ៉េអូ 100 25

ម៉ាស៊ីនចាក់ស៊ីឌី 100 28

ម៉ាស៊ីនចាល 37 37

ម៉ាស៊ីនច្រួតកាត 81 17

ម៉ាស៊ីនច្រៀង 100 18

ម៉ាស៊ីនឆ្លុះមើលឥវ៉ាន់ 56 11

ម៉ាស៊ីនឈ្មសដី 82 27

ម៉ាស៊ីនដេរ 101 1

ម៉ាស៊ីនត្រជាក់ 32 11

ម៉ាស៊ីនថកុន 100 15

ម៉ាស៊ីនថតចម្លង 47 18

ម៉ាស៊ីនថតវីឌីអូ 100 4

ម៉ាស៊ីនថតសំបុត្រ 83 24

ម៉ាស៊ីនធ្វើឱ្យកក 14 3

ម៉ាស៊ីនបញ្ជាំងកុន 100 16

ម៉ាស៊ីនបាញ់សក់ឱ្យស្ងួត 34 26

ម៉ាស៊ីនបូមសំអាង 53 14

ម៉ាស៊ីនបោកខោអាវ 35 30

ម៉ាស៊ីនបោសផ្ទះ 35 16

ម៉ាស៊ីនប្រាប់ថ្លៃឈ្មល 55 23

ម៉ាស៊ីនភ្លើង 80 20

ម៉ាស៊ីនយោងអ្នកលេងស្គីទៅទីខ្ពស់ 95 18

ម៉ាស៊ីនរោអាក់ស្បៃង 57 11

ម៉ាស៊ីនលាងចាន 30 1

ម៉ាស៊ីនលើកឥវ៉ាន់ធ្ងន់ៗ 58 4

ម៉ាស៊ីនវាយ (ចេញជា) អក្សរ 83 4

ម៉ាស៊ីនសរសេរ 83 7

ម៉ាស៊ីនហាលខោអាវ 35 24

ម៉ាស៊ីនហ្ប្សេត 57 11

ម៉ាស៊ីនហ្ប៉ីវ៉ុក 47 18

ម៉ាស៊ីនអ៊ីវ៉ិវ៉ី 59 12

ម៉ាស៊ីនអារឈើ 27 25

ម៉ាស្ហារ៉ា 23 28

ម៉ុនណោអ័រឌ័រ 46 18

ម៉ុនថាណា 73 26

ម៉ូដែល 86 5

ម៉ូតូ 53 19, 52 30

ម៉ូតែល 90 3

ម៉ូនិទ័រ 100 32

ម៉េកៀរ៉ី 74 11

ម៉េត្រ 54 B

ម៉េន 72 19

ម៉េប៉ុល 61 38

ម៉េរីហ្ជោល 60 6

ម៉េត្រជាងលើ 36 1

ម៉េត្រទាញចេញទាញចូល 36 21

ម៉េត្រសំពត់ 101 15

ម៉េរីហ្ជោវ៉ាន 87 5

ម៉េក្រូហ្ជ៉ិល 47 13

យក 17 10

យកចេញ 17 6

យកមកឲ្យ 17 3

យន្តបង្ហូរងរដ្ឋ 53 1

យន្តហោះទម្លាក់គ្រាប់បែក 48 2

យន្តហោះដង្ហាល់ 57 7

យន្តហោះធុនផ្សេងៗ 57 A

យន្តហោះប្រយុទ្ធ 48 1

យានចម្លងសុតគីល 75 C, 75 14

យានដ្ឋាន 27 2

យាននិងបរិក្ខារផ្សេងៗ 48 A

យានិក (មនុស្សទាំងអស់
-នៅក្នុងអវកាសយាន) 75 12

យុថ្កា 58 24

យូកីលីលី 98 3

យូថា 73 44

យ័ 27 6

យ៉ាម៉ា 66 15

រង្វង់ពងក្រពើ 79 18

មិនិក្រម

រង្គង់មូល **79** 11	រទេរុញ្ញកង់មូយ (សំរាប់ដីកជញ្ជូន) **27** 32	រានដេីរកំសាន្ត (តាមមាត់សមុទ្រ) **90** 1
រង្គង់ជុំវិញ **74** 16a	រទេរុញ្ញកូនង់ម៉ា **45** 27	រានហាល **27** 5
រង្គងវិល **74** 21	រទេរុញ្ញកូនង៉ែត **33** 14	រានហាលជាប់និងដី **27** 17
រង្ហាស់រង្ហាល់ **79** E	រទេរុញ្ញ (សំរាប់ដីកជញ្ជូនដី,	រាវិចាន **30** 2
រទេច្ចេទី **66**	-ឥដ្ឋជាដេីម) **82** 23	រាស់ **26** 10
រដួវក្ដៅ **26**	រទេរៀនដេីរ **33** 23	វិត **38** 4
រដួវត្រជាក់ **26**	រទេសេះ **55** 33	វិប **24** 3
រដួវផ្ការីក **26**	រទេអ្នកលេងហួលហ៊ុ **95** 8	រុក្ខជាតិជំពូក ដួង, ស្លា, ត្នោត ។ល។ **61** 26
រដួវរងា **26**	រនាស់ **27** 30	រុក្ខជាតិផ្សេងៗទៀត **61**
រដួវស្ឹកឈេីរុះ **26**	រនាំងប៉ាំង **32** 12	រុក្ខជាតិរមាស់ **61**
រដួវស្ឹកឈេីលាស់ **26**	រនាំងសំរាប់ឲ្យមនុស្ស	រុក្ខជាតិសំរាប់ដាំក្នុងផ្ទះ **61** 39
រណបម្ដាងសិលា (សំរាប់បុំ	-ចេញចូលម្នាក់ម្ដង **54** 12	រុញ្ញ **26** 12
-ឆ្អឹងបាក់កុំឲ្យរាំកំរេីក) **39** 5	រន្ធា **82** 7	រុយ **63** 18
រណារ **36** 8	រន្ធ **94** 8	រូបចិត **100** 11
រណារខ្យេភ្លើងផ្ទេតួចត្រង់ទៅក្រោម **36** 3	រន្ធច្រមុះ **4** 37	រូបចិតអំច្យុំរ៉េ **39** 1
រណារខ្យេភ្លើង(មានផ្ទេជាថាសមូល) **36** 20	រន្ធប្រស្រី **5** 48	រូបដែលគេកាត់ជាផ្នែកតួចៗសំរាប់យក
រណារមានម៉ាស៊ីន **27** 25	រន្ធទ្យេវ **101** 8	-មកផ្ទុំគ្នាឲ្យចេញជារូបដូចដេីមវិញ **33** 31
រណារអារដែក **36** 18	រមង **81** 9	រូបប៉ាក់ (លេីបន្ទះសំពត់ក្រាស់) **101** 26
រត់ **96** 6	រមស់ផ្សេងៗធ្វេីតាមប៉ុស្ត៍ **46** C	រូបប៉ាក់ (លេីសំពត់ធម្មតា) **101** 27
រចក្រោះ **48** 10	រមស់ធ្វេីតាមប៉ុស្ត៍ **46** 2	រៀប (ត្រ) **38** 8
រចយន្តធម្មតា **53** 15	រមស់សំរាប់ប្រេីជាមួយត្រៀងអ្វីមួយ **35** 17	រៀបចានស្ដាបព្រា (លេីតុ) **17** 8
រចយន្តប៉ូសសំអាតឆ្នួល **47** 1	រប៉ាំងចេកផ្លូវ **2** 24	រៀបតុ **17** 8
រចយន្តប្រេសណីយ៍ **46** 5	រប៉ាំងចេកផ្លូវវុល្លជាពីរ **82** 24	រោងលេងភ្លេង **87** 2
រទេដាក់ឥវ៉ាន់ **15** 19	រប៉ាំងដែកសំរាប់ការពារអ្នកប្រេីកាំភ្លេីង **48** 12	រោមភ្នែក **5** 46
រទេភ្លេីង **55** C	រប៉ាំងពន្លឺ **33** 1	រិពៃ **64** 4
រទេភ្លេីងដីកមនុស្ស	រប៉ាំងមុខ **92** 15	រ៉ាកែត **94** 2, **94** 18, **94** 29
-ទៅមកពីកន្លែងធ្វេីការ **55** 14	រប៉ាំងមុខអ្នកចាប់ **92** 3	រ៉ាគូន **68** 7
រទេភ្លេីងបេីកលេីផ្លូវដែកតែមួយ **55** 29	រមាស **66** 16	រ៉ាឌី **7** 29
រទេភ្លេីងរត់ដោយខ្យេទាញពីក្រោម **55** 32	រមាស់ **66** 16	រ៉ាឌីយ៉ាទ័រ **51** 56
រទេភ្លេីងរត់តាមផ្លួល **55** 30	រម្ហការ **79** 26	រ៉ាស់បេីរី **8** 16
រទេភ្លេីងរត់លេីផ្លូវខ្ពស់ផុតពីដី **55** 31	រលក **91** 24	រ៉ាហ្ម **18** 14
រទេរុញ្ញ **87** 4	រលាកភ្លេីង **40** 18	រ៉ុស្ស៊ីយ **15** 20, **55** 24

រ៉ុក្កែត **75** 13
រ៉ូដអែឡាន់ **73** 39
រ៉ូដអែឡិន **73** 39
រ៉ូតរ៉ឹនន័រ **64** 32
រ៉ូប៊ីន **64** 9
រ៉ូឡូដិច (ប្រអប់សំរាប់កត់ឈ្មោះ
-ក្រុមហ៊ុន ឬ មនុស្សដែលគេ
-ចង់ទាក់ទងនៅថ្ងៃក្រោយ) **83** 14
រ៉េស្ស៊័រ **52** 31
រ៉េស្ស៊័រពួក **32** 18
រ៉េអាក់ទ័រនុយក្លេអែរ **80** 13
រ៉ែធ្យូងថ្ម **80** 6
លា **67** 23
លាង **38** 16
លាត **24** 20
លាប **17** 11
លាបថ្នាំ **26** 1
លាស **11** 32
លាសសមុទ្រធំៗម្យ៉ាង **62** 10
លី **26** 16
លីលី **60** 3
លុប **77** 3
លុយ **13**
លុយទឹកតែ **55** 22
លេខតំបន់ប្រៃសណីយ **46** 12
លេខាធិការ **83** 11
លើ (កំរាល) **102** 5
លើ (ឆ្នាខ្មៅ) **102** 2
លើ (ស្ពាន) **103** 8
លើក (ដៃ) **77** 1
លេខសៀវភៅ **47** 7
លេខអាគារ **45** 24
លេងប៉ាតាំង **97** 9
លោកខែ **74** 9
លោត **96** 8
លោត (ដូចជាបាល់ ។ល។) **97** 11
លោតដាំក្បាលចុះ **97** 14
លោមមច្ឆា **68** 11
លំពែង **5** 71
ល្ពៅ **7** 26
ល្ពៅម្យ៉ាងតូចៗ **7** 28
ល្មើ **9** 23
ល្វីហ្ស៍ស៊ីយ៉ានណា **72** 18
ល្ហុង **8** 6
វក្កំ **5** 70
វង់ភ្លេង **99** 6
វង់តន្ត្រី **99** 6
វចនានុក្រម **47** 24
វីណ្ឌមណ្ឌល **79** 17
វត្ថុធ្វើឡើងដោយយក
-អម្បោះមកចាក់ថ្លក់ **101** 28
វល្លិ **61** 42
វ៉ាន **53** 26
វានរជាតិ **69**
វាយ **96** 1
វាយដាក់ទីឡូ **77** 10
វាយម៉ាស៊ីន **77** 10
វាលបរសេះ **95** D
វាលបាល់ចាប់ផ្ដើម ឬ នៅពេលប្ដូរវេន **96** 2
វាលលេងហ្គុលហ្វ៍ **95** B
វាលស្មៅតម្រឹមយ៉ាងស្អាតនៅជុំវិញរន្ធ
-ដែលគេត្រូវវាយបាល់បញ្ចូល **95** 10
វាលស្មៅ (សំរាប់សត្វស៊ី) **81** 6
វិជ្ជកោណ **79** 20
វិជ្ជមាត្រ **79** 12
វិថី **45** 31
វិទ្យុ **50** 18
វិទ្យុទទួលសម្លេង **100** 21
វិលឡូវ **61** 31
វិស **37** 42
វិស្កុនស៊ិន **73** 49
វីឌីអូ **100** A
វីនុស **74** 12
វីយូឡា **98** 8
វីយ៉ូឡុង **98** 7
វីយ៉ូឡែត **60** 16
វ៉ឺម៉ុន **73** 45
វេទិកា **99** 7
វេជ្ជបណ្ឌិត **39** 11
វែក **27** 21
វែកឆា **27** 21
វែកចំហៀង **4** 31
វែង **24** 2
វៀរហ្ស៊ីនី **73** 46
វៀរហ្ស៊ីនីញ៉ា **73** 46
វាំងនន **32** 10, **99** 1
វាំងននបង្អួច **28** 23
វាំងននបាំងកុំឲ្យទឹកសាច **34** 5
វីកម៉ាន់សូនី **100** 30
វ៉ាល់ **52** 27
វ៉ាលិស **56** 7
វ៉ាស៊ីនតោន **73** 47
វ៉ាហ្គុង **54** 9
វេស្ប៉ា **52** 29
វេសវៀរហ្ស៊ីនីញ៉ា **73** 48
វ៉ែនតា **21** 44

បិនិក្រម

រ៉ែនតាការពារភ្នែក **78** 12, **94** 28

រ៉ែនតាពាក់កុំឲ្យចាំងភ្នែក, រ៉ែនតាខ្មៅ **90** 14

រ៉ែម៉ុន **73** 45

រ៉ែ **31** 8

រ៉ែឃ្យូមិញ **73** 50

ស **95** 17

សក់ **4** 30

សក់កសេះ **67** 21a

សង់ដីឡេ្យ **29** 3

សង្ឃារ **63** 12

សណ្ដែកក្ដ **6** 15

សណ្ដែកដី **9** 28

សណ្ដែកបារាំង **6** 17

សណ្ដែកអង្កុយ **6** 13

សណ្ដែកអង្កុយខ្មៅ **6** 14

សណ្ដែកអង្កុយចំអិនក្នុងឡ្ប **18** 3

សណ្ដែកអង្កុយម្យ៉ាង **6** 16

សត្តុកករ **66**

សត្តុករ៉ែង **67** 29

សត្តុជ្ងួកបង្កុយ **65** 15

សត្តុជ្ងួកលាសខ្យងគ្រុំបង្កុង **11** D

សត្តុជ្រុក **67** 30

សត្តុប្រម៉ា **66** 11

សត្តុពស្រលម្យ៉ាងនៅទ្វីបអាមេរិក **66** 2

សត្តុឃុកក្ម្ពេ ។ល។ **63** 22

សត្តុមានក្រចកធំៗ **66**

សត្តុល្អិតខ្មា **40** 3

សត្តុល្អិតម្យ៉ាងដូចមេអំបៅ **63** 21

សត្តុស៊ីស្រមោច **66** 5

សត្តស្ឋាបម្យ៉ាងដូចកុក **64** 30

សត្តុស្ឋាន **69** 30

(សត្ត) ហ្វក **68** 12

សត្តុហ្រ៊ីរ៉ាហ្វ **67** 29

សត្តុតន្ទ្រី **64** 5

សន្តិសុខ **56**

សម **29** 12

សមស្ឋាបព្រា **29** 22

សម្រងក **33** 20

សមុទ្រការ៉ា **70** 31

សមុទ្រការីប **70** 20

សមុទ្រកាស់ស្ឋាន **70** 27

សមុទ្រក្រហម **70** 29

សមុទ្រខាងជើង (នៅ

-ខាងជើងទ្វីបអ៊ីរ៉ុប) **70** 21

សមុទ្រខ្មៅ **70** 26

សមុទ្រខ្ញាច់ **71**

សមុទ្រខ្ញាច់ក្រេតសាន់ធី **71** 55

សមុទ្រខ្ញាច់បេ៉ងតិត **71** 49

សមុទ្រខ្ញាច់តាខ្លាម៉ាកាន់ **71** 53

សមុទ្រខ្ញាច់ម្ថូហារី **71** 48

សមុទ្រខ្ញាច់រ៉ុបអាល់ខាលី **71** 52

សមុទ្រខ្ញាច់សាហារ៉ា **71** 51

សមុទ្រខ្ញាច់ហ្គោបី **71** 54

សមុទ្រខ្ញាច់អាតាកាម៉ា **71** 50

សមុទ្រចិនខាងកើត **70** 38

សមុទ្រចិនខាងត្បូង **70** 39

សមុទ្រជីពុន **70** 36

សមុទ្រ, ឈូងសមុទ្រ និងឧកសមុទ្រ **70**

សមុទ្របារិន **70** 23

សមុទ្របាល់ទិច **70** 22

សមុទ្របូហ្ម៉ុរ **70** 15

សមុទ្របៃរិង **70** 34

សមុទ្រម៉េឌីតែរ៉ាណេ **70** 24

សមុទ្រល្បៀង **70** 37

សមុទ្រឡ្ញាប់ចុហ្វ **70** 33

សមុទ្រអារ៉ាប់ **70** 30

សមុទ្រអ៊ុខុតស្ក៍ **70** 35

សររសេរ **77** 7

សរសេក្នុងឆ្នីងខ្លង **5** 58

សរសេឈាមក្រហម **5** 69

សរសេឈាមខ្មៅ **5** 68

សរីរាគ្គក្នុងខ្លន **5** F

សាក់សូហ្វន **98** 24

សាក្ស្រី **43** 13

សាច់ក្រកអាមេរិកាំង **10** 7

សាច់គោ **10** 1

សាច់គោកាត់ជាដុំតូចៗ **10** 4

សាច់គោកាត់ជាដុំធំសំរាប់ដុត **10** 3

សាច់គោកិន **10** 2

សាច់ គោ, ជ្រុក ។ល។ **10** A

សាច់ច្បៀម **10** 13

សាច់ជាប់ឆ្អឹងជំនី **10** 15

សាច់ជ្រុក **10** 6

សាច់ជ្រុកចងជាដុំ

-សំរាប់យកទៅដុតក្នុងឡ្ប **10** 8

សាច់ជ្រុកបន្លះស្ទើរៗ **18** 33

សាច់ជ្រុកជាប់ឆ្អឹងជំនីរវៀន **18** 15

សាច់ដុំ **5** 62

សាច់បីជាន់ហាន់ជាបន្លះស្ទើរៗ **10** 11

សាច់ពន្លះ **11** 28

សាច់ភ្លៅ (ភ្លៅជ្រុកខាងក្រោយ) **10** 12

សាច់មានជាប់ឆ្អឹងជំនី **10** 9

សាច់, មាន់, ទា ។ល។ **11** B

សាច់លុញ (ជាដុំ) **18** 11

សាជីឌាក់ចៃកផ្លុវ (បណ្ដោះអាសន្ន) **82** 19

សាជីជ្រុង **79** 25

សាតែលលីតគមនាគមន៍ 75 2

សាតែលលីតសំរាប់
-សង្កេតមើលធាតុអាកាស 75 3

សាទូន 74 16

សាន្រវិច 16 16

សាប្លិ 34 15

សាប្លិកោរពុកមាត់ 23 22

សាប្លិលាងចាន 30 10

សារពត៌មាន 21 48

សារានុក្រម 47 25

សាលាកាត់ក្ដី 43 B, 94 13

សារ៉ិ 59 7

សាឡ្យាង 58 17

សាឡ្យាត់ 6 6

សាឡ្យាត់ (មានបន្លែលោយ
-គ្រប់មុខឥតមានដាក់សាច់) 18 13

សាឡ្យាម៉ង 65 14

សិង្ហ 68 3

សិល្បករ 86 3

ស៊ុបសាច់គោ 18 14

ស៊ី 17 1

ស៊ីឌី 100 27

ស៊ីផ្ទេ 50 12, 52 5

ស៊ីម៉ង 82 10

ស៊ីរ៉ូ 18 6

ស៊ីរ៉ាំង 39 27

ស៊ីឡ្យ៉ាំង 79 26

ស៊ីឡ្យូហ្គន 98 31

សីបរ៉ៃ 54 B

សីរីហ្គ៍ 8 19

សុភាចារបុរស 43 17

សូវគ្រាស 74 10

ស្ងួត 5 63

ស៊្ងម៉ាក់រមាស់ 61 44

ស្ងួល 61 31

ស្ងួហ្គា 28 25

ស្ងួនសត្វ 87 1

សេីនបញ្ជ្រាំងភ្លើង
-(សំរាប់បង្ហាញផ្លូវនាវា) 58 14

សេីម 25 15

សៀវភៅផែនទី 47 20

សៀវភៅមានលេខថ្មីៗគ្នា 47 15

សៀវភៅមើល 76 26

សៀវភៅសរសេរវិណ្ណដែកល្អស 76 15

សេក (តូចៗ) 64 15

សេក (ធំៗ) 64 16

សេន 13 27

សេក 15 27

សែង 26 16

សែន 61 33

សែឡ្យ៉ីរ៉ិ 6 10

សែរៀន 94 17

សោ 52 13

សោទ្វារ 50 1

សៅការ៉ូខ្ទៃស្សណា 73 40

សៅដាកូតា 73 41

សំណង់ខ្លស់នៅមាត់អណ្ដូងប្រេងកាត 80 2

សំណាញ់ 27 19, 63 15, 92 23, 95 2

សំបក 8 8b, 9 20, 9 37b, 61 35c , 20 a

សំបកលោស, ខ្យង ។ល។ 91 40

សំបុក 64 31

សំបុកនាង ឬ សត្វល្អិតផ្សេងៗទៀត 63 2

សំបុត្រ 46 7, 55 16, 56 4

សំបុត្រអនុញ្ញាតឲ្យឡើងជិះ 56 18

សំពត់ 21 36

សំពត់ទ្រនាប់ខ្លី 22 8

សំពត់បញ្ជ្រាំងរូប 100 14

សំពាយ 19 4

សំពាយមានឆ្នឹង 89 28

សំពាយអ្នកបេងបូរេបប៉ុ 95 7

សំពូ 34 8

សំពោច 68 7

សំទ្បិ 39 23

សំទ្បិ្យ្សារ្របត្រ្យោក 33 10

សំអាត 26 2

សេះ 67 21, 81 23

សេះបង្កង់ 66 18

សេះសមុទ្រ 65 1

ស្ងួរ (កញ្ជប់) 16 13

ស្ងួាទ្បួប 62 10

ស្ងុង 68 8

ស្ងួ្នេត 19 15

ស្ងួរ 98 19

ស្ងួរបញ្ច្បូរ 98 20

ស្ងួរម្ឃ្យ៉ាងរាងដួចខ្មុះ្នា 98 21

ស៊្ងី 94 33

ស្ងីកាត់គំបន់ដែល
-គ្មានផ្លូវស្រួលឬូល 94 33

ស្ងួត 25 14

ស្ងួារ 31 16

ស្រ្ងី 2 1

ស្ងាប់ 77 6

ស្ងួេក 10 5, 8 21

ស្ងានិយតម្រត 43 A

ស្ងានិយរថភ្លើង 55 18

ស្ងានិយរទេះភ្លើងក្រោមដី 44 16

 មិនិក្រម

ស្ថានីយអគ្គីសនី **80** 20

ស្ថានីយអាវកាស **75** 1

ស្ថាប **77** 2

ស្តាំង **64** 7

ស្តប់ **52** 21

ស្តាប់ដេរ **101** 21

(ស្តាម) ឆ្នតម្រាមដៃ **43** 24

ស្តឹង **89** 30

ស្តុក **62** 1a, **65** 18a

ស្តូល **80** 14

ស្ទេង **67** 35a

ស្ប៉ាហ្គេទី **18** 10

ស្សេកជើង **21** 49

ស្សេកជើងកវែង **19** 21

ស្សេកជើងកវែងពាក់ពេលភ្លៀង **19** 25

ស្សេកជើងកែងចោត **20** 25

ស្សេកជើងឃ្លុបតមានខ្សែ **21** 42

ស្សេកជើងដើរព្រៃ **19** 9

ស្សេកជើងបាតា **20** 11

ស្សេកជើងពាក់ក្នុងផ្ទះ **22** 18

ស្សេកជើងពាក់ធ្វើការ **21** 32

ស្សេកជើងលេងប៉ាតាំង **94** 26

ស្សេកជើងលេងស្គី **95** 15

ស្សេកជើងសម្រែក **20** 19

ស្ស្រាង **20** 18

ស្តុក **16** 33

ស្ទីណាត់ **6** 8

ស្ទ័ត **37** 42b

ស្ទេក្តោប **63**

ស្ទេផ្ការខៀរ **6** 2

ស្ទេផ្កាស (មួយដុំ) **6** 1

ស្ទា **4** 5

ស្ទាក្តិចុងចោទ **43** 22

ស្ទៀន **43** 14, **83** 11

ស្ទៀ **27** 15

ស្ទៀនិងធញ្ញជាតិ **60**

ស្រកី **65** 3c

ស្រទាប់ **60** 18b

ស្រមោច **63** 12

ស្រល់ **61** 34

ស្រអាប់ **24** 10

ស្រា (ឥប) **16** 22

ស្រាទំពាំងបាយជូរ **16** 19

ស្រីបំរើស្រា **16** 32

ស្រី **2** 1

ស្រវ **60** 21

ស្រូវសាលី **60** 22

ស្រូវអារ៉ាន់ **60** 23

ស្រែ (ដាំស្រូវសាលី) **81** 16

ស្រៀវស្រាញ **40** 4

ស្រោមដៃ **27** 20, **92** 12, **94** 11, **94** 15

ស្រោមដៃគ្មានម្រាម **19** 11

ស្រោមដៃអ្នកចាប់ **92** 4

ស្រោមត្រច្ចៀក **19** 10

ស្រោមសំបុត្រ **83** 31

ស្រោមទឹក **26** 5

ស្រោមចង្កៀង
-(ដើម្បីកុំឱ្យពន្លីចាំងភ្នែក) **28** 27

ស្រោមជើង **22** 17

ស្រោមជើងនីឡុង **22** 6

ស្រោមជើង (ស្ត្រី) **22** 6

ស្រោមជើងស្ៀកដូចខោ (ស្រី) **22** 5

ស្រោមជើងវែង **22** 16

ស្រោមដៃ **19** 1, **92** 12

ស្រោមដៃពាក់ធ្វើការ **27** 26

ស្រោមដៃអ្នកចាប់

ស្រោមខ្លិយ **32** 15

ស្រោមសំបុត្រ (ផ្ញើតាមយន្តហោះ) **46** 16

ស្រះ (សំរាប់ទា) **87** 8

ស្ត្រីប៉ើរ **8** 15

ស្ត្រី **2** 1

ស្ទាប **11** 22, **57** 9, **63** 4a, **64** 1a, **64** 7a

ស្ទាបព្រា **29** 8

ស្ទាបព្រាចូកដី **27** 27

ស្ទីក **61** 36a

ស្ទីកស្រល់ **61** 34a

ស្ទែ **100** 12

ស្ទា **69** 14

ស្ទាក្រហម **69** 18

ស្ទាធំ **69** 17

ស្ទាយ **85** 5

ស្ទារអង្កុត **69** 19

ស្ទាឆី **69** 16

ស្ទាត **24** 6

ហង្ស **64** 28

ហាងលក់ថ្នាំពេទ្យ **45** 22

ហាងលក់សៀវភៅ **45** 18

ហាងលក់ផស័រ៉ាន់គ្រប់មុខ **44** 5

ហាន់ **31** 10

ហាម៉ូនិកា **98** 30

ហារ៉ៃ **72** 11

ហិបខោអាវ **56** 1

ហិបយួរទៀងយន្តហោះ **56** 2

(ហុង) អម្បៀះ **101** 2

ហុចឲ្យ, **96** 5

ហុតដក **18** 2

ហ្ឫល្ឃ 61 37

ហែក 77 9

ហែយ៉ាស៊ីន 60 10

ហោផៅ 21 41

ហៅ 17 5

ហាំញ្ញាក៏ៃ៩ (សត្តស្លាបម្ប្យាងតូចៗ) 64 2

ហ៊ាំបីហ្គ៊ីរ 18 9

ហ្គាឡ្បាក់ស៊ុ 74 1

ហ្គីវរីយ 69 17

ហ្គាឌីនិញ៉ា 60 14

ហ្គាវ៉ាស 27 2

ហ្គាវ៉ាហ្ឫចតឡ្បាន 45 19

ហ្គាស់ 80 29

ហ្គាហ្ឫ 50 27

ហ្គីតា 98 11

ហ្គីតាអេឡ្បៀចទ្រិច 99 26

ហ្គូហ្ឫបៃរី 8 11

ហ្គោហ្គ៊ីរ (សត្តម្ប្យាងតូច

-កណ្ណូរប្ប្រែងតែធំជាង) 66 8

ហ្គ៉ា 51 48

ហ្គ៉ីហ្ឫង 64 19

(ហ្គូង) គោ 81 20

ប្ហ្គ៉ាំង 50 26, 52 17

ប្ហ្គិសប៊ី 90 13

ប្ហ្គ៉ាំងដៃ 50 15, 52 24

ហ្គ៉ិវរី៩ 72 9

ហ្គ៉ិវរី៉ា 72 9

ហ្គាមិញ្ញាហ្គ្គា 64 29

ហ្គ៉ាស 100 7

ហ្ឫកហ្ឫយ៉ា 72 10

ហ្ឫក់តែត 21 33

ហ្ឫននិញ៉ា 60 13

ហ្ឫបកូ៩ 46 12

ហ្ឫបព'ីរ 101 16

ហ្ឫតីនី 7 27

ហ្ឫពីតែរ 74 15

ហ្ឫរណោរ៉ាទ'ិរ 80 21

ហ្ឫ៩ត 57 18

ហ្ឫ៩ប 66 18

ឡ្ប 30 32

ឡ្បតគ្រាប់កាំភ្ល៊ើង 48 27

ឡ្បតសម័យ 18 25

ឡ្បម៉ៃក្រូវ៉ៃរ 30 23

ឡ្បានកនុយកាត់ឆ្បារប៊ួន 51 E

ឡ្បានគ្គានផុងនៅពីក្រោយ 49 18

ឡ្បានឈ្ឫសទិកកក (តាមផ្ជូរ ៗលៗ) 49 5

ឡ្បានឈ្ឫល 53 20, 54 A

ឡ្បានដ៉ិកគ្រ្គៀងប្ប្រដាប់លត់ភ្ល៊ើងឆេ៩ផ្ជះ 42 3

ឡ្បានដ៉ិកដី 49 14

ឡ្បានដ៉ិកទំនិញ 53 25

ឡ្បានដ៉ិកប្ប្រងសាំង 49 3

ឡ្បានដ៉ិករថយន្ត 49 17

ឡ្បានដ៉ិកសំរាម 49 6

ឡ្បានដ៉ិកផ្ជ៉ារវ៉ៃរផ្ជះ 49 11

ឡ្បានគាក់ស៊ុ 55 27

ឡ្បានទ៉ិក (លត់ភ្ល៊ើងឆេ៩ផ្ជះ) 42 2

ឡ្បានទ្រុងតូច 53 26

ឡ្បានទ្រុងធុនតូច 49 9

ឡ្បានធម្មតា (ឆ្បារព'ីរ) 51 D

ឡ្បានពិចក៊ីប 49 4

ឡ្បានពេឡ្ប 42 6

ឡ្បានលក់ម្ហូប 49 8

ឡ្បានលាយស៊ុម៉ង់ត៍ 49 13, 82 25

ឡ្បានសំរាប់ទាញសណ្ណោង 49 15

ឡ្បានសំរាប់ទៅកំប៉េ 53 16

ឡ្បានស្ណាស្ឫងរ៉ាហ្គុង 50 C

ឡ្បានស្ឫច 49 2

ឡ្បានស្ឫ៉រ 53 17

ឡ្បានហ្ឫប 48 9

ទ្បៀនកណ្ណាល 53 6

ទ្បៀនខាងឆ្ច៉ង 53 5

ទ្បៀនខាងស្ជាំ 53 7

ទ្បៀរ 20 3, 101 9

ទ្បៀរកិប 101 13

ទ្បៀរអាវៃកដែនុប 23 12

ទ្ប៉ៃងឡ្បាម 40 10

ទ្ប៉ៃង (ឡ្បល) 103 11

ទ្ប៉ៃរស៊ុ 37 38

ទ្ប៉ៅ 99 14

ទ្ប៉ាងធំៗផុកផរ៉ាំ៩ 58 7

អគីដេ 60 12

អគ្តិសនិ 80 32

អង់តែន 51 46

អង់តែនទ្បូរទស្បូរ៍ 27 3

អគ្រ្គង 63 12

អគ្លប់ដាក់កណ្ណូរ 35 32

អង្កុលិលេខ 83 10

អគ្រ្គ៉ិង 27 11

អគ្រ្គ៉ិងឝតខ្ចៀ 33 26

អណ្ណាត 4 41

អណ្ណាតភ្ល៊ើង 29 26, 78 21

អណ្ណូងប្ប្រងកាត 80 1

អណ្ណើក 65 12

អណ្ណើកមាស 63 14

អណ្ណើក (រស់នៅៗលើៗគោក) 65 18

អតិសុខុមទស្បូរ៍ 78 30

អ្នកយកពត៌មាន (ការសែត, -ទូរទស្សន៍ ។ល។) 86 11

អ្នកយកសំរាម (ដីកយកទៅចោល) 49 7

អ្នកយកឥវ៉ាន់មកឱ្យដល់ផ្ទះ 49 10, 85 10

អ្នកយាមទ្វារ 85 11

អ្នករកស៊ីជួញឆ្វានឥវ៉ាន់រើផ្ទះ 49 12

អ្នករកស៊ីលក់ផ្ទះ ឬ ដី 85 5

អ្នករត់ 91 23, 94 31

អ្នករៀបចំបញ្ជី 83 23

អ្នករាំ 99 3

អ្នកលក់ 86 12

អ្នកលក់គ្រឿងអលង្ការ 84 12

អ្នកលក់ដូរ 87 3

អ្នកលក់បន្លែផ្លែឈើ 84 7

អ្នកលក់ផ្កា 84 11

អ្នកលក់រៃនិតា 84 9

អ្នកលក់សាច់ 84 13

អ្នកលត់ភ្លើង 42 10

អ្នកលាបថ្នាំ (ផ្ទះ) 85 7

អ្នកលាយស្រា 16 21

អ្នករលងគីបិត 99 22

អ្នកលេងភ្លេង 99 10

អ្នកលេងស្គី 94 35

អ្នកលេងស្គីលើទឹក 59 10

អ្នកលេងហ្គីតានាមុខគេ 99 25

អ្នកលេងហ្គីតាបាស្ស 99 23

អ្នកលេងហ្គុលហ្វ 94 10

អ្នករាយបាល 92 7, 93 14

អ្នករាយសូរ 99 27

អ្នករាយអគ្គលិលេខ 83 6

អ្នកសរសេរប្រូក្រាមកុំព្យូទ័រ 86 16

អ្នកស្ទីបអង្គែត 43 2

អ្នកសុំឡ្យានគេដោយសារ 53 9

អ្នកសំអាតរៀបចំផ្ទះ (ឲ្យគេ) 85 8

អ្នកស្គាប់ ឬ អ្នកមើល 99 15

អ្នកស្រែចំការ 81 7

អ្នកហេលទឹក 91 28

អ្នកហ្គឹកហ្គីន 93 21

អ្នកអាវិកាស 75 5

អ្នកអែបនឹងអ្នកប្ចោកផ្លួលខាងស្ចាំ 93 30

ពដ្ឋ 82 12

ពដ្ឋតូចៗស្ទើងៗ 34 27

ឥវ៉ាន់ដែលនាវាផ្ទុក 58 10

ឥវ៉ាន់ (របស់អ្នកធ្វើដំណើរ) 56 8

ឧទ្ធម្ភាគចក្រ 57 2

ឧបករណ៍កំណត់ម៉ោង 78 13

ឧបករណ៍ចុះលើលោកខែ 75 7

ឧបករណ៍បង្កើតអគ្គិសនី 80 21

ឧបករណ៍បន្លុតគេឡ្យហូន -ពីម្ចុយទៅម្ចុយទៀត 83 3

ឧបករណ៍សួង់អាវិកាស 75 4

ឧស 28 10, 89 32

ឧសថការី 84 1

ឱិពុក 3 5

ឱិពុកម្ចាយ 2 6

ឱិម៉ាល់ 63 20

ឱិទ្បិកក្រៀម 9 26

ឱស 61 35d

ឱកសណ្ណាន 21 45, 92 9

ឯ (បង្គុច) 102 1

និសចស្ថាន 45 22

ឲ្យ 17 9